THE Q
From This Moment Onwards

BRUNO ASIIMWE

Copyright © Bruno Asiimwe

ISBN: 979-8-9878940-9-5

First Published in 2023

Lisa Nicole Publishing www.lisanicolealexander.com

Author: Bruno Asiimwe

Foreword: Rev. Prof. Peter Kanyandago

Introduction: Mr. Tumuhimbise Mitchel

Genre: Non Fiction

Email: asiimwebruno49@gmail.com

Edition: 1st Ed. (released on 20th October, 2023 in honor of my late father, Mr. Besiga John who passed away on 20th October, 2019

Table of Contents

ACKNOWLEDGMENTS

I raise my voice to God in appreciation for His everlasting
love and power to make all my weaknesses grow into
strengths. Let the world praise Him; all is possible with Him.
Talents are for all human beings, and discovering them for use
makes God recognisable in us and in his creation.
I am grateful to the readers of my first two books for having
gone on to ask for the third book. You were even courageous
to the extent of asking for its title. I know you will soon ask for
the fourth book; I will write as long as I have life, and my
future children will possibly write where I cannot.
Considering the blessing that time presents, I thank the lady
going to be my wife, given that they will be ready to spend the
quality of time with me. With remarkable time boundaries, I
recognise my first editor, Christopher Ssebunya, whom I met
at Namirembe Hillside High School, where I attended high
school education from 2012 to 2013.

I am humbled by Rev. Prof. Peter Kanyandago, Rev. Dr.
Bonaventure Turyomumazima, PhD, Mr. Muhanguzi Justus
(Uncle), Mr. Tumuhimbise Mitchel, Mrs. Kyogabirwe Betty,
Ms. Atengorit Anne Grace; my siblings Mr. Byamukama
Bernard, Ms. Musiimenta Emily Besiga, Mr. Agaba Benedict
and Ms. Musiime Moreen. I reached out to you on short
notice, and your responses are visible in chapter 14 of the
book. Rev. Prof. Peter Kanyandago, thanks for writing the
foreword of this book as well, and cheers to my friend Mr.
Tumuhimbise Mitchel for writing the introduction of this
great book.

The overwhelming support I have received from Dr. Lisa Patterson, PhD can be traced in the work we shared at Domestic Peace Foundation Uganda. My second publication saw light in 2020 and the third book in 2023 is also here through Lisa Nicole Publishing in the United States of America. I also congratulate you upon graduating from Grand Canyon University with a Doctor of Education.

In a special way I would like to thank the following Japanese families for sharing quality time with me: Mr. and Mrs. Horiuchi Tomomasa (host family) and Mrs. Maekawa Hiroko (guarantor who doubles as my Japanese Mom) together with Mrs. Kazuko Fujita (my Japanese Grandma) ども ありがとう ございます。

The ultimate vote of appreciation goes to my parents, the late Mr. Besiga John and Mrs. Banooti Generoza Besiga, for allowing me to wake up as early as midnight (12:00 a.m) to write this book. I know I disobeyed you when you told me not to wake up again every other day; I pushed and pulled tables in the living room to make sure I was well positioned, thus making some noise. Thanks for the gift of education that has seen me enrolled in a doctoral program in Global Studies and majoring in Peace and Conflict Studies at Tokyo University of Foreign Studies in Tokyo, Japan.

Dedication

I dedicate this book to the woman of my heart in time: my future wife. In their upbringing is quality time with the reflections of my epitomised pieces of work hereafter.

FOREWORD

It is a privilege for me to write this foreword for the third book of Bruno Asiimwe. I got to know Bruno through his father, John Besiga, who was visually impaired. I have come to know Bruno better because he shares with me his personal and professional plans and dreams. Because of all this, I was happy to accept his invitation to be a member of the Board of Directors of the Domestic Peace Foundation Uganda (DPFU). This is a Community-Based Organisation which he founded and run for a number of years. Similarly, it is a joy for me to write a foreword for his third book, The Quality of Time: From This Moment Onwards.

In this book, Bruno invites us to take a close look at and manage well this precious resource we call time. If you have not yet started, or if in the past you have not managed time well, the subtitle is an encouraging invitation, From This Moment Onwards: this means that it is not too late to start.

The author has a particular style one gets used to. From reflections, he goes to some narratives about his life, his experience in school, and some philosophical observations about what is happening in society. In fact, each chapter can be read on its own, and even the sections in the different chapters can be read separately. That is one of the advantages of the style he has used.

In sharing with us, Bruno does not argue about things he is convinced about. He does not set out to convince, and some people might be put off by this. But isn't it time that we started sharing our convictions with others, leaving each person a chance to pick what s/he finds fitting? For example, when he introduces statements about God and prayer, he does not have to qualify these by saying if you believe or not. He comes out with statements and advice about how love, sex, and intimate relations should be handled.

This is an area that many consider to be part of private life, but haven't we been too shy to talk about it? Maybe we have emphasised too much the idea that "anything goes" and this has caused its own problems. In this book one can decipher some of Bruno's personal traits. He is adamant about what he is convinced about. He seems to say: If I have succeeded you also have to succeed, but of course, you have to take into account that he is disciplined, daring, and courageous.

The title of chapter 8, "Unfulfilled promises are inexcusable," is an example of what the author finds unacceptable. Those who know Bruno, it is not easy to get his laughter! He is a serious guy. But he can smile and have a good laugh. He is not a bore! But some of the things he shares with us could be turned into humour if he was not writing about serious things.

One of these is the first fourth-hand laptop he bought. It could only work when plugged into the socket, and it generated heat. Other anecdotes are about his "escapades" trying to find time to write at awkward hours, but in all this, he remained respectful. Some of these incidents, indeed, could send some of us roaring with laughter, but Bruno is a serious guy. Bruno is small but has a big heart, as any reader will discover.

For him, there are some non-negotiable areas, which include: promoting justice and gender equality and abolishing (not just alleviating) domestic violence. Regarding the latter, it was his wish (wish is not strong enough) that anyone who read his second book, A Family for Us: Together Against Domestic Violence, should fight or stop domestic violence. If you have not yet started, it is not too late: from this moment onwards! At the age of 31 years, Bruno has come out with his third book at the time that he is doing his PhD in Japan. As one reads it, one cannot but ask oneself how Bruno gets time to combine his several tasks and accomplish them well, and often with very limited material resources. This book seems to give us a key to how he handles time. He does not give recipes on how to do this. The book has several personal anecdotes which the author uses to make personal, general and philosophical reflections.

Don't expect a detailed exposé on how to manage time. But if you are willing to be shaken in your convictions about how it is not easy to manage time, if you are willing to question yourself on why you have sometimes failed to accomplish tasks you set for yourself while you had time and money at your disposal, or if you don't fall in this category but are intrigued by the subject, then read this book.

Rev. Prof. Peter Kanyandago
Episcopal Vicar for the Laity in the Archdiocese of Mbarara and
Deputy Vice Chancellor of Ibanda University

AUTHOR PREFACE

Every bit of the human life must face the test of time. This book gathers the entire picture of how time creates a better environment for us all. We are all different from each other and dependent on how one acts upon time and the changing events therein. It is therefore practically possible to see your time produce fruit right from the day of childhood to adulthood.

How often do you believe it should have been your turn to do something? Do you go on to feel remorse for your inability to act upon something? You have a lot to make of your reaction towards these questions. Your external growth tells a lot that people around you see and greatly explains what one may need to stick to for their worth. Undoubtedly, my interior picture of success has for long been hidden from the world around me.

You certainly make a part of the world around me. Through this book, there are intriguing cases of the origins of my success that you had never known, though you admire my strides in life. There is more confidence in my interiors of life than that you know me to be. That could be considered your own opinion, and you now have the blessing to hear from the horse's mouth; it is all the time I have solely cherished by going uncomfortable with my comfort every other day.

Furthermore, most people know who they are on the outside, and life ends there. Your time starts on the inside for us to see who you are. Do you know what it means to let people describe who you are, and you cannot believe it yourself? Absolutely. Our comfort zones have robbed us of the time to make self-reflections, where one would probably know their inner self.

From page to page of this intriguing book, the reader is set to analyse the cost of staying in their comfort zones at the expense of time. There is a price to pay by each one of us at the end of the day. You might be single for a reason and someone else is married too for another reason. Can you make your reason so defensive to justify what you do?

I do not intend to make anyone try to live my life but to live a better life for themselves.

My heart, through such pieces of writing, pours out for everybody ready to transform their life and beyond. If you are ready to be better placed and still keep your neighbour languish in wasting time, it is not advisable for you to read this book. From the word go, you should not waste your time with unsupportive agendas. In a broader understanding, the reader would not have room to change their life if I was selfish with the wisdom God continues to offer me.

This book is an act of making clear reflections on what you have access to that is a revelation of extraordinary milestones. Your age is your time to go on counting your life achievements. I will continue to zoom wider the view of what we shall attain in time.

In time, there is what you want to get to through seeing the cover page of the book on the shelf and moving on. Again, in time there is what you deserve to get to through opening up every page as you are doing to the last dot. The former is for someone who has not gone this far to read the book. The latter is a clear manifestation of the aspect of quality of time in the entire book.

Similarly, this is how life draws nearer to different people to tell of the difference between what they want and what they deserve. It is true that if I did not sacrifice and work hard to write this book, I would not deserve to earn from its sales. The message we ought to carry in our minds is to believe in the mandatory steps life must take us through to attain our destiny. What do you think you deserve as your endpoint?

In light of this, there is someone we intend to become the next day, and there is that person the world knows that we are today. Sooner than later you will learn of what surrounds you to account for who you are. The people you share a moment with could mean a perfect composition of such surroundings. It is true that you are doing things related to what they do. For a greater reason, you have chosen to have some time to read this book; I have read it before anyone else. On the other hand, you are meant to have a better day as long as you understand the writings in it.

There is no guarantee of success without respecting time. The sure way to success is only doing valuable ventures in the limited time you have to make quality time. There is a mark you are setting onto your chart that makes sense of where you are heading to and the life you are headed for. It is a great decision to consider a drive on a lane of better health, friends, family, wife, husband, children, girlfriend, boyfriend, career and wealth.

I know that these are things you want to experience from this moment of your life. This is not limited to what you will absolutely pay off in time. I have immersed myself in time; even for my wife in future to be the person I am dedicating this book to, tells it all. You do not have to take aim at making attempts to the present. Time will teach us to have trials way beyond today; tomorrow holds many more human successes than we imagined before. If you are not prepared for your old age, the winds of life are stronger to sweep you far away.

The title of this book, The Quality of Time: From this Moment Onwards is categorically explaining that it is not late for you and me to go where we ought to be. This is not the day to regret and think of having failed ourselves in the past. It is crucially the best moment of life to start where we are and believe there was no perfect work in the past. All for the truth there was, even no perfect person in us. Different from the past, today serves to be your turning point because time ought to be your best friend. Let us walk the talk of the best insights of this life-impacting book together.

Chapter 14 serves to honor my late father, Mr. Besiga John who passed away on 20th October, 2019 thus the occasioning of this release of the first edition of this book on 20th October, 2023. In the same chapter I recognise my mother Mrs. Generoza Banooti Besiga together with my daddy for sharing the most precious time of their life with their family and the world. I have become what you admire largely because of their unconditional investment in my life. It is time they started harvesting the freshest of fruits.

Bruno Asiimwe 2023

INTRODUCTION

Dear reader, within these words lies the invitation to reimagine your relationship with time, to transcend the boundaries that you have set for yourself, and to embrace the promise of becoming. Bruno, through this reflective and contemplative book, invites us to heed the wisdom woven into this narrative, igniting the spark of change and charting a course toward a future defined by the quality of our moments.

In a world where every aspect of human existence is subject to the relentless march of time, this book emerges as a guide to harnessing its power. "The Quality of Time: From This Moment Onwards" unveils a profound exploration into the intricate relationship between our lives and the unstoppable force of time. Through its pages, we embark on a journey to understand how time shapes not only our external circumstances but also our internal growth, ultimately shaping our destinies.

From the innocence of childhood to the complexities of adulthood, the narrative within these chapters delves deep into the interplay between our actions and the ever-changing tides of time. With introspection as its compass, this book beckons us to examine our responses to life's pivotal questions. Have you ever pondered the moments you believed should have been yours to seize? Have regrets ever cast shadows over your choices? Such reflections form the crux of this exploration, reminding us that our outward transformations are but reflections of our inner narratives.

Bruno, a hidden figure behind the façade of success, unveils the layers of his journey, offering a candid perspective on the triumphs concealed beneath the surface. Each turn of the page reveals not only Bruno's personal evolution but also the universal truths that underpin the fabric of existence. This book becomes a repository of revelations, inviting us to cast aside the armor of our comfort zones and embrace the discomfort that propels us toward growth.

Throughout these chapters, you will be confronted with the price of complacency, paid in the currency of unrealized potential and squandered opportunities. The narrative compels the need to evaluate the excuses that keep us within the confines of familiarity, forcing us to confront the costs we inevitably pay for our choices. As Bruno eloquently poses, are you ready to defend the reasons behind your actions, or will you rise above the justifications to forge a path of genuine transformation?

Yet, amidst these candid examinations, Bruno extends a hand of guidance rather than admonishment. The intention is not to replicate their journey but to catalyze our own quests for self-improvement. With each word, Bruno's heart pours forth, urging every seeker to break free from stagnation and embrace the possibilities that lie ahead.

"The Quality of Time: From This Moment Onwards" embraces you not only as readers but as a fellow traveler, willing to embark on a shared odyssey toward self-betterment. It is a rallying cry to abandon the shackles of indifference and embrace the wisdom that the passage of time bestows. As we navigate the chapters, we uncover the profound truth that success is intricately woven with our relationship with time. It is in the tapestry of our actions, intentions, and decisions that our destiny unfurls.

In this intricate dance with time, we learn that transformation is not a distant concept but a constant possibility. Each moment serves as an opportunity to reshape our narratives, to redefine our aspirations, and to sculpt a life worthy of our dreams. The title itself encapsulates the essence of the journey that unfolds within these pages. It reminds us that the present holds the power to rewrite our story, to forge anew from this very instant.

Mr. Tumuhimbise Mitchel
PhD Student
KU Leuven

CHAPTER ONE
Beyond Thoughts to Dreams

In the early days of my childhood, time was valued to be the greatest of imaginations. I vividly recall thinking about the big houses that would be put up using my own strength, buying and driving brand new cars and other properties one would love to own in their name. All this was presumably a build-up of a happy and great life in a vacuum full of thoughts.

Early childhood thoughts have oftentimes set young minds into a field of play specifically with what they admire most, love charitably, and even hate averagely. In a situation where a child looks on, only to admire something; there is less participation towards meeting their target. This cuts across to even adulthood with a clear example of men admiring beautiful women that happen to walk by the street and similarly for handsome men.

Very few of us register an achievement after admiring someone simply because this was not planned for, and there was absolutely no initial target. You may start to measure the instances of time wasted in selfish interests, especially to adults. Loving charitably involves sharing the small items in our possession. In human beings, expectations should be because someone invested in a specific venture and, to a greater extent, shared a portion of something with other people. On the contrary, most people build high expectations in life without an investment which does not arouse the spirit of sharing.

Considering an intimate relationship that carries within it the titles of husband and wife, throwing more light on this, let me call out to mention sweetheart, darling, pearl, and my love - all for love nicknames. The husband, in this case may expect to be loved in respect to being allocated to some time with the wife. This is very possible, given that they both consider their time to be crucial and worth sharing. Even a gardener will not cast millet seeds, only to expect sorghum grain at harvesting time.

A child cannot expect a toy car when you promise to buy them a piece of cake for their birthday. Unlike children, adults often have no limit in expectations since satisfaction is a mere question that no one wants to answer. Adulthood does not mean people attaining the age of developing new ideas. Creativity has turned out to be a miracle in my life, thus not necessarily effortless.

As long as I stand to recall, it was evident as early as thirteen (13) years of age. Flashing back, I truly realized that I was an average hater. This is common with stubborn people who are at the peak of trying one thing for the other. At such a tender age for an African child, I always developed a detestation for things I worked on and was never praised for. This meant that one must be lucky, contrary to such a position that is deserving of praise only for things worth of praise.

You clearly notice that a child rarely hates something for good, average haters. Every child at this stage should be in a position to learn and unlearn. There is a great degree of urge at thirteen years of age to focus on what is important to learn. The very focus in my life, to bless every other step ahead of me implied that colleagues, friends, and mentors occasionally pronounced a bright future for me. Saved by the thoughts of people around me, time was the only weapon used to monitor the great strides in my life thereafter.

You have the responsibility to live life to the fullest, from a day's thought to a lifetime of dreams. When do you dream of doing better in a situation that failed to yield results yesterday?

How To Objectify A Dream in Life?

Any dream is meant to be actualised based on the result attained at the end of work. Such results are obtained from a long-term consideration of hard work, making a lot of sacrifices, and taking very risky endeavours to a greater extent yet to be announced in a minute's pronouncement of success. I have typically experienced the two different settings of a dream that are manifested when an individual gets asleep and in a day's reflection setting before one falls asleep. All this requires a very calm environment for the mind to work out the dream phenomenon.

The interpretation of a dream;
D - Divine
R – Revelation
E- Encompassing
A- Artful
M- Minds

God is the author of life, clearly directing the impressive idea of a dream that is the true aspect of divine instruction. No human being starts a dream without a close encounter with God's love and guidance. Imaginably, who on earth would sleep and create a dream situation for themselves only to realise they were asleep at the end of the dream? Absolutely no one can do this.

In the middle of the dream, a lot of issues stand in question without clear answers since revealing the composure of its kind is quite sceptical at this time. However, it takes a brave spirit of an individual to believe this real life supernatural journey. Individuals who fail to visualise the possibility of something that has not gone evident in their life before, whatsoever will not continue to the heart of the now unknown success of the dream.

What is held within your dream ought to be very dramatic if you own the possible version of anything in life. We need to accept that there are great things hidden away from the human eye, only found in a dream. There is great potential in thinking through every event in your life, carrying the day's reading of what just happened. The artful consideration is remarkably fundamental because man performs ideally due to the ability to accept any results. The just God that you and I serve has given us only what we can handle at a time.

You may ask yourself how this comes to pass: look on please. It is bit by bit. Through small things in life, you are designed to build on and therein provide a ground smart enough to be relied on to handle big things and, later great things. Occasionally, many people, both young and old, want what they have not laboured for. This gesture is always not thought after, having earlier on rejected the path of hard work to account for the probable time spent doing something.

Indeed, this must be backed by the faculty of consciousness and thought, the mind to hold up. The sole reason for accepting a dream is not to ever go practical in covering up the human conscience. If you kindly want to taste events that hurt most in life, try covering up your conscience. In the event that we decide to cover up the sense of right and wrong, it is most likely to be a postponement of what will hurt the mind and body when life gets normal.

Most people do this knowingly, and a few act out of sheer ignorance of the interpretation of time for the next day. I have grown up seeing people drinking alcohol to forget tragic incidents of the day. In 2005, my teacher of the science subject in primary five said that people drink alcohol to forget problems.

In the African setting of the African Traditional Society, it was the men that always got involved in hard work that later meant family problems being placed on their shoulders. At the tender age of twelve (12), I did not agree to disagree over such thoughts since there was less time to internalise such situations. Truly, the party involved would momentarily tend to forget the problem for a while, say in the evening hour of the day. Evidently, in the minds of these individuals, the same problem will show up again the next morning.

Based on the above inscription, it is agreeably true you and I must respect conscience to see every person's dreams come true. A dream come true is objectified at the very end point of a seemingly uninterrupted situation next to realise someone was dreaming. Nonetheless, the uninterrupted scene ought to be interrupted at one gaining the bigger urge to put into practice what they are dreaming about.

A dream met when one is awake is the best, especially for beginners (first dreams). This is easy to recall at the end of everything, especially for one to keep a smart record of what actually got revealed. I personally first had two dream scenarios of the sort all at twenty-three (23) years of age while studying for a bachelor's degree in Human Resource Management at Makerere University Business School in Uganda. Honestly, I did not think about moving down from a triple-decker bed to search for a pen and paper in a bid to write down something.

All that moved my life the next morning was the self-confidence to wake up in the morning and start to write down the probable titles of the book in question; "A Family for Us: Together against Domestic Violence." The dream was the revelation of this title for the book I wanted to write. The spectacular part of your dream is at the edge of a number of trials you give it for everyone to really accept it. In other words, the time to work on the dream and the final product of the dream avail room for acceptability.

By God's grace, I had the capacity to recall the big dreams of my Life the next day. This may not be common to most people who are experiencing their first encounter with a dream. Perhaps one would be doubtful of such unusual situations in life. With an everyday situation placed in a position of the urge that builds on only means life is itself a dream experience. How many times do you think about things you possess that empower a hidden course of action in the mind?

You should, however, think of your position before what you want to possess in life. This enables an individual to anticipate only that in the measure of their respective capabilities to deal with a specific situation. Positioning yourself necessitates consistent unusual conduct that equips you with the weapon of acceptability. Very few people have had genuine dreams because of the willingness to believe in all they got revealed to. There is an obvious question that ought to linger in every person's mind at the end thought of the dream.

Who is Bruno to accomplish and perhaps actualise the dream? We are reminded of events in life that continue to remind us of who we are, given a clear perspective of what to achieve out of the dream.
Surely, this must be one of the occasions in life that call for maximum discipline to be able to shield the dream of every individual, behaviour of the dream. It is also the discipline of working out the dream without expecting a supervisor around your work.

Tame The Behaviour Of The Dream

On the night of Saturday, 7th January, 2017, at 2:30 am, I had a dream, "The Vigilante Dream." The dream is a clear manifestation of what it takes to tame the behaviour of any other person yet to dream. The dream involved nine (9) characters comprised of six (6) females and three (3) males. Initially, I had been involved in constant prayer, seeking that God reveal to me His mysteries.

A mystery entails a lot of things that my own effort would not reach at the break of a very busy day characterised by hard work. The best resource in this case is a sober mind, which re-echoes the need to respect conscience. It is from this ground that I felt confident of what was revealed to me in a supernatural mystery. This carried the meaning of a dream, though different from the past two dreams.

As a key player in this dream, there is a greater task ahead of this journey. A few days prior to this dream, I had listened to the moving story of Vigilantes published through The Nation (2015) in a bid to curb crime in Palestine. The earlier intention was to eliminate crime among Palestinians. With a clear image to the public, it was meant to contribute to making peace as a secret body aiding the police as a law enforcement body.

In a rational consideration, I vowed to apply a similar mechanism better fashioned to fight Domestic Violence and HIV/AIDS.

Over a gap of three days, after the story circulated into my entire life, it all seemed itching for the world against violence to swing into action. The pre-eminence of hesitation to pass the story to a better version full of action was quite unbelievable.

I kept at the back of my mind that time would not wait, thus gaining the urge to move on to face the challenge placed before me. The challenge of this nature is to date visible in a shape so identical for divine instruction. In view of my young age at the time, the issues involved in this challenge were truly a lamp stand to lift a specific beam of light in someone's life.

Actions drawn to bless other people turn out to be a blessing for the key actors in such a scenario. Acceptance was already part of my life's trail, especially focusing towards the direction of making peace in a high resonance to time. One may consider more unstable environments for the next path to realise the dream echo because they wonder over the instance of hesitation.

Coated with a prayer to always crown my day, this day, God proved His unconditional love to me. Whatever you and I start on in goodwill for other people is not our own but God's. The ultimate prayer that marked the start of the dream was from Ephesians 5: 1-2 on the previous day, Friday 6th January, 2015. "Therefore be imitators of God as dear children. And walk in love, as Christ also has loved us and given Himself for us, an offering and a sacrifice to God for a sweet-smelling aroma."

Important to note is that children and women are a great gift from God; thus, they do not deserve to suffer under the sour taste of domestic violence. At exactly 2:30 a.m., the dream started rolling in the pipeline of a beautiful mind while I was asleep on my bed.
Unfortunately, one of the girls named Macklin was raped as a young person and a pupil at the time of the misfortune. This could have appeared bad, but in the character of the dream, the right image of girls and women facing violence was very instrumental to deal with.

In the event that I was positioned at the view of one of my 2015 year's resolutions, progress for every life encounter meant a great deal of attention.

Every letter in the word 'PROGRESS' signified;

P- Positioned
R- Rightly
O- Of
G-Greatness
R- Relying
E- Entirely on
S-Selfless
S- Strides

This further triggered all my life to see peace for the girl no matter what it would take. With other family members converging in a quake of what everyone's eyes could not believe, temporarily, the whole environment circulated with a lot of confusion and fear for anything.

At the point when all characters involved the dream got silenced by the challenge at hand, I picked on my cell phone only to raise the police patrol department. Gracefully, the police patrol officers responded very urgently to the matter earlier raised to them, which prompted them to drive fast to the scene of the crime (my own family home).
The alleged victim of sexual abuse was then rushed to the hospital to crucially ascertain the rape incident and facilitate the acquisition of a medical certificate for the rape victim in question.

Later, at the hospital, a roll of quarrels unfolded among family members in a bid to justify whose responsibility it was to take care of the children back home. Different individuals started pointing sharp fingers into the faces of their colleagues in quest of the right answer to the ugly scenes of the day. You realise that every child has a right to be looked after at all stages of life.

Grooming a child would not necessarily require full-time attention from a biological parent, albeit might attract a community setting that holds the morality to protect every vulnerable persons. Have you and I not met some younger people on the way to work, only to offer a piece of advice for what is right in a specific field of life? This holds the smart detail of being a parent to a child or a younger person in this regard.

We need to weigh the magnitude of protecting a child from a stranger. Quoting the example of the dream, the girl child for heaven's sake or for humanity's sake, alas to the alleged perpetrator of sexual abuse. Join me in imagining the kind of thoughts that went all around the mind of this young girl while aboard the police patrol pick-up cabin. This must have been so undesirable to the future in a measure of time to come. Very many girls and women face the same challenges that seem unanswerable.

To the young boys, young adults in tertiary institutions of learning, and old men, rape is not part of the stages of growth that a woman must go through. Your girlfriend or even your wife is not positioned for rape or marital rape, respectively.

"The caretakers of the child in question ought to have been apprehended for child negligence to a great extent," one would say. The preventive measures of anything bad are in the way you and I use the time given to us in life, as far as balancing work time and time spent with our children at home.

On return from the hospital, the innocent girl that represents millions of girls and women facing sexual violence lay on a hospital movable bed that was lowered off the police car. Inopportunely, many of these cases go unreported to such agencies on a day-to-day basis. The now survivor was covered with a white bed sheet stretching from the feet to the neck area. This served quite controversial to the onlookers with my elder sister, Emily Musiimenta, who exclaimed, "She has passed on!"

Further detail of what the bed held was a pile of drugs on the left side of the pillow, Antiretroviral (ARV) drugs which shocked my sight. I screamed up to say, "Why all this for this young girl?" She was infected with HIV/AIDS! Who on earth would want to see someone go through such an ugly situation? You must surely see the value of time ahead of this girl; the quality in this time should be fronted against violence.

The life of this girl was moved from the lane of good health to a lane with drug dependency for life. Take time to identify yourself with such a girl's life getting to realise at their youthful stage, a stranger raped and infected them with HIV/AIDS. We may never feel what unprivileged people go through, not until there is the same issue around us, with our family members or people we love. In the bigger picture of this situation, hope for justice was restored by a courageous remark from my younger sister Moreen Musiime.

She empathically suggested, "Take the survivor of sexual violence to your organisation (Domestic Peace Foundation Uganda) for further assistance."

As I exclaimed, yes, this should be done the next morning first thing before anything! My biological father, the late Mr Besiga John, dishearteningly added, "Where on earth will you find the perpetrator in this case, the man that raped the girl and also infected her with HIV/AIDS?" Indeed, this was a very disheartening remark to make before the victim of sexual violence. This did not appear in the dream by accident; it carries the evidence of many people meant to discourage troubled individuals, victims of domestic violence from attaining justice against their alleged perpetrators.

It is how girls, women, and a few men suffocate in their bedrooms, schools, workplaces, and recreation centres due to one discouraging voice. At times such discouraging voices go unrecognised due to the disguised shape in their appearance. The environment in which crime happens may solely discourage victims of sexual violence. Hidden places, dark corners of the bedroom, and board rooms of very important organisations serve as a curtain to tell someone of whose concern it should be.

You and I should stand out of such crowds to encourage the masses in our communities that justice covers shame. Why does a perpetrator of such violent cases feel confident to walk in the corridors of a specific street in town today? They believed that the victims of the circumstance would not say anything. The thought after implication under marital rape means that men are entitled to having sexual intercourse with their wives at all times. This has, on other occasions, crossed to house boys raping their female bosses.

The result has always been that their husbands should never find out, implying that everything in the house would be set ablaze. This reminds me of a story I candidly listened to in a queue at one bank on a Saturday morning back in 2011. Three men met outside the bank in Mbarara District, Uganda, and entertained themselves in the idleness that purportedly engulfed the situation of waiting for the bank to open for work. It seemed these men shared some characteristics of relentlessly chasing after girls and women for sex.

This was yet to be proven beyond doubt under their filthy conversation that was made up of perverse utterances. One of them had, in the past years laboured as a housekeeper at one of the most prominent people in their area; a Member of Parliament of the Republic of Uganda at the time. In the absence of the Honourable Member of Parliament (MP), who always left for the busy district of Kampala where he spent over two weeks, the housekeeper admired the wife of the MP.

Day by day, the man intentionally drew his feelings closer to the beautiful female boss. With respect to time, there was a better relationship between the housekeeper and the wife to the MP that was yet to turn out unbelievably true. All in the sight of the woman was a hard-working housekeeper and a very special, innocent man who was believed to prove all time well spent at work.

One fateful day, it was the innocent woman and the ever hard working housekeeper left at home. In the event that she watched the television, leaving the housekeeper to go on with his mundane business, the normal business ended at seeing this man close the back door. However, there were no big questions to ask as she continued with her best position to satisfy what her eyes saw on the television.

The well-known humble housekeeper sat next to the female boss like there was a secret yet to knock her ears.

The secret was indefinite, not until the man had his boss suffer rape. Things of the sort have happened before, but it is our responsibility to stop their reoccurrence.

The other two characters that were listening all along made click sounds with the touch of the middle and thumb fingers. I was a very young adult at nineteen (19) years of age back in 2011. I truthfully did not believe my ears. As I lay in surprise at what such men wanted for the next hour in life, the alleged rapist happily remarked, "She instead developed fear and told me not to say this to anyone." In a clearer description of what this meant, the female boss felt that if the husband got to learn of the rape case, all tables would be turned upside down in the house.

All was assumed that the MP would consider the wife to have been cheating on him with the same man or even other men, thus the call for silence. It is believed to be the environment that surrounded the scene of the crime that perhaps hindered the wife of the Member of Parliament from seeking justice. Someone has been in the same situation before; today marks the end point of this with them, but for the world to value the quality time of seeking justice.

The situation you are in today is not your fault, but the future should be your concern. Let no one determine your destiny by discouraging you from making the next stride in speaking out the truth of a bad situation. Having heard the discouraging and disheartening comment from my father in the dream, I angrily responded this perpetrator was not the best athlete in our area (hometown in Mbarara District), literally meaning that he was not so fast to escape the arm of the law in Uganda. "He would be brought to book," I added.

There is not any human being that has stood to discourage me in life, especially claiming that it is not time for something. Discouragements can only materialise where you have no capacity to take on the challenge.

How will you fail to take on the challenge when you believe something is possible? At this point of the dream, the vigilante is needed to report such cases of domestic violence and HIV/AIDS. At every village level, one individual should be positioned strategically under a Community Watch Mechanism to curb such incidents of Violence, specifically domestic violence.

Aided by a toll-free telephone line, there shall be fast and speedy mechanisms to envision successful reporting in a world full of Domestic Violence and HIV/AIDS. Women in this dream signify a blessing to humanity and hold the capacity to watch over the growth of humanity. Unbelievably, most women have been put down and left with less love and no peace. With facts embedded in time, start to love your wife, your girlfriend, and your daughter to the extent of fully empowering them for a reliable future, and we shall live to recount their good deeds. Children re-echo the position of being silent victims of domestic violence and HIV/AIDS.

With the involvement of six (6) women of the nine (9) characters in the dream this clearly showed me that women should accept to champion the Campaign of fighting against Violence worldwide, including girls in schools. Objectifying the dream started at 2:40 am when I realised there was a great need to start working to shine a light on the face of women and children as silent victims of Domestic Violence and HIV/AIDS.

This dream was actualised the day I founded a community-based Organisation, Domestic Peace Foundation Uganda (DPFU), on Tuesday, 21st December 2015. This dream also served as a mystery of peace that God revealed to me. By 21st December 2021, DPFU had directly supported 1,085 lives to combat domestic violence in Mbarara city, thus directly impacting the lives of 212 men, 211 women, and 574 children and indirectly impacting over 5,000 people with free services.

Acting To Meet The Archive Of Great Dreams

A great dream should signify that you are closer to something greater than you think. In other words, you are not yet at the finish line of such a race; however, there is a measurable distance to run through. Start to live a life of prayer and positive achievements. Though these achievements may appear small at some point in life, there is never a bad start for one to achieve great dreams.

Great dreams come to unveil the most possible solutions to life's challenges that are exceptionally meant for those that live a faithful lifestyle in particular fields. Most things that appear in a great dream mean some part of one's life encounter and experience in the past. This opens up a calmer atmosphere for the fulfilment of something that earlier appeared in your life. Based on this fact, God is ready to open you and I the treasurers of any dream that is considered great only if we trust Him. In other words, if you and I struggle, God will use us.

You do not need to trust God for a dream in Life, though God wants you to trust in Him for a great dream in your life. This sounds fundamentally uplifting to only people that are willing to work passionately to see positive change in life. You must have built the capacity to sustain the practicability of a great dream for God to reveal such a mystery to us. We hardly learn of our full capacity not until there is the self-realisation of what our hearts cherish most.

Dreams answer the how part of things to anticipate in the near future. It is how you want to do something that initially steers up greatness in it. Ideally, if you and I want peace, what is important is how to make peace and not who made peace and when they made peace.
The philosophical meaning of PEACE is:

P- Place
E- Every
A-Answer
C-Coated with
E- Empathy

You will do good things because you prefer the same to be done to you. A dream is positive and portrays the need for those around you to pay attention for them to see its roots.

To trust yourself is to do that based on to mean trust. The ideas most people rotate around mean a lot to them but nothing to everyone else. This is very okay in the pursuit of putting the idea to work, and so is a great dream. People have dreamt greater than we have done before, but what they dreamt about in practice is the biggest question to answer. Holding to mean the right thing to do; tell someone about the dream, put it in practice for other people you did not tell to notice and believe you one time dreamt great in life.

Let every dream be a representation of a better life ahead of us, a perfect reflection of who you are and the shape you have put the world in by design. Several minutes away, people monitor the dream of life for self-interests, yet the people dreaming qualify themselves for a second position. Through this, I have had all my great dreams position other people in the first seats as I go for the second seat; so remarkable.

CHAPTER TWO
Ruled by the Human Shadow: Failure to Start

You cannot run after your own shadow, suggestive to say you have no excuses for dwelling on the past to say the future. In the projection of what your shadow holds, the future should not be a mistake of unfolding events. Specific situational events appear to rotate around human life, and given an ear, they protrude into the playing field of human success. You may have never asked yourself a question like this: why does someone anonymous to my life decide to judge me ahead of time in the event of limited or no knowledge about my past and present life?

Well, guided by the 1995 constitution of the Republic of Uganda, Chapter 4 Article 29 Section 1 Subsection (a) holds the inscription: Every person shall have the right to freedom of speech and expression, including freedom of the press and other media. To this fact, human beings know of the protection offered by the law for anything therein as also inconsiderate of its worth. By this guaranteed principle of the law, allow someone to speak against your life because we have a clause that protects them in the 1995 constitution of Uganda.

Perhaps other countries have a similar position on the law. Nonetheless, stand to protect your dreams by being mindful of what certainly makes sense for you. People who know your intentions get close to you and start to draw the curtain of fear away. I have lived to make peculiar strides in life because I hear all speak but listen to only one among the ten people I may have heard from by the break of the day.

Time has often defended me to reaffirm this quotation that I have relied on: mental discipline is positive indiscipline. In most cases, you ought to do your best against your neighbour's questions and strange remarks simply because they do not believe something is possible. In other words, they have not been in your position before and will never be in that position because you are younger than them; nothing beats time in the backdrop of human work.

On Friday, 1st September 2017, my life got excited about the presumably unfair intentions of man for the future I already have tested. Casting my mind back to the memories of the day, I had had a long day of discipline guided by a specific work ethic like other days have previously manifested in my life. With a clearer vision of the best things I want for my wife and children in the future, more resourceful information is the order of the day. This has always been gathered considering the different sources of information one decides to listen to.

For my sake, the British Broadcasting Corporation services, commonly referred to as BBC, is the radio station that carries out research and has reliable information for my heartbeat. Supported by a brand new smartphone branded Techno W5 Lite at the time, accessibility to listening to BBC became as realistic as recording that piece of information my ears fell in love with. In anticipation of a better walk from the office at 4:30 pm in the evening, my hand that had gone through a long time laid on the table appending signatures to different documents grew stronger.

Supported by the break in my working hours, I hurriedly stretched my hand into a packed bag only to get my earphones ready to set off for an evening walk. This (trekking) empowered me to live better with the meager resources in my possession at the time.

I had completed my Bachelor's degree in Human Resource Management from Makerere University Business School, awaiting graduation due 18th January 2018. With all that in mind, the money needed for my transport to and from the office was not fully spent since I only boarded a boda-boda in the morning and walked back home in the evening.

In the event that all this had become the routine of my days out for work, within my mind while walking on the road was an unclear image of who keeps their eyes around me. It is such a pertinent response for any persons to recognise that they have got only one pair of eyes on their face. Nevertheless, many other pairs of human eyes and animals are watching over and around your head with one pair of eyes. I believed so.

Truly, you and I have only two sockets in the human skull. Therein, our intentions are to draw our focus on things we can afford to see and defend using the human brain. Appreciating time with things we see, the eyes that see, and the brain in control of sight in there. Extraordinary gains are absolutely met by extraordinary individual steps to go where other people have never gone amidst being monitored by people you hardly know.

We continue to live seeking pieces of advice from our superiors who did not do what we are doing at our current age. Considering this evening walk with earphones directed to my ears, someone believably superior watched over me without my knowledge. I acknowledge the possible dangers associated with the long-term use of earphones amidst compromising safety on the road. His superiority grew with intentions to communicate to many people against ways for which his own conscience were vices.

The day I received a piece of information pertaining to my conduct was on Friday, 1st September 2017, as my elder brother Benedict arrived home from a tiresome journey from Buhweju district through Bushenyi district to Mbarara district. On reaching home, he exclaimed to my sister Emily as he put off his shoes from his feet: "Emily, are you similarly using earphones like Bruno as I have just been told by a friend of mine!"

This grew into a bigger discussion as Benedict looked into my eyes to reaffirm his position for what he indeed was told. "My friend clearly informed me of your bad behaviour to have opted to use earphones while walking on the road, wondering what you always listened to," remarked my elder brother. I am certain that my brother's communication carried good intentions, especially for my safety as a pedestrian. Ahahahaha, I laughed at him and spontaneously got bitter having had from him. Very many questions started running in my mind about who their friend could be and what they do.

The confidence of my response was if he knew I was listening to BBC radio after a day painted with unbelievable achievements, he would never judge my actions. Scenarios like these could have manifested in your life before. Some people recognise our presence in society only when we appear in the realms of glory.

To date, the anonymity of that character in question is believed to be like the individual that we ought to open booklets to determine our fate. In these booklets, we shall tell the whole world and put on record their uninformed and ill intentions for our success. Things that were not happening in the past included listening to BBC with a smartphone that was bought using proceeds from sales made towards the second book I authored in my early days at University back in 2015. The book was entitled A FAMILY FOR US: Together against Domestic Violence.

I have for days wondered the reasons someone would consider never to identify us in bad times but want to judge us in our good times of the day. Unfortunately, the friend of my elder brother never told people of my bad conduct on the road where I was using a small phone branded itel with numerous buttons on it. He perhaps never realised I did not afford to buy one for myself. Your beauty is in detail in your mind, and a few facts appear on a reflected mirror to your face. Today, many people are superior to you in reference to age, and you are superior to their achievements at your age.

Humanity should build on set targets to focus on matching with the greatest achievers in respect to social, political, academic, economic, and transformative change. This shall deter you and I from chasing the shadow of the visible achievers in the world, not to perform their way but rather perform better to be record breakers and achieve things our way.

Simply A Try Makes You A Victor

Offer ten minutes of the weekend, holiday, or honeymoon to make the rest of your life's journey admirable to all people. It is as though a young man met a beautiful girl at their workstation as their first client. He most likely says a lot of sweet words, trying to penetrate the life of this beautiful girl. Time and time again, such a young man has had their success story told at a wedding ceremony with that girl in their future that we may be witnesses to.

Unexpectedly, the young man will have done the needful, only leaving their future love to build the image of the probable man in their mind. Conscience would demand to know who these young men really are and to detail why they chose to say certain words to them.

In a real sense, the young man had never met such a beautiful being but had always envisioned such a great day.

There is something for a few people in acceptance to sit in the pavilion awaiting a football match to start. In the closely comparable event, there is anything for all people that await the results of the most anticipated football match back at home. The spectators in the pavilion choose to be fun to different teams as they selfishly wish the win for their respective teams. At any occurrence of a loss or win to the game, all will have seen and believed in what happened then.

Anything to land in the hands of all false believers back home, doubtfully, they will go with the results of the earlier missed football match. Victory unfolds for reasons among which the achieving hero is covering up the time they failed to reach the peak of success. Even for the fear that oftentimes builds up in your mind, the most important will be trying to go over something.

In 2005, at the age of 13, in a school setting, food that was not served on the dining tables from the school kitchen was illegal for one to consume. That in question guaranteed that even external food meant for individual pupils never had smooth entrance into the school compound. This situation opened up every other pupil to demand for materialistic items from their parents and guardians.

Brave a pupil I was to swiftly gather the courage to answer my classmates given they had problems which I today perceive as challenges. In the power to solve their problem, we all took on the challenge. By far, this crossed from life outside class to the subjects I pursued in primary five. I wanted to read and excel as a medical doctor, that I insisted on reading textbooks articulating mathematics and science theories at the helm of failing like I never attended mathematics and science classes.

Through giving in to struggle for what I never was, time opened the best mechanism to identify peculiar things in life for an African child. The demand for a voice to reach out to parents on occasioned school visits sprung out of me. All was to vie for a leadership position that would allow me to communicate with parents and pupils congregated in the school's main hall.

Democratic tendencies appeared too harsh like dark clouds in the sky on the days of choosing class leaders. I prayed for such glory, though I never saw the light of the right leadership paths in my class. Trying occasion after occasion proved no positive response from the young delegates; however, pupils in class simply did not want a strict and principled leader. It is always early to give up on making your voice heard. I tried speaking multiple words in the English language in class where other pupils kept silent, on the playfield and in my environs.

This reaffirmed the courage to lead before my classmates to the extent of having trust among many built-on expressions made in the English language. Deep within my heart, confidence engulfed everything I lay hands upon for success. Every time pupils realized the visitation day for our parents drew nearer, ceremonial friends were made. Many of these pupils identified with me in great trust of my English speaking prowess, which convincingly meant I similarly would write in readable English language. The greatness in me that the world has continually been astounded by credibly started then.

Since then (2005), I have always gone to school for talent realization and skills development, never lovingly for academics. Can you imagine such a revelation at a point when I am currently pursuing a doctorate degree in Global Studies and majoring in Peace and Conflict Studies at Tokyo University of Foreign Studies in 2023?
People will deny you many chances and push you for a life opportunity to lean against for the rest of your success.

These pupils to date as adults have what I had discovered but have never discovered it in themselves. You are a unique being given that you try out that you never ever did. Certainly, I did not know the best of English language but I was better than most of them; they never accepted the challenge to reach victory. All of them presented problems which I made challenges to easily face and go over as a victor. Writing became timely and part of my life in the event that pupils around me lived to communicate to their parents.

In a few minutes, one pupil at a time met with me to present an outline of what they wanted from their parents, from which I drafted letters. In life, people might fail and continue to offer a starting ground for your success. Every human being is pertinent to the realization of a brighter day ahead of us. Without this outline of materialistic and scholastic items like football and books, often written on a small piece of paper, I never would have discovered the talent of writing as far as being a philosophical writer.

Having gained fame in such a field of work at that time, the capacity to build on the few words in my English vocabulary grew as I tried to write more letters on their behalf to their parents. It is not enough to stop where you are; someone better and in the making is getting set to go for a similar race; my actions the next day sounded thus. The acceptance to go wrong in existent imperfections sets the human ability for any trials in life.

There was no grammatical correctness, no paragraphs that rounded it all for true imperfection. The door and room for the world to correct me lived then at a time I tried my luck. Tomorrow is no time for failure; rather today is the time to try.

Many parents read good pieces written in the English language but went on to understand believably it was their children at school. Hardly did they recognise my presence in ink on a piece of paper. Honourably, I improved my writing skills, and unimaginably parents thanked their children for the remarkable improvement in articulating words in the English language through letter writing. We are meant to answer the call to time every day we live.

Your greatness carries away the imaginations of grounded efforts in trying to do things everyone else has disregarded to be possible. Many people have told me of the times I had a hand in what they see as successful, I have to work extraordinarily to prove their point. The next year (2006), I was promoted to primary six, where the teacher of English language used to pick on seemingly absent-minded pupils to read texts in English.

The day he served me with the book with inscriptions in the English language authored by Ogundipe to read, the whole class went silent. This was not for the worst, but awaiting my moment of trial to read. Quite fascinatingly, I stood and held the book ahead of my eyes, thus taking the reading. There was a comment from him; tried. Thereafter, a pupil and classmate, Felix Mutabingwa Bwikizo, who happened to speak fluent English, touched my left hand as I sat close to him only to remark, "Bruno, You read excellently with a good piece of accent in the English language."

Above all failing grounds in the past, for this reason forth, I started to try speaking good English. The teacher of English language gave me a push to start speaking good English, supported by encouraging words from Felix. Many people around us have been shown the right direction in which to take for necessary moments of trial. Moments full of trials without resilient and constant reasons to try again are simply empty.

The emptiness in some trial endeavours is not far from pride. We deservedly should accept good remarks for what lies in our achievements, keeping in mind the limit of motivators in life. Every rich man and woman has worked to get more money day in day out. Nonetheless, after getting the money targeted for the day, the money seizes to motivate them. They would rather work harder to get other sources of income.

I challenge you to try more times for any remarks made towards the day's achievement for you to keep the current trophy of victory. The world is like a competitive arena where credit is given to the first record-breakers because they are the best we know today. The only aspect in human life that determines individual success as far as being a new record-breaker is time. Human beings younger than me by a year outstandingly serve as the only positive and biggest threat to me in life. S/he will stand in a better position to try out all I have done and, by far perform better than me.

Exposing performance based on making a stride to try out something brings this into perspective. My friend was one year and nine months younger than me at the time. Considering what I did at her current age with limited bandwidth for the internet to do research, limited resources to support my cause, the rigidity of society to accept my ways, and no one to look up to for the groundbreaking activity. There is a possibility of making an assessment of the challenges I met then and possible solutions to them today.

In support of a more open and welcoming society with a greater bandwidth for the internet to do research people to look up to like me, s/he absolutely will be a better record breaker. Notwithstanding, that it is harder to surface on today's billboards as the new record breaker without trying more occasions than you have failed to succeed in.

The Person in You

You seized to be an empty vessel the day you were created in your mother's womb. Without question the environment before, during and after birth supports the mental ability of human actions today. The environment around humanity ranges from what they eat to things that go on around them.

At the age of eight (8) the environment around me guided my reasoning to recognise myself as a spitting image of my father. To date, I resemble my late father by looks, that most people also associate the work of my hands to be a resemblance of him.

I believe this was even a hotter discussion as early as the time I was born, confirming to my visually impaired father that I was his biological child since we looked alike. Remarks and questions from the public on whether I was as intelligent as my father were not obvious remarks and questions. Being an ambitious young boy, the best response served to satisfy every other demand from the public: yes I am as intelligent as my father. This meant that I would start to compete to be better than my father, though not evidently so.

Working around the clock to see myself as a better person than my father was a waste of time. He had his life to lead, and most importantly, I was different from him. Competing with my father was the worst thing to ever do, and I have stopped doing it since then. You probably share situations where, even in your adulthood, competition lies between you and your neighbour.

Forgetting I was all around a different person was a losing ground in the first place. We always waste time and start to camp in other people's lives, leaving our life unattended. It is even better to compete with yourself than to compete with other people.

Appreciate the position of life in you, view life with your own pair of lenses, and tell of the changes that go on in your own life. In a scenario where an athlete competes with himself, they will be the best. Daring to compete with other athletes, they evidently admire them and want to be like them. We should always want to be better people, not like other people, by considering the identity in us. The inner being in us are the roots of small things that are the sole difference that we really are.

Our roots explain the virtue of holding the truth in depth of paying small debts in life. ROOTS
R-Reality
O-Of
O – Owed
T – Times
S – Symbolically

These debts are due for payment on principles of time, with a given period of time accepting to multi-task and score positive results in all fields of work. These small things include allocating time in fractions of the whole day to pay time predefined debts. There is a debt to pay to your parents, friends, children, siblings, workstation, strangers, wife, girlfriend, boyfriend, husband, and children, and home chores like cooking and washing clothes clean.

Time ought to be given to all important things around you. Through multi-tasking in a day, we learn what we do best yields passionately to prove who we are. There are many gifts that we are born with but possess because we know them. It is ideal to interpret a specific gift in your life and more importantly, to use the gift to make a better day.

G - Granted
I – If
F – Found
T – Today

This meaning suits what a gift practically goes for. The gifts of life, like love, hard work, and victory, enable men to believe in themselves for whatever they set out to do.

Whoever has the intention to emulate such gifts in their work, there are considerably more things to put in place. Associating with everyone you encounter may not necessarily build up a supportive effort. It should be an in-depth analysis of academic achievements, learned practices, and considerable dynamism to achieve that you both admire. Comparability of specific associating factors builds a bridge of a unique relationship to support the innermost being of an individual.

Growing incidences of falling short of what is the right thing to do shows the outermost expression of human weaknesses being an inevitable aspect of life. You are not weak to collapse alone, and you should never be strong to stand with a friend leading you into a messy life. In the past, human weaknesses lived to test the time of every day, unlike today. What case is committed in facing inabilities in us and with us to find stronger leaning sides?

The sensitivity of going wrong has seized to be a fact to many young and old people today, aligning their mess to human weaknesses. Different means of friendship call for change in outlook views of the image one seemingly tends to portray. This happens for genuine intentions to appreciate a friend as a product of individual gifts. Close networked friendships and open networked relationships vary from distant networked friendships in factors embedded here.

Relationships attained through channels made by relatives within identical family backgrounds qualify to be called close networked friendships. Most of these relationships hold their foundation easily reversible from bad to good, though individuals in them hardly contain the mess around. Family meetings are called several times to have sanity prevailing over such relationships.

On this basis, joy is oftentimes short-lived to thereafter create room for distant networked friendships to emerge. At this lasting challenge of the relationship, individuals find a way to reach out to everyone else they come into contact with. The first character they find in the new party rules out a failing being in them to desperately meet a new life. Such relationships tend to last but are full of hatred and misunderstandings.

Hope is the only gift that keeps the relationship of this nature thus far. The uniqueness of open networked relationships is that individuals stand on the true merit of who they are. It is like standing across the bridge on a mountain peak where a bright crown of future successes appears. Then, everyone yearns to climb the mountain, so they walk away with the king or the queen in question.

Nonetheless, oftentimes, we do not consider the life one has led to climb the mountain as far as the mountain peak. Such an unintended friend ought to be extraordinarily patient with changing factors of the probable relationship as one climbs up the mountain peak. In respect to answering the choice of a remarkable king or queen, the patience of the intending friend is in itself an answer to all ever-existent questions.

In it, there are renowned virtues of restoration of the ideally missing facts with close networked relationships and distant networked relationships.

Comparability resurfaces to vindicate the paths of life ahead of these people in an open networked relationship. With it, manifestations of foresightedness stand real to all the people therein. For either the king or the queen at the top to resonate with the earlier intending friend, self-esteem, love, courage, hope, hard work, and patience are gifts that lie before, during, and for the future in perspective.

Notwithstanding, that now this relationship ought to attain more uniqueness, thus leading to direct other close networked relationships and distant networked relationships with time. The achievement in them holds a hidden agenda in two words: God fearing. All reignites the empowerment to wake up and work for the same cause, striving to meet life's demands.

In every human being, there is the desire not to feel belittled by life's situations. It is amazing that individuals possess desires to go for the best. As you and I continue to grow up, parents have lived to see a lot of things in us. You probably should be something is the statement of every parents' lips. You also see yourself for the same things, well, that ought to be a blessing rare to find. In most scenarios, we see something else in totality different from what our parents made of their anticipations.

Setting everything aside to tell of some things we have hidden from the eyes of people that bore us! It is strange an idea to consider but only a decision taken by courageous and unfailing minds of this world. Again, mental discipline is positive indiscipline. We ought to value ourselves before other people consider us valuable. In a greater sense, you and I should value ourselves more than any other people do to us, keeping all unfolding events constant.

Expounding on mental discipline carries with it a depiction of moral worth for individual minds, though rarely considered for groups of people. Feeding on a balanced diet does not absolutely incorporate beef for vegetarians. In the same vein, mental discipline does not call for adherence to every voice. Positivity of indiscipline with mental discipline rallies to defer what millions of people want for you to initially consider that you want for yourself.

Defensively, the attitude to call indiscipline positive in that nature holds its sensibility in yielding immense results at the end of the day. For in such instances, we dispel points of regret in life even when we could have trekked the paths of regret. Regrets elevate humanity in times of change. In anticipation of regrets, building false confidence lies in the hearts of many to say; she cannot make it there, or he will now start to fail, and they have lived for fate.

Emphasizing the pivotal point of regrets to be changed clearly tells of limited or no support in the past from family, friends, enemies, and colleagues. Holding to the fact that you accepted room to take your own path, diverting from the highway roads, unique things go with you. In us, dreams shall be born and nurtured for one to insist on walking alone. This does no harm to the world but uplifts the most ignored individuals and blesses them with a unifying image.

Worry not, at the time many people went against your will; but you set a precedent by keeping an open heart for the world. Someone you never considered your supportive pillar stands ready to celebrate the landmark of victory in the journey most despised but worth taking. You now start to get a following of two different groups of people, though all rally to support your cause. One group of people fear you for what you stood for, and respect is in question since they do not easily reach close to the person in you.

The other group of people respect you since they have the capacity to reach you but have nothing much to change in the person you are. Facts of such nature assist us to believe in the trueness of our being. There is something we never share, you possess and cannot lose, but by far, you have not discovered as of today. Go for that in you accredited to self-worth for unbelievable things many of us are capable of. The person in you speaks, and it is high time you listen to that voice; even the deaf hear such re-echo to beat time to relate, impact positively, and change the posture of civilization.

Young People Should Hold The Measure Of Success

In prospects that lie in the future of every young person, there is full anticipation of who they should be. It is all reliant on who we are today, starting with the moral aspect of life. In a range of thoughts to define the way most young people choose to conduct themselves will create the way for their future. It is in the morning of every day that you choose on the activities to undertake for the day.

Clearly, there are a lot of things that will make this day all a unique thing. Today is an event marked with its uniqueness that should be measurable. Situations may dictate what we decide to become in the near future; however, working through these situations matters most.

Physical strength is evident in the life of any young person you may have come across. It is meant to be used adequately to build the moral views of society. This appears hard to realize for the youngest generation in the world. The moral views of every individual are proportional to their health. The future is stronger based on your health as a young person.

Unhealthy lifestyles are impatient, which ultimately goes against seeing something grow from a lower level to a higher level. A youthful mind embeds room for patience to allow small things to expand. Patience is a virtue among young people that should stand all tests of time to contain frustrations, thus being hopeful of the true measure of success.

There are numerous ups and downs in life where every day's expectations may not turn out right. Working to fit a lifestyle painted with challenges puts you in a position full of possibilities to have a life designed with measures of success. Every day is a design you and I have laid down to show the world our enormous beauty. It depends on what is involved in designing the success measures in life, contrary to depending on who takes the lead in making designs.

An inspirational life of any individual young person is subject to a condition to tell of what was involved in doing today's product. Sustainability is all I value for any product of the actions to live the test of time.

Death is the most understood factor to inevitably win over the battle of earthly life; young and old, death is true. The success of a young person should be seen as early as they exist. Small things matter in every person's life to the extent of being the foundation for bigger things.

Continuity agreeably stands with sustainability which carries the only meaning of success in any ventures in life. You may continue doing your work and never sustain its success. I have always accepted that someone younger than me stands a better day of doing greater work to pave their way to success than myself. Through this, time mirrors the challenges I could have gone through for today's success which is all the younger person uses to beat me. There is no success without you giving in your moral views towards facts of the life you project ahead of today.

It is being morally upright to start with, realizing that someone better than us is always in the making. Certainly, without this consideration, you are living in a selfish and lonely world of thoughts and perhaps sitting on perceived success edges. There are more births in your locality than there could be deaths registered. Imagine you knew that every younger person stands to be a better success storyteller than yourself.

Impliedly, you support the younger people around you to see your good works live for the next day in a better environment. Young people, ensure that good ideas do not live and die with you. The future is most likely to be lived by the young people who work to see better developments beyond their vicinity.

Visionary minds carry with them stages of development at a vast scene for the minority of generations among young people. This is the perception of many people who have for long tried to keep away young people from doing what could publically be appreciated. The enemy of the success of a young person is an individual who lives in fear of their own perceptions. Going by your own instincts of success indeed makes you successful in that field of work towards landing on your career.

Success of a young person should rather be owned than possessed. In view of many failing platforms young people could have taken, the on-lookers insist on remarking; that it is unsustainable. Actions have oftentimes been put to the test on whether they are intentioned for success or failure.
With the societal setting of what is perceived to be individual or collective actions by young people, morals are the pivotal issue of notation. Our moral standards inform the environments of our lives to explain the paths taken towards success.

It is not a one-day activity to build the moral standards of a young person though it carries just one second in time of moral decay. Categorically, parents greatly create a moral stepping stone into the actions of young people today. It is, nonetheless, not to acclaim that as a young person, the success of your life depends on what you go for as against the possible indoctrination one could have experienced hither to. I would prefer young people jumping out of every nasty environment to living for frustration, abuse, crime, and laziness.

The world of success all over is an open venture, though for which a heavy price ought to be paid through hard work. Time demands every young person's mind to be put to task to think far beyond today. The planet I live on is a moving planet and possibly the same for you, young and old people. Make your movements heard through undoubted pieces of work and redefine successful endeavours in life.

It goes to mean that you divide your time for what lies in the priority zones of life. Only accord time to what brings profit at sunset unbelievably that even no other person believes in. With what I have always considered pertinent and accorded most of my time, results are way enormous. The passion and spirit to be successful is pre-eminently for fresh minds of a young person. It is then that one concentrates on doing the right thing instead of suffocating trying to do what was intended to be perfectly done yesterday.

This is possible given that you can measure the actions of your mind and heart in a moral beat alongside the consequences attached therein. Human life is by such implications a way paved with possibilities both good and bad. Young people are all successful albeit the difference lies in what you value to be the success of your life. Most importantly and preferably success built on individual principles reaffirms ones moral standard to be believed in.

The measure of such success is reliable and should be consistent no matter what goes around young people. Every success in its true image breeds challenges that matter for life to appear true in its ways. Your success is your challenge, though the world still calls it a landmark of success.

Contain The Situation Because It Is Purposeful

Sail through what appears to be a landmark of success, holding the truth of its existence to lie in the journey of maintaining it. The situation in which we are exercising time creates a difference that truthfully happens to go beyond measure. 'It is not possible' is a remark most people will make for them to refute things you meet in every situation. Having accepted to set the ball rolling in a specific career, activity or field of work, go for your destiny.

Take possession of every challenge in your life's career and start to look out for the purpose built therein. There is a position of chances in taking on difficult situations to arrive at the incense of containing them. The very first instance of working around the clock to keep moving given a business venture one could have undertaken, suggests a whole smart approach. Working to see the next day of any business, more currency points may be given out to a customer during the evening hours of the day. Later on, one tries balancing financial books, and they realise there is a shortage created in the business.

Ideally the customer in question may not be known to anyone in the business centre. The difference lies between the business books of accounts and the business attendant. In the earlier reasoning, the entire day was a smart event for the completion that lay ahead of the busy and hard-worked features.

Wherever you could have previously gone and whatever could have been embedded therein, tough times push for relaxed minds. Start to grace the achievement before you with a pure relenting mode. An achievement worth celebrating is built on bit by bit, where in between the specific bits of achievement, one should relax. This supports a self re-energising mind to identify what contributed to the success at scenes in the picture. It leaves us never to underrate what we go through that marks our success.

Every achievement in its likeness is sided with difficult times, which are a learning point. Learning is evident because of a problem you are aware of before your finish line. However, do not learn from the problems around you rather learn the preparedness of tackling every challenge. It is the preparedness that paves the way for us to work within actual environments of yet realizable purposeful situations. Having to live to test good and bad times as business opens up room to detect possible threats that may be hidden in the game of time.

There is no day you shall wake up only to live under false pretence of non-existent success expectations. Surprisingly, even people intending to commit crime, they largely anticipate to succeed in their endeavours. With this expression we all strive to do better than yesterday as light opens up to break the night's darkness. Success should not be the strategy to achieve sustainable measures of accepting the face of such a vivid situation.

Success holds a greater understanding of a prepared journey meant to see its destiny in active actors. I continue to reaffirm my role to anticipate a lot of changes leading to success based on the time invested to meet these changes. Certainty of these changes in changing times strongly demands human effort to contain.

You will be pleased to appreciate jubilations grounded in strides made over and above what seemed a cluster of impossibilities. It is far much by your purpose to live that you believe in what is challenging us. This points out the power to contain success with what has often times hindered other people from going where you are. It is believable that someone wants your position of success, however; no purpose to contain that they want. Determine the purpose of that you admire.

CHAPTER THREE
The Surpassing Power of Love

Every thought rooted in love shows bright colours in the most preferred faces of intending parties to love. It mounts on day after day, drawing two unique abilities of sight and attraction. One day away from your loved one would soon appear as the first night in a desert detention camp. Love is sensibly different from what most people have gone for; love for tomorrow tells it all. Through possibilities of the future to be lived by generations, there is a future destined for us.

The human race wants to live longer than ever without understanding the capacity to be loved more. It is so much in consideration of the invisible things could mean to shape the future. In view of sight, there is vision, and for attraction there is a point of common interest. Today, there is no choice other than to be a leader for oneself prior to serving other people as their leader. You want to go somewhere other people cannot go by themselves even when it is their dream to be there.

For them, it would most likely be in the blink of an eye that things of the sort would happen: peace to love, marriage, happiness, education, and good health. For many reasons, I decided to spend sleepless nights to think for and on behalf of human-led challenges. Well, it all carries the suspicious plan of supporting specific human-led and well thought out challenges. In this marked guise of support, great thinking emerges at the apex of work in a bid to understand the challenge in question.

Domestic Violence, for me, is one of the challenges to win over simply because of its systematic approaches, though severely hidden from overwhelming numbers of victims and survivors.

Unfortunately, counts of people distinguished by employable responsibilities and employer strength oftentimes dressed to question my intentions; for a challenge they never ever deemed a practical challenge. These ranged from my biological parents, siblings, civil servants, and then classmates from Makerere University Business School. "Why are you clearly coming out against domestic violence? You are a young man", they said on many occasions.

This is about age; supposedly to them old people had all it necessitated to make and enable peace. Beyond the age, the questions directed to me seemed not enough to limit my abilities. Secondly, my marital status that would soon face the litmus paper; preferably, it would be that only married people had to dance to this tune of putting an end to domestic violence. I, for one was not interested in young women for an intimate relationship at the time.

Over and over again, I wanted to see a happier generation where women would be respected to the extent of being believed for excellence, children being appreciated for work well done and men justly loving themselves for the sake of oneness in family homes. To put forward all this, implied that previously people who labelled themselves in a mere count of numbers to mean age of wisdom, time for me held something extremely different. I believed in my own practices to move an agenda guided by principles of love that re-echoes as the surpassing power of love.

Where they were married and could not stand for peace, Ideologies of posterity based on peace for others would then serve my right occupation. It has always been love for men and their material wealth over love for their wives and children. This often times propelled men to judge every woman only when bad omens took the stage in society and family.

With only the good times being viewed as great, a contribution made by and meant for men. Love was used as a tool to discrimination and so it was evident only for present days. Time demands from all directions continued to fall on deaf ears of gender inequality.

You would take a moment and want to see the fruits of your works; forever to be enjoyed by posterity. Love looks over to people around you for the identity they hold and does not yell at strangers who should deservedly live with us. Listen to your wife, husband and children at all times of the day and the night.

Measurable Love

Love is measured through our actions, especially based on places of first encounter with receptive hearts of these actions. There is no doubt that it is by chance to meet hearts ready to receive what you do before them for love. It is in great consideration of first impression that matters on whether you are to be loved back or not. In view of two men holding different identities, Jack and Adams who choose to meet many people in the same location.

On the first instance Jack arrives in a Mercedes Benz car for a party where Adams had previously arrived in a Land Cruiser Toyota car. The two had their invitation cards to the party without inscriptions of Mister and Missus (Mr. & Mrs.) put before their surnames. The organisers of the party already tell us that these are bachelors. Who knows the real intentions of every guest at the party? Most presumably, Jack and Adams could be the very guests set to find a girlfriend because of their actions.

Certainly there are female guests believed to have attended the party. One would be keen to conclude of whom between Jack and Adams best would assume a position of their future husband but to start with a boyfriend for now. The tool to use in measuring the suitability components of either male guest shall absolutely turn out to be the visible materialistic possessions to suggest riches or wealth.

However, this wealth placed in cars could at the end of the day not hold water. You and I may not rely entirely on such visible wealth with less proof in the eyes of a fragile girl. "These cars could have been borrowed from a car wash station in town", the unlucky girl would say. In a long wait this does not happen on the look of things, rather many girls get disassociated with the party as though they had made appointments with Jack and Adams.

The truth of actions is a reaction that later opens us to the consequences thereafter. In a few minutes contact addresses would be shared between the earlier mentioned two male guests and those who affectionately had luck. Such acts mean that the first steps taken in measuring the love yet to be lived and seen by the new girlfriends could emerge out of such scenarios. Wishing the best to such a relationship is important and could have produced some of the married couples we see today.

It is greatly important to further learn of what has become of such marriages and the characteristics under here. One of people that subscribe to this notion shall give things like food, material wealth and spiritual backgrounds for the full nourishment of the soul perhaps they intend to conquer. The other party receives that given to them and thoroughly digests it to the full capacity of satisfaction only to return more or part of the same to the giver.

Evidently enough is what has become of lovers where love stands a measure as far as what you choose to do for people you love in an intimate relationship. Over actions taken on by one partner in an intimate relationship; returns will most certainly sway our minds to living a life free of expectations based on love.

Listening To The Heartbeat Of The Oppressed

I woke up every day of my life only to notice many people making their way on the street. Without further concern to know who they are, I believed they all have issues that greatly bother them. For one reason or another we all want to meet specific targets in life, some set to solve daily aching challenges and others drawn to impress solutions already arrived at by people we hardly know. This could be in the name of achieving deadlines to the smallest of thoughts. For the sake of other people experiencing the dark side of life manifested with problems like death to mention.

Death of loved ones stands in the way of joy to find the extreme sense of where such people go. You now start to realise things that genuinely oppress human kind wherever in the world. It is death mind you not the cause of death. How many of us ever concentrated on the cause of death more than the dead themselves? Few of you could have respected hindering death in the future not to assume the strength of God.

It is not meant to please the atheists of the time, however; only for those that want to listen for the survival of the rest of humanity. The sensitivity of being oppressed also may fall on the other side of modernity to steer the wheels of family, most importantly for me to believe that such is happening even today. Well, let us mind of where the wheels are systematically leading the world in this capacity.

They at times have exposed who we are against women, children and limitedly against men. It is true that human beings have very tight schedules before they leave their bedrooms, within their living rooms and seemingly outside their family homes; man is indeed for himself.

Catastrophic missions get to register success stories over news on Televisions everyday though committed by busy people, men and women. These missions are intolerable to humanity and create an image of wild animals in people.

No and No for me!! The wild animals are beings with no respect of their capacity to influence positive achievements in life. The value imposed on every human being if they were to be sold off for shillings on stock markets; undoubtedly the exchange is unbelievable even for the worst economies today.

Stand alone to show a direction worth taking and keep moving for someone. One or two, they will follow you for a reason. There is always a reason for an alarm notwithstanding, where it is sounded. It is more understandable even for one that makes the alarm in the wilderness in quest for a saviour.

You can be saved by people you do not know and we are best saved by strangers because they did not attend village courts where strange vindications were put up against us. Trials in a wilderness often times save someone you did not know was living for previous days of their life.

Level your thoughts to this encounter with an old man you met in a wilderness where they had no food at all for some time. In the picture of a young person you have the strength to move around the bushes and pick on fruits for the day. It is not obvious that you will meet this vulnerable man. Impliedly the mind plans on how and when to consume the fruits gathered earlier on.

To save the life of the old man your mind stands on a balance of giving out of passion and receiving out of survival for the young man and the old man respectively. It will always be trivial to keep money in my wallet; not to have lost its possession as a result of the wallet falling out of the pocket but its inability to save someone whole life I am able to positively impact. People in need truly want the smallest share of the small things you possess, for it is to enable them survive for a day and could lastly appear a day of renewal in life. What is more important in life than to acknowledge the paths we took yesterday as turn to start afresh?

Humanitarianism is earned by many yet a few ought to sacrifice their little blood. In turn of things that triggered me to say it was important to say no to domestic violence; this did not mean that every day of my life carried with it the vivid manifestations of its wrath. Honestly, one would say I for one did not stand to perpetrate and be a victim who dared to lose their life every other day.

I wrapped up the small and different pieces of courage within me as a young man then at twenty two (22) years of age. Courage moved me to abandon my bed, friends, colleagues and family but for a journey that was yet to be covered in two months and thirteen days. It is then that I run down the valley and climbed up the mountain of passion to write my second book entitled, "A FAMILY FOR US; Together Against Domestic Violence".

In every aspect of truth, I had nothing of my own but the passion and love to influence the world around me. It is not a smile of your enemy that will change the day around, for they might intend to blind fold us. My enemy was never allowed to smile again because they started to see me grow to be the game changer to that effect. It all started in the mind, the reason I will tell everybody that nothing was but something is.

Humanitarianism is worth accepting as the best risk for me to take in life. This literally points out the sense of investing in people who have life and they will produce more life in other things a hundred times fold. One would consider the only property then in my life: an ox as vividly to serve a source of wealth today. I sold it off not because there was a need for money but rather a want for peace in life.

Peace will forever be peace considering one understands how it was achieved for others, they will want to keep it given they cannot improve it. With a few shillings in my pocket, there was room to change my mind on where to invest the money. I never dared to change my goal for my own sake in future. This tells you there is more in store for me because people around me will be different from who they were yesterday. Risking became the order of the day now to purchase a fourth hand placed mini laptop computer.

The little you have is what will impact on society and more of what you have will not be your own possession; more will always be shared amongst your wife and children. The computer in question did not store power for the next one minute. In a simple expression it was only powered on given that its charger was plugged into a powering socket. In light of this, a lot of heat was immediately generated from day one to the last day of writing the book. It was within the same time of writing the book that I was attending to my research for the book and class assignments commonly termed as field attachment.

My fellow internes often times wondered why I spent all my time on a computer and subsequently advised that I would stop. Why should you fail to listen to people around you at times? The answer is simple; they do not know where you are going and from an informed point of view they cannot trek with you.

I ignored every kind of pieces of advice both from my superiors and colleagues. You must be consistent with your actions for someone not to acclaim; it was luck or mistakenly done. I did not give up to hearing comments from people but gave up to taking all their pieces of advice. Why not listen to them? You would ask. My actions proved different because at the end of the day, work was done even much better than other students that attended field attachment days.

Suffering manifested every day of my life getting exposed to direct heat generated from my laptop then, escaping from my childhood home to spend nights in a silent room that was rented out by my classmate one Rashidd. For me mental discipline was positive indiscipline that I believed even escaping to use my God given gifts and talents was great. The result of my work was yet to vindicate the earlier paths used in escaping from home.

Having finished writing the book in its image as a manuscript, no one believed me right from home except people on street. People will always expect us of less value not until we position ourselves for greater value. At this point I still stood alone and had to offer myself for a risk greater than that I ever per took in life.

I merely did not have any money with me to have the book published in the publishing house. I offered to sell my only property again and this time it was the mini laptop that was used to typescript my 305 paged book for two months and thirteen days. I had to first ask the person who was to take up the purchase of the money so I would buy a flash disc to store the soft copy of the book. The little money I got could not push me to the publishing house but a way was yet to open. I opted to visit a printer where I was to get the hard copies of the book at a cheaper cost.

Young people and old people are all human; just do things your way not because old people did different.

They did things their way and you must accept being a unique person short of that, accept to settle where you are. Within my mind I did not go negative about risking my hard earned manuscript as far as being attacked by a computer virus or even being misplaced and the worst case scenario being stolen because negativity will derail continuity.

Ultimately, the few copies of the book were ready to be sold off to different people. How was this to impact on society where more people were illiterate? In my own thinking as a philosophical writer, even the literate masses would not easily conceptualise the message considering the shaky reading culture in Uganda. Dreams served to support the next step on what decisions there were. I did not take a second thought but decided to found an organisation that was to interpret the book that contained information intended to end domestic violence.

I founded Domestic Peace Foundation Uganda on 21st December, 2015 now at twenty three (23) years of age and in my second academic year at Makerere University. It is the proceeds of the sales made out of the book that I used to have the organisation take off. All seemed against me because people around me started to worry.

Source: Domestic Peace Foundation Uganda, Founder – Bruno Asiimwe talking to Kirehe community members on the 1st Anniversary of DPFU on 21st December 2016

Life Longevity Dwells On Happiness

A life long-lived is in your current age matched with events unfolding because you have done a great deal. It is absolute that you and I were born and do not know the day everyone shall breathe their last. Very many babies die, teenagers die, youth die, middle aged adults die and old people die. You have room to say he passed on because you are alive, nevertheless; there is a number of good deeds counting even when they are long gone.

Why don't you take the only opportunity to start counting your achievements today? There is need to move on to another level where a specific record is set. Not to even worry if someone is running behind us to break our records in life; most people don't live long even when they are breathing. You are not young or old not to start living again a life long-lived. Allow me to say, it is most likely that if we do not admit to such facts; there is a possibility of being the only centurions in our village and our work shall never be traced.

Wake up today and start to live long everyday you realise you have breath to stretch on the bed. I want to help you and help myself to say, we ought to distinguish between fun and happiness. It is fair to have fun and excellent to enjoy happiness. In this understanding fun is there because you are not feeling okay with a situation, people and yourself.

The force to pretend to be okay makes you associate with things that follow the direction of the wind on that day. It may happen to be a party where you received an invitation card considering one attendant, however; you well know it is not a healthy one where your wife is not. There is a bigger picture back when you smiled at your wife than pretend to laugh with other people out there.

Similarly, a situation where one happens to be in a peer of drunken people, they will easily follow each other where the alcoholic drink would be served. This is not because someone is capable of purchasing the same alcoholic drink but simply because they ought to have fun. Sooner than later the eye witness would perhaps wish they were those people having fun. You may never enjoy the past of someone having fun today if you cannot derive the meaning of individual actions. Did you ever notice that people having dirty fun rarely leave at ago?

It is not satisfying and we shall always try out different things month in month out in search of satisfaction. Happiness is so identical to making a step by step movement in life though the eye witness keeps appreciating your achievements. Happy people work hard every day and cannot easily see that they have accomplished; they are to a greater extent limited to evaluating themselves. They want to have the whole of their life a full accomplishment thus leaving other people to say well done, great commitment and future acclamations like they will be rich people. It is at this point of life that you are living long enough whatever the age in number.

Given that there are people in your life who are not placed to help you improve your happiness, tell them to help you maintain it. In instances where one falls short of that expectation I will ask you to keep them at a distance. Today your age is your own source of pride considering things you have done therein. If you can risk exposing your source of happiness first, do it to yourself for some time. This is meant to guide you on how to measure the wrong characters intending to demean your status of happiness.

Furthermore, you will notice the ups and downs you previously met, the struggles you are going on to accept as positive for sustaining the happiness and the uncalled for struggles in life. I have experienced this and someone will tell you how you cannot make it and emphasise that you stand room to fail. I stood a calm response for them since they were my colleagues, classmates, parents, elders and people with authority but made firm decisions to keep up a correspondence with my actions.

It is important to let someone have the fun of what they may want to hear and deny them the opportunity to enjoy the happiness of stopping your actions. In light of hope, it is being sincere to take your own path when the other nine hundred ninety nine (999) people are taking a different path. Seemingly confusing to many people is such and seemingly regrettable will be someone yarning to have been in your position. For happiness to manifest in your life, sweat will be seen more to yourself than the onlookers. I personally recall the positive struggles of the first two years of the founding strides made towards Domestic Peace Foundation Uganda.

As a University student then pursuing a bachelor's degree in Human Resource Management from Makerere University Business School; peace for other people came first. With titles building up around my life to mention as a philosophical writer, researcher, feminist and blogger saw external expectations also grow. I did not live to meet external expectations because 99 per cent of them held shear negativity. Believing in myself I accepted the inner expectations to rule my life. This triggered me to preparing a time table I had to respect amidst university demands, family demands as a child to someone and human weaknesses.

In the composition of a time table, I humbly highlighted my weaknesses that would later direct my mind to focus on the strongholds of my being. Unfortunately I started looking unusual and more different because I never met external expectations from the world around. Such expectations included being a student that should spend their money with reckless endeavours, student that would fail to graduate and a student that pretended to be serious thus making an honestly proud young man.

Once again negativity was never dwelt on to make decisions but positivity rather took centre stage. Why would I start blocking myself on my way before I meet the road block intentionally meant for me on the same route? In the broader sense of my time table, there was room to enter the lecture theatre only when the lecturer was in for the specific sessions that run from 8:00 am to 12:00 pm.

Since I was a commuting student, to and from my parents' house I ensured that I was home for lunch by 12:30 pm. This was a short distance of a half a kilometre that allowed me to reach home fast. After taking my lunch I would watch television till 1:00 pm getting set to trek to my office which was four kilometres way. You cannot rule out the scorching sun that shined on my bald head. I had to wait till late evening to walk back home making it eight kilometres. Mind you, I always had some money on me but which was on budget and never on budget for transport.

It was out of the book sales like I earlier mentioned which was to be used to run the day to day office activities. Shortly I would be asked why I did such to myself leaving out time to consistently have fun with colleagues. Evidently the answers were to be manifested in the fruits of my work.

My earlier titles shifted from a lower stair case to a higher one; now Founder and Executive Director Foundation (EDF) of Domestic Peace Foundation Uganda.

This happened as late as twenty three years of age for my own picture. Many people will want to rephrase such to as young as twenty three years of age. It is within the same time that the class social status attracted those that tried to work hard and again believed they were the best. Friends out of my age bracket came around since my actions attracted great men and women, struggled to maintain my dress code and improve my attitude towards my own public image.

All this went as far as believing in me and for whatever I did to have been the best at it. Intentionally these events unfolded to bring out the unique capacity for the competitive world. Try competing against yourself, you will instantly grow humble and start to appreciate you are worth being the best at it. This would prove that as far as the organisation was concerned, I did not look at the neighbouring organisations to want to be like them.

Keeping in mind I was the founder, there were many unique things that other people did not offer to me. Some people will have the courage to tell you to stop where you are given that you may not have enough resources for them to see. In times like these, I knew the first and by far most treasured resource would for every human being be their brain. Physically the human brain is not at the forehead where such a person is seeing but at the back of the head. They do not know the effort behind your head can change the entire world around given that we respect time. Luck is true to someone ready to do things that are not illegal and against humanity.

The organisation was six months old with meagre resources and I realised African Evangelistic Enterprise (AEE) had run an advertisement seeking organisations that had interest in benefiting from global fund.

The AIDS Support Organisation (TASO) was the principle recipient of the global fund in Uganda, and AEE was the sub-recipient of the global fund in Uganda in 2016. Who was to be one of the Sub sub-recipients of the global fund in Uganda and specificity Mbarara District? The press note seeking applicants to show interest carried with it specific eligibility criteria.

Key to this was that applicants should be two years in existence and above, seemingly discouraging to go on making an application for the global fund grant. I knew it was not illegal to submit an application showing interest in taking the grant. Less experience in this field of work appeared to be a weakness, which I admitted to, and subsequently found the strength therein being confident of decisions I was to undertake. So it was a very competitive atmosphere where over one hundred and fifty organizations participated and I was lucky to have won from the first stage of submitting applications.

It is pertinent to keep in mind that all this was happening for a student in the evening hours of my second year at Makerere University Business School (MUBS). I vividly recall that I was the only Founder and Executive Director Foundation that had not completed their studies. Considerably not a single person questioned my academic qualifications. It is true that the weak-hearted people did not dare participate because they could not meet certain requirements in the eligibility criteria.

Never give up to a system given that you can improve your inner abilities as a human being. This re-echoes the position of not listening to external expectations and concentrating on the internal expectations of life, the extraordinary capacity to be myself. A capacity assessment for the organisation was done considerably close to one year upon which I was turning to the end of third academic year.

Two months prior to this time, I received an email inviting two representatives from my organisation to participate in a capacity-building program. This was prepared by the probable funders in Fort Portal city - Kabalore district at St. Joseph's Inn Hotel. I was preparing for my final examinations at the University as well which were two weeks ahead. This was yet another day to risk my education because I knew the best part of my life was not necessarily being the best in academics.

Source: Domestic Peace Foundation Uganda. The capacity building workshop where Bruno attended prior to winning the Global Fund Grant. He was still a student at MUBS.

Self-discoveries tell of the amount of energy needed for every activity one per takes. There appears a glimmer of hope but to be reminded that the organisation was now one year and a half old. To the capacity building work shop I carried with me academic notes that I entirely depended on every evening of the busy day. Key among the topics covered during the day was financial management of the organisation, monitoring and evaluation of project activities, leadership and governance.

As a student of Human Resource Management there was relative comfort to always practice what was theoretically articulated in class.

After one week off the school campus, there was still only a week ahead to sit the final examination upon which I was to graduate with a bachelor's degree. My mind carried an image of readiness to sit the papers with students that had remained behind and settled for class work.

With a calm mind I sat my examinations and on the last sitting that occurred on 24th May, 2017 there was a message on my phone at switching it on from the examination room. "You are requested to check up on your email for details asking your organisation to submit a concept paper with a budget attached" read the email.

I had no room to absolutely jump over the school compound to have finished sitting my last paper like other students were doing.

I packed up my bag and set off for office work with a resilient spirit to being a winner. I had never prepared a concept paper seeking funding but I never dared to tire myself as far as stopping my mind from trying out to do things my way. Experience is never the work you present; it is rather what one has gone through in the current field of work. All through the time of work that changed my life every day I pre-eminently exhibited patience, hard work and prayer.

From that time on, expectations grew and it was not later than two months to be announced as a Sub Sub Recipient (SSR) of Global Fund round ten in Mbarara District. I understood the achievement therein than any other persons could. Your work will defend you and no one will ask for your academic papers to be where you want to be. People will only ask for your academic papers for you to be where they want to see you.

It is today that every human being should choose where they should be in life. On the day of signing the Memorandum of Understanding between AEE and DPFU, I was the youngest Founder and EDF in the board room.

I was neither asked about my age nor was I questioned about my academic credentials. My actions projected a bigger picture to the wall as a self-led person ready to change myself and influence the world at reasoning the best paths to take first for other people. I preferably considered changing myself before thinking I would influence the world around me. That required the independence of the self-worth that was hidden in my reasoning capacity. It is good to go where other people have not gone given the choice of reasoning for being there.

This rimes with the purpose upon which you and I are set to exhibit at the end of the day, influencing other people's way of thinking, believing they can and reasoning to be the best for themselves.

The Founder and EDF of Domestic Peace Foundation Uganda – Bruno Asiimwe signing a Memorandum of Understanding with African Evangelistic Enterprise for the Global Fund Grant round 10 on 11th July, 2017.

CHAPTER FOUR
The Way You Reason

Under scrutiny is our behavioural shock absorber; the brain. Every living creature has room to influence what they see that is also living simply by the use of the brain. Your brain is strangely other creatures' source of survival based on the way you reason. Choose to use reason for either decisions thought after every day.

It is clear that by your actions analytical minds around us will definitely tell whether it is death or life after us. These most likely are the actions, words and findings about us recorded to have enabled their survival or even their death. I will tell of a man who meets a woman with an intention to make them their wife and thereafter take them home. They become part of a bigger family and the relationship goes beyond the two people to their children and other relatives.

All that is done on wards is first tested in their own conscience, believable and most reliably not for the dead but living no matter the state of mind. The young couple to be put to the right context of their now very intimate relationship; one must have chosen to bear children. In the normal expression of such instances, there is preparedness of the society to receive children. How prepared is the mind for what is to come; the children most likely?

Very few of us take time to reason as a very important part of life. Proper reason gives self-worth for survival and such is said to be putting the brain to work. However; given that you and I decide not to avail time to reason we shall still reason but pay dearly.

Look in this context of the earlier sighted couple, on where to start reasoning for survival or death. I started being busy as early as the day I was formed in my mother's womb. Believably, the busy schedule kept on changing as I developed in a real person in the image of someone's likeness; God's image. To date I am busy as a thirty one (31) year old and I will hence forth continue pretending my way as a busy person. This is meant to inform the living man and woman that we all have been busy before and will still be busy by the fact that we have life in us.

The difference lies in the level of work to be matched with the current age computed in time spent being busy. Commonly, it is that you have previously been told to wait till 10:00 am in the morning since they are still busy. By far of this explanation you stand to believe creatures with life in them are busy as long as they live. Will it be true to say that some people are not important to you and for that reason we are not busy when meeting them? The meeting of husband and wife sounds a gong to tell us, great things are to happen because they are together.

Absolute answers would have it that these two people will achieve things that could never have been achieved if they stayed individually. Events unfolding suggest that most likely for such a young family, they agree to have children. In other words they stand to get busy and further enable other people to be busy. Plainly the two will have a sexual encounter for the man to get the woman pregnant with a baby.

In a situation where the two parties made themselves busy for the sake of their future baby and family, time for reasoning will be considered vital. Most important to note is that in Uganda men tend to assume being busier after making women pregnant. It all stands of the weak pillar of reason that they are working to meet family demands. It is the responsibility of the two parties; husband and wife to meet these demands.

Men in a different expression are distancing themselves from actual responsibility of defending the amount of time earlier accorded to reasoning. The denial men continue to embrace to think of money as a basic consideration for the nine months where their wife is pregnant and forget that it is rather a basis for denial of love vested in time. Time spent with your lover is basic to making money that will facilitate medical bills. It may look unlikely to be that practical because you have never considered reasoning it out as important to be accorded more time for future actions.

On Tuesday 6th February, 2018 I happened to pay a visit to Mbarara Regional Referral Hospital and Ruharo Mission Hospital all in Mbarara city in the south western part of Uganda. With specificity I proceeded to the maternity wards for the two separate hospitals with obvious expectations. Also growing expectations of love started to manifest in the wards I entered. The obvious expectations meant that the females were the expectant mothers therein, everyone waiting for their own minute hand of the clock to tick at giving birth to a new life.

The growing expectations on the other hand came with tension on who was responsible for the pregnancies in question. Over 99 per cent of the expectant mothers had with them female caretakers which appeared to my dismay.

Where are the husbands to these beautiful expectant mothers in the maternity wards? This question grew a lot of tension against my brain to wish I had reasoned on their behalf prior to having their wives pregnant. Shame upon such people, for they did not accord time for reasoning of the probable future for their children and family.

Men were purportedly busy looking for money which was to look after the new born baby. Under proper reasoning, prior to giving birth, the couple will be working together to make money and not wait on looking for money.
It may never be found until your wife has got out of the labour room. Proper reasoning allows a husband to be by their wife in the labour room and the female care taker who in most cases happens to be a relative is there on invitation.

One would want to ask as to why the men in question adamantly deny their family such a sign of love and commitment. It was not the tree in the back yard of their home that this woman turned to and got pregnant. They slept in bed with their husband and got pregnant for their family. It is not in any way being considerate of others to forget the power of reason. In all the labour pains this woman agrees to endure without your presence.

Where should the false assurance emanate from to tell if they will endure further pain in the name of struggles within the family setting? There is room created for these people to face Post Traumatic Stress Disorders which must cross to the new born baby at some point. The limitedness to go forward in family business is worse and uncontrollable where we sit in the driver's seat of failure to reason. Your choice of reason makes other creatures different from the way you saw them yesterday. The way you and I reason is a gesture of life or death for other people not to mention your child, husband, wife, girlfriend or boyfriend. It means having enabled such a situation we die an internal death prior to killing other people by poor reason.

Dare To Live And Influence To Die As Thought After

Time passes by without human control and it is naturally existent off human hands. Ever since you learnt of this, what controls have you put into your life to work with time? We need to work diligently with time considering the boundaries set by our own hands.
In a rational and workable manner, I want to express time boundaries set by man to be lines drilled on a rock in the wilderness.
Given the conditions of the rock, weathering is part of its life span measure; a reason for us to never tire in following the same boundaries time to time for further drilling. Lest of such checks, there will be no boundaries and it will in turn tell that no man has visited there. It is a must do endeavour for you and I to control time within our settings.

Ultimately, man will have no control on time and its principles but will develop self-control. Life is daring us to understand the purpose for its manifestations. Time has life in it that is constant because of the checks in life directed towards our actions. Leave alone the limit of time at the passing on of man. You shall be limited of your actions by time, good or bad actions in that painting left to a sales man; some buyers may never take a copy for themselves or even one buyer may decide to buy off all the copies for themselves.

There is an assurance that every day of your life, you continue to make your painting look appeasing or disgracefully disgusting. Look out for the best actions not for yourself but for people around you to carry on when you are gone. Things we have continued to take for granted in the image of human actions have held us back to speak volumes on earth. There is a fading line of humanitarian achievements among us in this changing environment.

Humanitarianism is an outward giving force to other people not because you have a lot but for a purpose built in love and peace. What do you give out to people around you and far beyond the boundaries of your perimeter wall fence? I have considered living a life that is shared by other people every day. The manifestations of sharing the small piece of cake with them on the ground started great in the mind.

It is accepting to share the good to reduce the burden your community is facing for the world to see light. In several means of having your own life true other people deserve to live a hundred fold times. They ought to support you the same number of time considering your hand earlier placed their transformation for who they are today. As a human being grows older, the minute hand of their watches seems to be shiny depending on what they did when they were strong to deliver. Living a life yet daring goes beyond yourself to the possibility of your situation from turning around for the worst.

The shape of your health, education and relationships can change without other people noticing; for good or for bad. It is crucial to get ready for possible changes in your life by changing the way other people perceive life to be today. The preparedness to carry on should serve to tell how much you want to invest in other people. The people in need around your house do not need your money per se, they want your time. It is believed that through stretching your hand to create love in them; the same feeling goes on to be a source of life for the entire community.

Our communities need only one individual to think and perceive life different from other members in the area. Milestones are met by extraordinary measures taken on by ordinary people that work to meet a level of being extraordinary people. Men and women in our life that consider tackling a specific challenge in the community; they want to find solutions to specific challenges through sacrifices made with the little money on their bank accounts. You will notice the challenge that is crippling families and the entire community because someone has interest in making the challenge fade.

It was a responsibility I took upon myself to notice to have seen a challenge in my community. Many women had no more love in their family homes from their husbands, children went to school late and gradually dropped out of school and a few men went without meals in their own matrimonial homes. All these experiences were not learnt from a class arranged by a professor.

Life has to be put on a weighing scale for us to know how much a price to pay for watching ugly scenes unfold and still go silent. Whenever young people tend to show out their love for each other in public, the elders want this condemned. Why do most people detest the aspect of life where one grows from one level to another? Problems surrounding you have roots mainly hidden in abrupt takeovers. Time is no longer valued to mean patience and allowance for maturity and growth of what one partakes.

Human achievements appear on a set of stare cases and someone influential in society is stepping on them as they go up. I have noticed that death is a thought after event of bad actions that have a following of influence. Watch the space and tell of things that carry the meaning of influence for your actions. Having gone as far as experiencing this, the mind does not effortlessly get over such things. You think of withdrawing your decision and live the reality of your passion or keep rigid to live in the vacuum world.

It takes a principled and wise person to any change of decision in the real world. There you choose to defend the path you believe is worth taking rather than standing the most remorseful experiences of day to day life. At some point of my life I was to join priesthood and live a celibate life.

I involved myself in making a decision to join the major seminary and days counting, soon I revised my conscience; it was not the best of thoughts for my heart and life in general.

On the other side, there was a vocation where married people serve God as husband and wife; through taking matrimonial vows. In that position, a decision was changed around for me to be set free of my own actions ahead of life. I chose criticism from a few people and had to live my life considering that there were no people to get into my shoes and feel the heat therein.

  Always be a winner of the choices you make; they will be your first property. At this point someone will set off on a journey they truly love to climb up the mountains and slope down the valleys. It is all up to you to live before death comes or to die and live forever. Small achievements will convince you to stop work and enjoy that seemingly great time. Big achievements will prove the many people at the top so you keep running.

  The human mind is ready to be put to task for whatever appears desirable. It is more daring to understand why you deserve to live again for the next day meant to be your birthday. What do we have to offer that people did not see yesterday? In light of your age today, it is enough for life to evolve and the world to look bright; just start on believing your next step. Accept to conquer your realm of exposure to positivity, growth and change.

University vs. Career Readiness

Multitudes of students at the University are eighteen years and over thus the match of understanding where they are; as grownups. To be specific and carry this issue into context, most students at the University are in the 20 year bracket. Right from the start I want you to ask yourself; why do students have a future before they join these prestigious institutions of higher learning and clearly lose it on the day of graduation?

Well, let me open your eyes to the fact that you are reading with my mind to save half of this generation and posterity. I attended my undergraduate degree program at Makerere University Business School from August 2014 to January 2018. This inscription was clearly put out on my School Identity Card, to say I was aware University time was a project with activities based on a specific timeline.

For the three years at the University with over four thousand graduates every year in different disciplines; no student attained 100 per cent for all the academic papers they sat. Zeroing to my own class, lecturers and my colleagues believed there was always the best student. Can you imagine calling them best students when they attained 90 per cent in an academic paper? Yes, that is the tradition. I only knew that such students were better students in class and never did they attempt to be the best. Young people at the University are verbally encouraged to be greedy and not get the realities of being better people.

In instances where one of the students attained 90 per cent in an academic paper, where do they find the difference of 10 per cent? As a mediocre not necessarily self- proclaimed in class, I often achieved a 60 per cent mark in an academic paper and believed I was better. In the quest for being a better student I offered a lot to look for the difference of 40 per cent. This was not in the school library but outside the entire school premises. Such a practice would soon make me the best person.

Why do you want to be the best in your village? Think beyond the village and delve into the world to be better outside your hometown. You ideally start to recognise the loop holes in what we do different from who we are. Given such a mind like it is to date in all higher institutions of learning, the competitive edge is gargantuan right from the doorstep of lecture theatres and staff rooms.

In the dilemma that most students and a few lecturers live, high anticipations grow for them to see every day a better day. Where is the competitive edge among students and young people? Believably, all students have Identity Cards awarded by the school authorities. "Does this make individual students novel?" I often asked.

Never, so I stood my ground and took my own direction even when the ninety nine took a different one. Within my high school days I already discovered I could play football, make a prayer, and write articles and poems. Discoveries are important for us to know the purpose for which one is Jane and the other is Bruno. We are different people all through but the difference is that we do not know not until they have told us.

The unfortunate incident of most young people in their 20s is that they start to shade off their discoveries earlier met in high school because they want more. You must believe there is enough for you to start on instead of playing a game of scrambling for more. Simply accept that you have a number of friends who are enough. Work out your ideas around them and one of them could lead you to the next step. They most likely will encourage you to grow bigger the sales of your pieces of work by investing half of the proceeds back into the business to sharing the money amongst them.

Believing I was a better student did not satisfy me to settling with the School Identity Card alongside the National Identity Card. It was never time for me to shade off my earlier discoveries in high school. I made my career start to manifest in talent realisation and skills development. "You must get prepared for life outside these lecture theatres," my mind shouted. Every day I knew my School Identity Card held an expiry date too reading January, 2018.

All would soon mean that the world owes you quality time spent at the past station. This meant school, place of work and job title. Among my three talents earlier mentioned I would take on one for a priority; writing. As early as a month old at the university, I made writing my thing to have it over flow the red margins drawn by my parents, siblings, school authorities, classmates, onlookers and the general society. It still re-echoes that one good thing grows from small and never starts big. I wrote my first book entitled "Speaking Volumes for a Moment in a Seminary."

There were a lot of personal experiences attained in preparatory and minor seminaries covered in 16 pages, just imagine the size of the book. One would choose to call it a booklet; it is a book for me. I vowed never to block myself on a journey I consciously set out to lead. I never bothered to look for an editor, all was seemingly okay for my readers. Students that learnt of this called me beyond my name to saying he is a writer.

I was yet to keep away my Identity Card that other students kept as a treasure since I had started to get self earned titles. This made me different before the school administration and the students' body. Remember I was not desperate at being the best student but standing to be better than all of them. In 2015 I wrote my second book entitled "A Family for us; Together against Domestic Violence". Believe me that I am still attending every lecture every day and thereafter getting engaged in discussion groups with a few classmates.

For this one I looked for an editor and it was a 305 paged book. Considering the knowledge poured out into the manuscript, the right person for me and given the topic of choice as domestic violence; Sarah Rukundo as a lawyer was suggested to me to have had relevant expertise as a potential editor.

Upon striking an agreement for her to start on editing the manuscript, I would go back to school a happier young man. "A week was enough given their expertise in editing," she said. After one week I made a phone call before I would walk into their office on a given Tuesday.

This was to ascertain the readiness of the editor to give me the work done with editing and awaiting completion of my payment. She relied to the call and asked me to avail more time and come in on Friday the same week. At such a point the agreement ceases to serve its due purpose; the atmosphere also suggests otherwise. On reaching their office where she sat at Human Rights Regional Offices - Mbarara, I was offered a seat. She told me it was not possible for them to edit the manuscript given that I am not a good writer.

In sincerity, she was so calm and respectful to my opinion of the manuscript before her desk. Within our interaction she noticed there was a missing gap to believe her words. Therefore she advised me to wait on as she calls after the other colleague with whom they shared the difficulties of reading and trying to understand the manuscript as a piece that would yet fail them.

"She is also a lawyer and together we failed to see the flow of your story in the book" Sarah said. The scene looked very ugly and discouraging by their words. They further told me that it was not the way writers articulate their words and I perhaps needed to read more books of other writers for me to entirely rewrite the 305 paged manuscripts. Within me, I already noticed I was in the right place meeting wrong people. I was intentionally hearing them out and listening to their pieces of advice.

I believed their remarks were baseless and frivolous. The journey ahead appeared scary and it was a silent evening for my outlook.

People may label you a failure, worry not for you have the quality inside that the highest bidder would go for. The day in conflict is a new year. Never to tire, the day after came with a new moon alongside the colours of the rainbow. Through a certain printing house I was availed a contact number of one experienced editor, one Abraham Ahabwe.

Within the lines of a phone call I could easily grow happy noticing the prowess in their editing paths. He informed me that he had ten years of experience in editing articles in the New Vision newspaper and Vision group at large. "How many pages is the manuscript?" he asked. I strongly responded 149 pages of the manuscript. At once he said it would take him two full working days to have it edited.

After three days of anticipated work, I made a follow up through a phone call to get the manuscript ready for printing. Retrospectively, he was aiming at the goal posts. Abraham also requested that we meet over the weekend to chat the way forward for the book and added that I was a great writer. At this point the analogy between the two editors was clear of who would yet discover what they had never seen. I soon would know my other identity as a student from Makerere University Business School.

One Saturday morning in 2015 I made a first call to inquire on the meeting place with a bigger sense of achieving a milestone. He made a few words through the phone call, "Bruno, you are a philosophical writer and so we have to edit this manuscript together for you not to miss the writer's intentions" he said. This was the reason I wanted us to meet today. I grew humbler as a young man at 23 years of age at the time.

Within our communication, we agreed to meet at Rwizi Arch Hotel in Rwebikoona trading centre, Mbarara City. On arrival at the hotel, the first sight was at the reception desk.

The receptionist directed me to where the blessed editor was seated. There he sat in one of the corners of the room and the greeting was suggestive of a trajectory of success as a young writer.

Two weeks down the road, the book was ready for publication. At this point I valued time so much that no one would stand the ground of delaying my next step. I visited the office of Fountain Publishers in Kampala and only to be told their interest was in academic manuscripts for primary and secondary schools. Giving up at the time seemed too early and on consulting my maternal uncle, Mr. Muhanguzi Justus who happened to double as a journalist and the author of the Eyes of a Journalist, I was asked to search for the proprietor of Fountain Publishers himself.

Over one weekend in the company of my late father; we run into Mr. Tumusiime James at Igongo Cultural Centre in Bihaarwe, Mbarara City. In his busy schedule I made a quick self-introduction and informed him of my interest in publishing my book with Fountain Publishers Company. Staring at me he put forward a few queries:
1.   "Which topic have you written about?" James asked. I easily replied, Domestic Violence.
2.   "Do you have a family to write about domestic violence?" James added.

No, with strong analogy in my mind of what he was yet to say; may be discourage me and tell me it would not work out! To allay his fears over what he was starting to hear about was that beyond having a family is being a child to someone. He was also a child to someone in this regard. At this point I grew stronger to mention that according to the research carried out and reflected in the manuscript, men are more of perpetrators of domestic violence than victims.

Women are more of victims of domestic violence than perpetrators and children are openly silent victims of domestic violence. Nonetheless; for his stature in the publishing world, he ought to let me be the first child in this case that I did not own a family (mind you I was above 18 years of age) for my sake to break the silence of children facing domestic violence.

3.   "Where do you get the expertise to write a book?" James asked.

Considering the grounds of discourse, I narrated having started writing as early as thirteen (13) years of age during junior school days. It was from writing dates on my books in class as words, to phrases, sentences, paragraphs, articles and to now to writing books.

4.   It is expensive to publish a book, where will you get the money at the end of the day?" James asked.

All for the day would soon lie in the hands of the beholder; I told him that given room to publish with his company, I would serve my purpose right to solicit for money from my parents and friends. With prior knowledge of my uncle one Mr. Muhanguzi Justus, a journalist and writer he made reference to him. From this point I would forward the manuscript to him for further perusal and he would be the one to take it to the publishing house.

The day appeared in roses following the trajectory of meeting my uncle. I later made a phone call and would further submit the softcopy and hardcopy of the print for a read-through. On the pieces of advice from my Uncle, I was a good writer but clearly guided me on how he would arrange an appointment with Mr. Tumusiime James.

Through a few trials and after making appointments, their busy schedules at a point collided thus explaining the challenges that lay ahead. I offered a great appreciation to him and revisited my timelines for the first issue of the book. Time was catching up with me; I now had to do things my way including perhaps self-publishing the book.

Within one year the book was readily out for the lucky readers though at a high cost. Young and old as one may happen to appear, they ought to have many options among these; never to think of giving up as a rational option. I want to tell you that there are always lazy people awaiting the non-resilient men and women to fall and give up on their life careers. Living for my race as a student carried me over other people to be better as they sought being the best.

At the point of making sales from the book I was referred to as a philosophical writer with guidance from my editor. Being you makes a novel man and woman. Career demands grew within me eliciting where I would invest most of my time as far as setting priorities beyond class.

This was to support making sales and keeping in school to meet the academic destination. Truthfully, most class mates spent all the day at school to prove they were students and wanted to be the best performers. Emphatically, they wanted to be positioned best for class and worst for career readiness.

It was not time to settle with fewer achievements in talent realization and skills development. God is ready to use you as for the agenda you involve your life for. Given that it is a good one he will take time to push you through and considering it is a bad agenda, God will also take time to pull you out of it. Choose your fate at arriving fast or not arriving at all.

On 21st December 2015 I started up a Community Based Organization as earlier noted in the capacity of the Founder and Executive Director Foundation (EDF).

I named it Domestic Peace Foundation Uganda (DPFU) envisioning a domestic violence free community with the work therein. My fellow classmates now called me Founder. It seemed a joke and prestigious but hard earned indeed. The competitive edge was gradually being met for me.

One year down the road leading the organization as the Chairperson of the Board of Directors of DPFU, Mitchel Tumuhimbise communicated to me through an email; "You are the man of the year for 2016 for me and to this note you are a philanthropist." I vividly recall rushing out of the internet cafe so I could go make a reflection of the meaning this held. With consultations from my dictionary in English language, I thanked God that other people saw me work, evaluated me and told me what I was from being a school pupil to a footballer to student to writer, to philosophical writer, to Founder and now to a Philanthropist.

Indeed it means being better than others for you to be fitting of criticisms. The last title of a philanthropist remarkably followed my stand that DPFU would offer free services to the community to intensify the fight against domestic violence. For that matter, the illiterate people and the literate that had no access to the book were meant to end domestic violence by benefiting from the organization.

People can best evaluate you to be a better achiever, sincerely start on your work and leave record files open for others to critique and bring everything under your hand geared more for light ups than praises. By this gesture as portrayed never seek praises; simply go for criticisms ahead of your work and you will live.

My career path was well spelt out at this time alongside being a final year student. In these days of work and sleepless nights I was only putting my mind to task; Why? Within me lay a compelling word of courage to see a better community where community members enjoyed themselves.

This is described in what people see in themselves; realise they possess. You also have the capacity to see beyond people around you to justify why you do perform better than them.

It shall no longer be the concept of being the best performer but rather a better performer. Ideally you are meant to position yourself for mighty achievements which call for a wakeup call from what you are doing today to be there. Sacrifice is greatly part of a journey we ought to share on as a life solution to better solutions.

The seemingly good is not good enough to account for the struggles of husband and wife for their children. In the same sense the seemingly bad situations are not bad enough to cover-up the realities of life as being in itself a situation of ups and downs. Today is a preparatory avenue for your life's career that lives in us today.

Sacrifice Your Oridnary Life For an Extraordinary Life

Ordinary life involves simple things on your to do list every day and every year. This would involve sleeping on a big mattress before thinking of planning to buy a bed. I for one vividly recall living a life where the year determined who I had to look like, the kind of people to make friends and the kinds of food to eat. In other words I had never thought of drawing a year's resolution plan as late as 2014. Every New Year's celebrations determined my fate for what the year would look like.

In this scenario one will prepare to look for an alternative source of light where the moon starts to disappear in the skies. We shall not think of believing the night has come but be prepared with alternative sources of light beforehand.

By my actions we would absolutely vow to live life different from a year's determination towards humanity getting involved in causing life positive change.

My brother, Bernard being the eldest of our siblings; asked me if I had a resolution plan for the New Year 2014. I wanted to jump over from the ordinary years into extraordinary years. The response thereof seemed jokey and unserious of my words. "I now have a three year's resolution plan though there was never a year's resolution plan before", I replied. Mindless of what you have not had done, if it is gone the time left should be spared to concentrate on that in your court yard.

This purely extraordinary plan was to see me write three books while at the University. Amidst numerous challenges, this plan has been achieved to pave way for my extraordinariness. There shall always be record breaking signs for a life worth cherishing and living. This carries with it the sacrifice of time. I have sacrificed my time to also mean being selfish with my time.

It is pertinent to say, all things in life do not call for your attention and all people do not deserve to share all your time. Accord time to priorities in life and mean saying no for no. Choose who a friend is and who a colleague is to sacrifice bad people around us for a much better company of friends.

The better company of friends shall not encourage you to move on not because they have it all; they know our every weakness. Even in the picture of weaknesses there are people to remind us of the work in progress. These men and women are working as hard as we are; they possess time for cleaning up their minds before an encounter with other living creatures on earth.

Several instances happen to serve a time of reoccurrences of great things we have done through our friends, times we offer for personal reflections on what we do and labour to achieve for a better mark. Your year's to do list or plan in this case stands to reflect numerous activities.
In the limitedness of time while at Makerere University Business School I associated with fewer people and embraced life beyond school. It is in the same kind of life that hopes for tomorrow could not rely on the simple things we did for the day. It was rather for the extra things that mapped out the aspect of sustainability of resources, peace and love. The ordinary people did not choose the harder part of life that demands patience, commitment, self-control, aggressiveness, positive mind change and attributing our successes in the hands of God.

CHAPTER FIVE
The Only Time to Live Is Now

Yesterday is gone, and today is the only hope for people to show their worth. Learning from the past is relevant and expecting from the future is uncertain. In anticipation of the future, today serves your mandate to own the likelihood of tomorrow. It is time we gathered courage to bless every other day of our life by sticking to personal and societal values. Something great is in the making without worries of where life shall end, who shall control them and whose day it will be to celebrate.

With absolutely no assurance of our existence for the next day, you perhaps had better take control over some things in your life; crucial ambitions. Hidden in every person's ambitious encounters is the want to see a milestone achieved. How much do you offer on grounds of achieving milestones of the sort? It is clever enough to note the trail of living your ambition bit by bit. There is a foundation upon which every ambition grows from stage one to stage two and stage three.

In stage one of human ambitions, the environment in which we are tends to trigger the mind to think different. All first stage events are wishes to both your mind and the other people one will have informed about their ambitious plan.

A wise person easily shares out their ambitions at this stage for relevant support. Keeping any ambitions to yourself makes the subsequent stages unlikely unique.

We should be open to information, resources and ideas. Some lazy people will try to play about with what knocks their ears, forgetting they do not own the genesis of the idea. Every ambition you have seen and heard about from an informative avenue is a great idea.

Development is being open minded and centred at breaking the silence of its picture. In case you meet a selfish individual who decides to keep us in a dark corner of their idea; falling alone shall be justified by self-denial of the good suggestions, compliments and possibly a highlight of bottle necks ahead. We all would want to identify the worst situations so that we prepare ahead of time.

We need to save our own time today leaving out those individuals that may want to disguise in foretelling our fate. Position yourself like a footballer; they will pass the ball to the opponent and realise they were wrong to do so. They never look on and sit back for the other side to easily sail through. The play field will fully get occupied to withdraw the lost pass to their teammates. Worry not; for you can believe in owning that idea to building with other beneficial persons.

Contrary to what human eyes see, the truth may hold that people around us are against us. Stand alone and walk in the very crowd for criticisms hoping to gaze at the suggestions therein. Every idea is small because people have less to anticipate as they would still stand to block your path for their own undefined reasons. Keep moving as opposed to wasting time on thinking again about stopping the motion of things you believed in at first hand.

Stage two involves actions directed towards one's ambitions. The actor steps forward in making the ambition visible for what is better interpreted by their conscience. In other words you have the original piece of it yet to manifest as you want. The earlier sharing suggests that one is at this point well versed with the possible maladies thus solutions are a must. In a causal exposure of the idea, more knowledge is brought out in a beam like medium for oneself.

This means that by far the ambition explodes into a bigger picture from the original one just held in thought. There is consequently no harm to have told them of what we own. The people you may call supporting pillars in one way or the other start to demand the results of the idea. They are a compelling body to seeing something out of the furnace; however hot it might appear. The rationality of work based on time is a must stick out reality.

Time demands that we do our performances and wait for other people to get on stage when it is due. Start to score yourself out of timelines set with an overall goal and targets for you to deliver. It means work based on time which provides no go zones like respect for every other person's opinion especially saying no to the project working cycle. There is no reason whatsoever, as to why we listen to people set to discourage our way of doing things. You choose where to start and they determine where to fail given that you believe they know better of the idea that started solely by your single mind.

It is not to disregard people for what they offer, it is rather to say that they want us out of the race so they are rendered part of the elements constituting the no go zones. Avoid direct influenced parties as opposed to the indirect ones. Visiting a library and picking on a specific book in a given shelf is not deterrent to one's success. You read and choose what suits and falls in line with your own agenda.

Have Control Of Your Journey

Stage three of a working ambition clearly puts it that we have control of the journey earlier agreed upon. The make-up of how the idea has been packaged should not be brought down to the ground. It takes pre-eminently patient characters to unwrap what has been in the pipeline at some point. You know of the ingredients in the cake and further baked this cake, take reasonable time to slice it for the target buyers out in the market.

It is incumbent upon us to know of how much to yield at the end of the day. Wait on taking it all for the same price since it is clear that the costs incurred in the first place should be paid off through a higher price. Similarly, we ought to set a price to ourselves as we believe setting foot on more journeys in life. While at the cross roads, the price is initially the same for all human beings; something different must get to the surface of the roads. I am trying to make your life different from yesterday by adding value to it.

With more value and believing of what it has taken you to get there, the price must go up. You have got to position yourself as a very expensive issue. On the road we control our work from losing value at the hands of wrong people. Human beings deserve to gain fame on the road of life and most profoundly, have value that is appreciating. It is for such reasons that we want to control the way we are packaged for the other part of life.

Even under circumstances that provoke value for their life, think of your own image on the road. What have you designed on your fore head for other people to accept trekking with you? Many people make a mistake of not telling the bitter truth to their own hearts. It starts at things you and I have had go wrong and undesirable that we learn of specific weaknesses and strengths. The unpleasant things mean a more pleasant situation if we accept taking the blame.

In a second thought, people better correct their differences because something started to show up in their life. It is completely a bad thing that they want to correct the image portrayed because it has appeared to other people. Give yourself a pat on the back for saying no to more shame and reconciling your position should sound great again.

You may have not thought of what it is to carry shame on your face wherever you go. The good in us is intentionally hidden away from the smart people that would have come in to walk this journey with us. The best resource to controlling the pivotal stretches on this road is not money but people with value. Those that stand on principles of moving forward alongside the challenges involved. Given who you told the world around that you really are, people shall also treat you thus.

It is not by surprise that man loses their money to the people around them and it seems normal. To a greater extent you now are getting light that it is pertinent to make a friend on the way you intend to take than looking for them. Making a friend is being friendly to oneself in a greater sense of love, honesty and believing you can. Well over you is the sense of attracting someone to share the same, they however; have less of these in most cases but have confidence in abundance to meet you. Offer the best practises for them to stick around given that they would not survive at daring to abandon you.

This kind of friend is supportive in all aspects of your life hence forth and productive beyond yourself as time passes by. It is possible that they are going to be better at revealing to them how hard it has been and when the problem started. Ultimately they will add a lot of value on to your life from the initial successes made to them. On the contrary of this, it is even easier to look for a friend since they are not bothered by what you add to them. Consequently, they shall not add anything to you simply because they do not have it.

As personal expectations grow there is always a source upon which one draws the distinctive expectations of value. On this understanding, your friend will advise you to go and they will catch up with you on the way up. They want nothing to appear bothering and so consider making us feel free of our actions.

At the end of the journey certain things must go different from the initial plan and it will be you alone. They will not be there to blame but will be watching with ease as one falls off from the road. Desiring to be focused is one thing and being focused is another. With desires in life things are not in the actual and one anticipates that regret could surface. It covers the vulnerabilities of the situation itself to opening up room for false declaration of what it will be like.

Get out of what it will be for your journey. Get to be the first player on the football pitch to attempt scoring in the opponent's side. In the other sense it is never easy to go there and so is holding on to be a focused being. Save it all with actual work and mindless of what could be a bottle neck that has not come your way. With actual work you know your destination because you are moving towards attaining a well spelt out vision.

The path shall forever be slippery in the rains and dusty in the dry season. Nonetheless; we must get to the destination in question with a few people that deserve rising up to the occasion with us. Controlling the current situation demands of us to go true to set the boundaries and other rules should be kept away to reverberate reasons for struggling thus far. We can still lose it not until we have attained it which makes it worse when we have attained it that all can seem empty. The signs of victory that we see are believed to have been hard earned and so choose jealously to guard them off the trail.

The End Is The Starting Point

Time does not break off for a one week's holiday to sort out anything as we often wait on someone. You have waited enough to see your age and believe it is not just a number but oldness. Making age true maturity is paramount for everyone especially to explain that where we are today other people were probably there before and have left for other things. We cannot afford to hold back on reading from another angle when there are no reasons to justify such a position.

Imagine we agreed to stay behind when every other person aboard the ship that is already in motion on the sea; sinking down to the bottom of the waters would appear as the headline over news. Who else would want to lose their belonging on the ship to strangers there? I will not want to sink with you then. Strangely it is the picture we see and ignore by allowing our work to stop somewhere.

You did the same yesterday to keep out there and think it was not your time to excel at starting again. Giving up today is giving a green light for good and bad people to prove their worth. This is not being a Good Samaritan by the way, you are just not ready to get better and have everything slip off your hands. I want to think being served with food that you laboured to prepare but you still hesitate to eat should get one thinking that time is catching up with us. It is the only hour, day, month and year to live.

Agreeing to nonliving things to have a life span with clear expiry dates should be amplified to human life. With such knowledge it is not wise to keep waiting for death to strike to think we did not complete the journey with an unknown destination. Often people think rationally in light of death striking a friend, workmate or noble man in the community.

If you have not started you will soon relent and let life continue. We are often shocked and keep asking if they (our friends) are really gone that after a week of grief people hurriedly reorganise their life to the normal work schedules. This set of practices is fantasised by things that appear to be there for us today as parents, intimate partners, friends and strangely property left behind by the deceased.

You are one person and your neighbour is another person with clear differences. We have limited time to choose between being true to ourselves and being false to the world we live in. Just like it happens in a twinkle of an eye so is how swift you lose yourself out of a bigger crowd of falsehoods.

Life demands that we observe a going concern principle for achievements already realised. It sounds great to start where we ended yesterday because someone already has told us it was amazing for them. The guidance one may need is given by telling us to go on with the responsibility that was earlier on started by ourselves. It is in our favour that people choose to set us high above everyone to make us appear very important. How relevant are you at going against numerous attempts by people who prove being there for you?

It is time we respected other people to show how far we can go to have respected ourselves. Considering this in the context of listening to their voice, it makes a debt to clear ahead of time. Pay off such debts by embarking on business that you have for years abandoned in the confusion of excuses. It goes without saying that a man or woman left to explain their position and does not make it right perhaps wants to say they are guilty.

What if we explain our stand beyond one's expectations that most likely lie in words to go acting? The result of your actions shall immensely supersede guilt for the world to follow you.

When People Praised Me, I Heavily Felt Indebted To Do Better

Success is reached by many things that one person engages in and many things they choose to stop doing. It carries a neutral ground at specific engagements where we are judged and evaluated by other people. Any human actions prompt people to walk with you, suggest that you have been used inside and out. I start to see how important it gets to be for one to defend them.

Besides the neutral position of being sympathetic with us, we ought to make our pieces of work defend us beyond boarders. I am not seeking praises for things I lay my hand upon but I intend to fulfil the obligations for which I stand to live. These are things we are supposed to do; perform better in what we choose to do, provide quality time for family and yourself.

Work starts at self-approval without thinking of who would want to approve you and the work therein. Life is viewed as a weighting scale where one side accommodates positivity and the other negativity for and against us respectively. There is treasure hidden in self approval where exploitative people will tell you it is bad. You know yourself better than any other people in society.

Live alone scientific evidence of which we are that requires separate tests to be carried out; they can also be compromised at some level thus loss of confidence in testing gargets. Everyday a human being wakes up and they preen themselves through the mirror ahead of being a public figure. There are two things we do in the morning of our everyday that make us go wrong for the rest of the day. It is dreadful to take double standards by seeking self-approval and external praises. You already have taken on inner praising sessions and scored to the climax of it.

The only trap you will forever get into and never think you deserve to regret is taking such a dreadful double standard. Every girl and woman you have known is beautiful out there and all boys and men you have seen are equally handsome.

Men and women, girls and boys need to go defensive of what they go through in life. It feels strange to leave a mirror home and psychologically carry it in the mouths of strangers on the way, workmates, classmates and elders in society.

I am gender sensitive in all my expressions believing women have the same capacity like men do. Every woman you tell they are beautiful; it is externally true according what you have seen. This is wrongfully and always intended to deprave you of your beauty. Why do you think you are more beautiful at hearing external approvals towards your beauty? The wrong side of being praised will soon manifest if not understood with reasons for its existence.

The woman that so much believes these words beyond the beauty they recognised while preening themselves through the mirror: takes on self-exploitation and to be specific sexual exploitation in most cases. All things good and bad have a starting zone where we are meant to discern of the paths to take. It is never embarrassing and confusing to change your mind towards external approvals and for this matter overwhelming praises. It calls for vigilance and being extraordinarily careful of assessing your position.

At least fear for your milestones and make an assessment of where you are and what you are doing. In the early days of drawing achievements in life receiving external praises seems to demand for something. Given positivity weighing out negativity, you are called to do more of what you are currently partaking. You are encouraged to produce more results and not to stop there.

Among human beings stagnant growth is considered a health problem. Equally being stagnant with life achievements is a waste of time and a bigger problem. Why do we move from one year to another and forget to celebrate new achievements?

There is heavy indebtedness in receiving praises from people when deep within you; stagnant growth has taken on the stage of achieving more. In other words people who raise praises for us seem positively against us; with huge demands to see a life we may lead better. More to what we had previously done that now they praise us, means it is high time we had more of it. Can we indeed stand a chance to live in other people around us because of the work we put on their table yesterday?

On making the first sales of my first book many people purchased a copy of the book to support my project. At a later date they all demanded that I should write more books having met an interesting piece of it. I was simply selling myself to them through the book and they realise that they deserve to have more of me and the bigger mind therein. "When are we having your second book out?" they asked.

I gave an answer that pushed my pair of hands back onto the keyboard of the laptop. "I am already writing," I replied. Furthermore; the book will be ready for purchase by December next year. Hope for them to have more of me and growing demands on my side triggering like a sting, "work harder", my mind sounded. Also you boost the level of investment in business and further reinvest in forth coming projects.

Your financial discipline is so much tested for whether you are ready to eat up all the income and proceeds from these sales or stand to make bigger investments. It is beyond today that we want a better tomorrow, enjoying less today promises more for tomorrow. Again having had a bigger book with a thrilling though most feared topic to be discussed among family members in society; domestic violence, where is the third book.

This suggests that you have hot cakes on the market which many other customers want though with limited reach. "I will soon have it out, take heart" I said. Then it seemed easy to breathe in and out but time lives to give the right measure for every one of us. If you think it is time to promise and sleep back, there is more to be desired not until the third book is released. This piece of writing accounts for my third book.

Since most of you people have not visited the bank to access loans with collateral upon your property, the best loans manager is time. You shall pay at some point in the same currency or even a heavier one. The loan of presenting more quality work is really demanding but worth it.

I personally noticed with inner pain that this book was supposed to be printed out by the 18th January, 2018. This I noticed with key concern coming my way earlier in the calendar day of 24th May, 2017. I have involved excuses to justify the delay in having the book ready for print as having a lot of organisational work at table. Strange indeed, I simply did not want to sacrifice myself with sleep to make haste of the writing in question. You will most undesirably have a lot to present as an excuse and forget it is your life today and not the people you expressionlessly make promises to.

What is the whole night time being used for in your life? Think about how you spend the night time in account of the day time. It sounds funny if really the night we have should depend on the same day of our life. Again it is a continuation of activities of life justified by only keeping time over the day and respecting reasonable sleep over the night.

Have time to work and rest during the day which suggests there is a great deal in having time to work and sleep over the night. With keen interest in keeping productive by my work ethics and for my customers, the third book would soon see the light of the day. Truly this goes often practical by spending sleepless nights writing up the manuscript.

It is a lot of trouble within the night that I realised intended to tell my conscience to stop in the middle of the two hours offered from the night to write. Dozing off was evident and by the way not once and not twice but several times. You greatly believe you are working within time and it makes everything real to two hours of work.

Thinking it is time to move on counts a great deal of completion of actual work. I vividly recall my parents telling me to stop waking up very early, "Bruno, you ought to stop waking up in the middle of the night to write", they said. Oh I plainly knew it was not going to be easy and calm. The next night I insisted on waking up, the issue was now about a high electricity bill probable by the end of the month. I devised means of writing without advance complaints.

It was rethinking on how I used my laptop over the day time; it needed to be charged to the full earlier in the day so I could have battery saved for the night. The urge to accomplish what you have set out to do is how far you may want to go than how far other people want to see you go. It all starts in us to be resilient with the situations placed beforehand. My parents had no bad intentions; they simply could not imagine what I was trying to do.

Being resilient is contributory to self-seeking support to see the work of your hands come to pass. With less effort we shall achieve commensurately to less gains as justice demands to serve us right of our actions. Soft time pays off easily to your friends and hard time on the contrary pays off in principle to supporters. The team behind most of the human work is that in support of the ongoing work. This serves to mean that given our supporters notice stagnant growth in our current work, they seize to walk the talk of having met great things in us.

It is crowned by them as just one had luck to have the first product of their work ready; "it is certainly no more" they will say. Time does not demand to maintain what we are capable of doing rather it is clear that we improve what we have today. Grow the talents and gifts you have to own them. These talents and gifts are not our own, holding the same picture of their occurrences. A day of idle talents and gifts carries no distinction from other days thud an undesirable account of our time.

It is a lesson from which resourceful learning ought to take place; people want to see a better part of your life. More yields are recognisable to serve a life worth living and people worth following. What do you do to have a following that wants you to feel the demands placed before you? All we have chosen to be our label in business tells our customers of the identity we want to carry.

It moves to bless the work of our hands and prompts a resource network that shall offer their time too for your success. Success is built for other people to emulate and grow in a greater dominion of your spitting image in them. Feel cheated to wake up on a journey where no one follows your footsteps to raise the image you portray to the rest of the world. You and I have chosen to go on a new route which qualifies everyone around us to make a genuine turn for a life blessed with respect to time.

CHAPTER SIX
A Renewed Person

Time to make a U-turn in life is just the right moment of life. Decisions are possibly new for the sake of a life fitting to live for every human being. Do not delay to go your way because it is you to lead that life thereafter. Whoever has been there is right and should not be blamed for that. Contrary to their situation you shall be blamed in the near future since time still accommodates a change in mind.

Carrying an optimistic venture is only prudent with your actions being viewed to be less intentioned to satisfy your other people like parents, siblings and friends. It is a great stride when we satisfy to our hearts before we can gain courage to satisfy other people's intentions for anything in life. Did you know that you shall never give what you do not have? True, no person can love others before loving themselves. It is the sole reason you choose a marriage partner you love thus the match with who you are to a bigger extent.

We have often fallen short of making any reflections about the life we are leading. In the same sense think about today before you dare think about the next day. There is breath in us to simply know our worth which lies in God's love. Personal reflections are crucial on a day to day living basis to purposefully regain positive focus of the capacity in us. Everyone is great and has the capacity to change things around. Give it a try today, for you have given many things in your life a try.

Within such a setting, you draw life at the centre of what you think you are today, and within, a deeper ability arises to say; start there.

My personal weak part of life is better known when I am silent about the wrong and look at each part with a positive attitude. The decision for that you have for the last one, two, three, or seven decades relied on, can be the focus as to why you are there. Your life and mine are totally different beyond human breath. Go on, and do not take a second to look back at who could laugh at you.

They are sad to be against you and happy for who they are and where they live every day. Yours is simply harder to take on and very true, by the way, for they happen to be walking because they trekked yesterday. Start to trek this early and keep the courage as the shining rays on your face of life. You will have time to walk on your journey too and even have picnics there. Your life should be a picnic on the influential path of life: change of mind.

You really weigh a lot of kilograms, given you are to stand on a weighing scale. We are not ready to lose ourselves at having got up the aeroplane without using stare cases. Even then you must start it off by lifting the left leg onto the first stare case. Get in motion and someone will meet your struggle to see you through. Stationed objects shall fall on any side of the direction of the wind without prior resistance. I should then allow the on lookers to help me lift up the right leg to level-up my standing posture on the second stare case.

Keep in mind there are more stare cases to enter the plain; it is not about the people already aboard the aeroplane. It is about you first, and other people must be following you. They might be ably stronger to get up past you but the width of a life stare case demands they should support you given you choose to be in motion.

The sick discover what made them bedridden while in the hospital and choose to live for more days because quality life is worth a change of mind.
"Stop smoking cigarettes, drinking alcohol, sleeping with multiple sexual partners and please stick to your matrimonial partner" the doctors often emphatically put it. He further adds, you have to decide to live before your health deteriorates again.

Tomorrow wants us stronger even on our deathbed because we must die at the right time. Again you are mature to die today and old to live. Your age is only important in number but most importantly is to elevate our maturity consciousness. Maturity consciousness is relevant to accepting to live a better life for you. Why not me?

Have you at one time disguised to be in someone else's position because they are not around, you really felt uncomfortable there. We can change best in our current positions without the help of witch craft to deprave other people of their capacity so that we see ourselves there. It is simply a waste of time and money. Evidently crafty things will be sought from people in a worse state than we are in.

Impliedly, discipline is paramount in making the better decision of the day. It is critical keeping on the right trail of change from what was not meant for you. You were not born a sexist, drug addict or even a hater of your neighbour. Hold the discipline cycle with care of people around the sphere of your change not to inflict pain on them unnecessarily. I stand stronger to this effect; pain shall be faced by someone because they were your role model in wrong or for things preconceived as good life.

It could be your girlfriend, parents, or marriage partner that pain is moving to. Be careful not to fear what they are going through. Stand a solid ground to explain why you want to go the other way. What is building you beyond their expectations is harder even to believe but worth accepting.

People might at a given time want to suggest you visit a psychiatrist for what you are changing to take on; if it is positive keep a deaf ear and move on. Your actions thereafter shall defend you. Decisions made in such circumstances mean you want to work differently from yesterday. A good decision matches our actions and silences verbal utterances from wrong people. Consider measuring the actions of the changes of our mind to fit inner feelings, something wrong could still be hidden around your personal spheres of control.

Remember you can only control your heart and nothing else not even your children, wife or husband. One of the red flags that prove your spheres of control are in danger is the feeling of self-isolation. It will grow day by day and become dreadful in a while but we can always keep away from being too late to realise it that we have taken today. Being isolated with your decision means you are not meant for it, and later on, the other red flag shall be the feeling of being restless. Your life may now be in a blink and so you ought to relent because of the decision earlier made.

You could have moved away from the main goal having run after the reflection mirrored in your personal life. You absolutely could have crossed into someone else's life that you have admired for so long. They could be your mentor, lover or even subordinate at the place of work. Revisit your initial goal to appreciate the difference between you two people as being with indelible differences. However, we are always better than those people we admire so give yourself a pat on the back and move on.

It is normal to miss a step in your work and better to realise you had soon better get back to see the source of what you are missing out on. The source of missing that step cultivates a better seed in us to be positive again. The root cause of the problem is gradually getting to our nerves and we shall soon say enough is enough.

To this point, every player in decision making probably because you have now consulted them appears worth a source of support. They still are not the implementers of the decision so be mindful of keeping it at that level. How ready are you to answer a question from one of these people in context? Honestly it is very interesting to say; it is always a healing tool kit to concretising our decisions in life.

It is about reaffirming the inner position for some people and to other people you are declining for what is to be conveyed to their ears. They at least want to hear something, so the ball is in your hands. We must stand warned not to dare please someone for what they always wanted to hear but rather what our hearts want; it is the heart that should take control of our decisions. You will indeed grow stronger by honest expressions, time favouring of what is your choice. It will be yours to own and use to the maximum without regret.

Renewal of who we might want to really be is now guided to accept a life with challenges thus facing them. This is based on full participation of the heart and mind in making a life changing and impacting decision. The maturity aspect of our existence beyond age resurfaces to tell of our worth. Your choices in life tell a lot on how mature you are today without the question of age.

It is now okay for life to push you and you have something in return to offer, just fight back. Take a firm stand to resist falling back to losing in facing the challenges set before us. No one has forced us to be where we are today and so there is consent to every single moment there. It cannot be that easy to see ourselves renewed in action of self-denial to the past events, believing it is about taking on new principles in life.

The biggest principle for everyone here is making up their life. Today every woman has to apply several make up fashions from time to time on a daily basis.
It is excellent to see beautiful people. Men make up too with a slight touch on their faces and more work on their beds. I thank you too and appreciate that it is excellent to look handsome. All this is a very short story full of sweetness without substance; makeup your life instead.

In other words it is time we worked out for the decision we have taken up in life. Every decision carries with it multiple responsibilities. It is the onus therein that will point us to the consequences of failure to perform. You pre-eminently defend things you know people around you must see like the face by applying a lot of makeup. If this makeup does not start in the night till you finish up in the morning and it is just done in the morning; sorry, it is just temporary.

Permanent makeup will start in the mind and most profoundly, it seeks you wake up out of comfort and write its ingredients down so that early in the morning you have a list set.

Since you never knew this, the list has on it five (5) questions:
1)   What do you use your time for?
2)   With whom do you spend your time?
3)   Why do you spend your time with them?
4)   How do you realise you are losing out on time?
5)   When did you fight a losing battle to regain your lost time?

These are the only ingredients you ought to have on a shopping list set for makeup to apply on your life. They are the most expensive ingredients on earth in simplicity of debt which is only payable by the individual. It is not worth a risk to offer a loan to a defaulter in this case so that they pay out their debt of time. How often do we think about the five ingredients in the context of far-reaching benefits?

I spend time loving myself by working hard with my match to create an impact for ourselves and others. For heaven's sake you cannot love yourself every morning and hate yourself for the rest of your life. It is ridiculous of us to behave thus. It is better to leave the bed without makeup and go makeup your life.

For us to stand on the path of success it even more evident that these questions are asked to the mind as we perform the day's work. Following the order in which they appear is not a design but rather a formula of getting the right answers. If we mix them up the results for which we intend to get must be different at the end of the day. They guide us not to mix up this key principle for the new decision in life to change as influenced by our own life.

It is now a journey worth setting foot on to trek a thousand miles of better times. Believably, the uphill tasks and downhill tasks are clear and accepted to shape the road on which we are trekking. I want to assure you that on this route very few people are trekking. The many colleagues around you gave up and so could not make it close to the starting point. Count the few on the road as your true friends because you share a lot in common and definitely match at some point away from the difference in decisions unfolding.

Yesterday Was And Today Means Yesterday

We all want to believe that yesterday was quite messed up but look, it is gone. Make sure today does not turn out to replace the very events you had unfolded yesterday. It is time we changed the tactics of the game to prove to the world that we are better than someone. It is a simple tactic, nevertheless; with critical guidelines ahead for us to reach our intended destination. Be careful of what it is that you portray in your work today keeping in mind that the next day demands many answers to that effect. There are no perfect human beings but there is perfect work in the hands of the most imperfect.

This is because they know where the problem was the last day they messed up in life. They do not pretend things shall keep all right on the way. Throughout a day's work, there are measures in place awaiting the change of times such as a generator for load shed and fire extinguisher for a blaze.

We are called to keep awake and alert in executing our duties for it only takes a while to step back. Specific measures need to be aligned to your work for the very best of today, thinking it will turn out to be a better activity. Have all the hopes in your hands right from the mind. In a stronger sense work out the possible excuses to failure of things you are engaged in as work. How do imperfect people produce perfect work?

They start on something not because it is their role but for the wellness of the entire day. They are not partial performers to enter a class room and score with good grades in mechanics but fail to fix their door back home. They live life to the full and let actions move other people's thinking about their work of the day; "they have saved it all", people will say. Did you ever triumph over that work well done that attracts people to say good about your work? It starts in small pieces of work in an hour's count to something bigger where people around us develop a smile.

The smile soon grows to laughter and the whole room appears a scene of play to make us believe we have done it. All this creates an impression that every human being deserves that time in their life; attracting others to the cause of a smile. Shall we rise to this cause, for it does not come easily without commitment and a renewed spirit of work? Like I have always said, every day is a sought for accountability.

You and I have a choice to make today worth accounting for. Taking the onus to make full accountability, partial accountability or even no accountability at all for the day we live. Whatever the choice, it must be reflected in the next day we timely exist. Life is genuine to all humanity when it comes to vindicate of full accountability for a day lived, people will want to associate with us. In a sense of partial accountability people will seemingly dissociate from us following multiple questions.

It is strangely true in instances where no accountability at all can be traced; life is full of emptiness. It is not going to be anymore of wishes hence forth, it is definite to actions that prove the work at table. The master has done their part and the servant is only to finish up the entire business. Take three things that lead to full accountability. First accept to start on work believing you are the only performer on stage and the world is behind you for survival, so do not let billions of people die today.

You have to be a better performer than ever in history and rather new history is created by you today. I want you to start to feel what this means in life. Secondly with your brain, do the performance your way not based on other people's ways. This makes a remarkable record and creates more of the right work. It is you to swing the world of human expectations to where you want to see them.

Human expectations will hence forth bench mark what is in the real performance of the day. It is rare to meet such expectations but forth coming to have done things our way. There is no principle at making stage performance for what everyone in the world is waiting to see or hear of. Pre-eminently, you have to be your own boss who is hidden inside the work of your hands prior to meeting stage managers and cheer leaders among the noisy crowds of people.

Thirdly, fight to protect your dignity among the crowds. The end of your work has power to mark the loss of your dignity. You try to always regain the strength to keep you healthy and safe on the road to attaining full dignity. Indeed human beings are forever imperfect but their actions can be perfect.

The three fold principle mandated to seeing us through as life goes so demanding, have more to cling on. Few people in the world live by this and the rest have kept on the other side of the book. Fear has engulfed their paths and attitude towards work has made them think they must never be slaves again.

Holding ourselves to a better day has nothing to portray we are our own slaves. In a bigger picture most people are part time slaves to fear of starting on work and attitude towards work. Are the owners of casino halls not the true masters of our slavery since we think fun must be the order of the day? I want to make you understand where slavery ended and where it started again. It ended on trade routes where most people were physically handcuffed and opened new trade routes in the minds of lazy people.

It is absurd today that most people want to live free from work and again be able to account for the day. It is very true that we cannot have the cake and eat it too. For work to be realised in this changing moment of life, time must be allocated to work without strange remarks; it is improper to work thus. This has greatly affected both the old and young people in today's society.

Nevertheless, we have now chosen a new path to take and set the earlier mentioned three fold principle. It is all possible that life is fresh and new with our effort to realise change and admit to changing times. We just need to strike a reconciliatory tone for everyone to believe in us again.

It is much easier to hold the important part of life than play about with the future as manifested in the things we do today. How do you drive fear out of the work you ought to put on table as accomplished? Do not fear to fail as you execute your duties. This carries with it a sense of labouring to do work several times. It is in trying to stand that the baby gains the stamina to walk on and everyone believes they are walking.

If the baby gave up on trying to stand they would not realise that other people who tried standing up are now walking with ease. Similarly, given that you and I keep where we are with fear to start the day's work, it will be late or even never a time to start. Wiping away this fear means you have greater capacity to go where other people never dared to gaze at. It is hard to go where they did not gaze; to say they only realised it was a dark side of life. I want you to feel privileged that you can now shade light there.

Make people do what they never thought was possible because you have had to be a part of the start. This reminds me of what it means to be the Founder of Domestic Peace Foundation Uganda at twenty three (23) years of age. Older persons have engaged themselves elsewhere and still go on settling there. It is time for you to take your own direction as opposed to developing fear to go there. It will absolutely pay back in the strongest currency on earth tomorrow.

Better returns for work made today are never to reflect the better part of the day's work today; tomorrow holds a lot for us. We have a measure upon which rewards shall be placed even when it is being different from what we were yesterday. Now that there is no more fear to start you are well placed to have money work for you because you have made it. It is no longer man working for money in this context.

New inventions start to hit the road to the market centres today and more shopping centres are operated on with new ideas directed to defend work better done today. It is close to the end of the day that we have seen time being spent with no fear to start great things, adopting positive attitude towards work and entirely accounting for it. Did you ever think of the force that previously held you back? Can you think of the force that can push you forward? Every bad situation should put the mind to task of tracing the way of a good situation in life.

Being knowledgeable about self is what has always hidden away the truth not to think that we have it already. You have what it takes to paint the image of your friends with the right brush. In a greater sense you have what it takes to paint your future with the most attractive mixture of paints. Tomorrow shall no longer be in your hands. It is in the deeper understanding of who you want to be exclusive of what you see in yourself. You better can say who you are by what you do today.

Know Your Instincts Better

I have believed in talent realisation and skills development for a better happy being. We all have talents and gifts from the point of birth but lack skills at that measure. It is hard to think that there are people without talents and no skills at all. Life pays us well by the way. Talents and skills pay us better. It is the context of the natural alongside things that are artificial.

What does it take to discover the natural things in our life? People should be free to exercise their brains every time they want to do something. I want to discourage you to stop thinking about what you want to do. It is all a waste of time and yet done with the first resource.

The first resource that we all have is the brain. Given to you and me, we have the brain free of charge but have to exercise at a heavy price. That is the reason billions of people today have not known the natural in them. On the other hand I want you to do that you want to do. Those that thought of doing that they have for long wanted to do by yesterday are still thinking about the same today.

They just think more now that the time is moving so fast. People who were doing something yesterday are doing more of it today and starting on other endeavours every other second of time. My birthday message having been born on 18th February provides that I have everything in the natural that other people I admire have.

It is a cross cutting issue beyond myself to other people; we already know who we are but it all stands in question. What are we missing on starting with the natural things we have; talents? Human beings have turned out to fail themselves by vying for more than they deserve to take on. We simply must go for our match. This means that you must start very small or where you are today. Often people will ask me where they should start to get to where I am today.

This is an enormous mistake one should ever do even when they cannot do their own grades in life. Once again you are better than me if you choose to go there. Clearly it is a hot scene given that you continue to tell me you are not worth self-development. We are unfair to ourselves when we take more time to think and take no time at all to do something valuable.

Why do people want more in the event that they have nothing?

Greed and desire are two draining paths most people have strangely discovered to suit talents and gifts respectively. I will continue to show you the picture you are in as long as you go for more than you deserve.

Greed is portrayed further in things we do not know and desire is portrayed in things we do not have but have known of. It is vital to agree with me that small things grow big and later bigger. Without starting small you are destined to fail from where you are.

You will not go anywhere with greed and desire. Rather consider covering a specific distance from the bus station where you are standing today even without money. People should have earlier learnt the importance of reaching where they must go with simplicity of who they really are. It makes no sense to disguise as a master when you are a servant. The master will soon discover the artificial path you are taking and deny you the chance to serve him.

In a greater sense it carries no good in praising the petty skills embedded in stage-managing your life. You may lose a skill that is petty in light of competition. The prowess at disguising life denies us time to do the right things and later it is all regrets. It is as simple as doing yourself a favour for a new person in you.

It is not enough to exercise the brain you have but most important is where you exercise from. The truth remains that most of us will still take such issues for granted. If you want to know the worth of your husband or wife, tell me where you first met them. This carries the same interpretation of how much the environment influences discoveries of what we have as talents. You will discover you probably can write and read exceptionally from the rest in a given group setting.

It is impossible to do better than yourself. You will better be a hunter given that there are animals to chase in the nearest environs than is a writer. Something pivotal in making personal discoveries that both natural and artificial is choosing where to go. As most young people have noticed, it is harder for young people to make such choices by themselves.

It carries with it the impression those older persons especially parents hold that every baby should live by the choices of their bread winners. You may have realised that you are living in a specific place today with full knowledge of your bread winners. Do they go ahead to note how we adapt to the current environment? As the baby grows their environs change and subsequently the brain composes itself to suit doing things that resemble where they are.

Unfortunately most parents control their children as they grow into adults as opposed to directing them. Taking control of your child means you often go negative to the extent of telling them never to do something or go somewhere. There is a great deal of hope in directing young people on which route to take and what to do. This does not mean to say that you never inform them of what is wrong to pursue and the bad places not to visit.

The distinction lies in events where most elders tell you how you should not walk alone in the night but go silent about the vulnerabilities with the young people in such situations. With better direction these elders are positioned to further mention that the next day starts in the morning and with it a lot of light protects the young people for the good routes to take on.I am bringing an open mind towards making young people responsible for their renewal though a bigger margin shall be met by the environment.

Even for choosing where you might want to belong tomorrow, it will not be as easy as you think to stand alone. Your attitude and thoughts are drawn relatively on the same page with most challenges in the same environment. It is never your fault for the challenges you faced without your own conscience making specific decisions as a child. Having started to discover the talents within you and to a greater extent guided by your environment. Full responsibility remains to tell how you choose to use them.

It is limitedly a choice to know your talents but greatly a choice to decide where to go with them and what to use them for. Today every person is challenged to use their talents for a greater cause that portrays them as people with renewed brains. It is not dependent on your current age to start where you are with the talents you have just discovered in your possession.

Take it upon your control to delve into serving oneself with working out the novel talents you have been blessed with. Your talent is not good if you choose to keep it to yourself. After all every other person around you may want to be true to you as far as the talents they have. A talent is nurtured and people see it grow into a bigger pillar for your life.

With time talents lead us into being wealthy having known how far we should go with these talents. You now have courage to better your instinct and project possible gaps in life for you to maximally utilise the time at your disposal. For us to better understand the character that drives the brain to better the use of talents; covering the gap hidden in skills is important. You most admirably will attain skills through constant practice in that you love to do.

The prowess considered by people that share your work makes us new every time they meet us. This is the reason a talent added to a given skill will enable you to sale like a hot cake. Everyone wants to associate with us day in day out and they never seize to keep your meeting points memorable to them. Like I have lived my life to realise my talents and develop my skills so you can go questioning about the happiness my friends derive from meeting me. Many people will call you a brilliant person because of the actions you put in line of your work.

Simply tell these people that they can be better if they choose to start on believing success lies in talent realisation and skills development. That is all about your instinct where you should better know that we all have it though with a difference in exposing it. Some people will show it and others choose to keep it thus living as failures for the rest of their life.

Respecting Money

In the first place money deserves due respect for what it is. It will hold us back or push us forward as long as we are not at good terms with it and respect it on the other hand. Money has the capacity to be put to use by any human being as long as they will access it and not necessarily from the ideal sources you are yet to know. Why are you told to respect money before you have it?

Money is never yours in the event that we must use money; for we individually do not take ownership for the money we have on bank accounts, in the pocket and in the business. Time will certainly limit you from holding it for a longer period of time than you can make an investment, expenditure or even lose all of it. There is great need to handle what does not belong to you with care so that it keeps its original value. For money, the way you keep it and the reasons aligned to keeping it thus, tells if you have chosen to respect it or not.

I want to bring to your notice the two sources of money that guide a person to be renewed as far as respecting money. The initial source of money is what most of us have had in the early days of life. The other is a self-made source of money where people are making money by themselves. Someone will tell you it is their hard earned cash at the end of the day. Keep keen to mark the analogy between the two sources of money in people that seek renewal of respect for money.

It is all about being rich for this matter. I would want to simply put it that way so that you stand where you want to be for you to make riches worth your effort. We wake up seeing a case situation that involves a bread winner or for specificity a parent and a school going person. The parent is the initial source of money for this school going person in the early days of their life.

The pupil or student in question is at the receiving end of the money from their parents. People whose practices tell that they truly want to keep poor have to date never told their children how they get their money, reasons for spending it on them in that way, places to get the money and when to spend the money. These are the four questions they not only have failed to answer but also are not aware that children deserve to know of.

This is geared towards respecting money for a renewed person in life from their past:

1)   How to get money?
2)   Why money is spent on them the way it is being done?
3)   Where to get the money?
4)   When to spend the money?

The middle class are the bridge between the rich and the poor. You will find most business people, professionals and skilled people. They also have children going to school and this is what they opt to do in explaining whether they respect money or not. Their children are never told how they get their money and when to spend the money. The questions that still go unanswered are:

1)   How to get money?
2)   When to spend the money?

The rich are extraordinary people in the world who also have children going to school. All they have is financial literacy in practice and it is not about the number of degrees you have or asking why one did not attend a business school. All questions are answered before their children set off for school in the compound both affront and at the back yard of the family home, on the dining table, living room, rest rooms and in the bedrooms.

We all want to be like them; the rich. Honesty and Sincerity are paramount, how many of us have answered these four questions before and are still poor or categorised as a middle class person? None of us deserves to be rich then. It is very possible to renew your respect for money today and gradually we shall refer to you as a rich person from a humble background. Here it is not the question of where you come from rather the answer to where you want to go.

I want to answer the earlier four questions with you.

To being with; how you answer the question before us carries a lot for us to easily get there.

1)   How to get money?

You better get money by making it than getting money by looking for it. You will have understood to sustain money in circulation by making it and you are not certain of having money if you are looking for it. You might keep looking for it and never find. If your child realises that you are making money they will take a firm decision to go where life pushes them into making money.

This involves one's mind to work beyond the normal to an extraordinary encounter with financial discipline. Life for them is in the reality path of uphill and downhill tasks that make a confident and resilient being.

All for this child is going for assets rather than liabilities in life. In the event that you tell the children on how you look for money, they will know it is that easy and someone has money to dish out free without work done. I tell you most sadly; people who are looking for money work harder and still earn peanuts but they never give up.

They must live the next day and so they must go out to look for money every other day. The person looking for money at some point will lose the little and their children will still be demanding for money. This is how the children will share the blame at the final point. Why don't they ever ask the parents as to why they have accepted to be slaves to money given that they work for it? Money works for the rich as the poor work for money.

I recall disturbing a house maid at home at nine years of age that they had to report to my daddy later as he came back from work. The house maid informed him that I had told her she was not part of the family as a child but rather a house maid, simple. My daddy grew angry with me and asked; "how sure are you that you are my son?" Having heard from many people that I was his spitting image, deep within lived the confidence of him being my biological father.

However; I went on to know the importance of believing to always ask how things happen. You should better answer how you make money for a greater cause.

2) Why money is spent on them the way it is being done? It is not a must that money must be spent. It is with a number of reasons but most important it is better you tell them to make investments answering why it is spent. We need returns and recurring returns of money for us to be rich and stable with financial discipline. Your children ought to work hard to make returns in the near future.

3) Where to get the money?

The places where to find money are characterised with sacrifice, commitment, persistence, prayer, measurable patience and determination. Short of this many people will look for money in good companies and organisations. The rich are making great companies and organisations to make money for them even when they are not around on specific days of work. Guide your children on the better path there for them to jump out of the current painful lifestyle in their possession.

4)   When to spend the money?

Budgets and work plans are not entirely for organisations and great companies. You must identify when to spend money based on a given budget that has a budget ceiling as you get out using the money. This strongly implies that you shall only spend the money at a given hour or day. Time is the biggest rule to keep our money working for us and making a lot of profit.

Relatively you should learn to spend money on planning to make a specific expenditure. It is prudent to visit a super market and pick on seven items when you initially planned and budgeted for only four items. You will be working outside the budget which ultimately will push your pocket to the wall. You have room to make your money respected by other people especially your children or let yourself respect it alone and lose everything in the children. Your life will be short even when you are a centurion by age and hence no legacy to be inherited.

Having gone losing money, this child will look back to the source of the money and find it no more. Self-made money or hard earned cash is that made by your children. If you did not show them the way, most of these children will also disrespect money and carry regrets all over the place. It is not mandatory that people will respect money because it is made by them.

Though, we are hit hard in times we spend money and realise it was wrongly placed. It is incumbent upon every person to respect the money in their pockets. Have full responsibility for that money and make good use of it. I want to again say that small things will grow big and later bigger. With the concept of using money to renew you, by all means avoid having financial losses because you cannot risk reflecting on the four questions earlier put in the context of money and time. In return you will run away from the cycle of a collapsing initial source of money.

The Cycle Of Collapse Of The Initial Source Of Money

Systematically, money will come into your hands and leave your life since you decided never to respect it. You should all learn from this and start to see where you lie. Are you a parent today or a child in this case? Either side you should be a better parent or a better child in order to have money serve us better with the current changing times. Silence to the four fold questions highlighted means people are in the blink of having nothing good about money and the future of their probable investments.

Expenditures should be made when we must spend on budgeted items. Previously, you could have always taken on a different path characterized with extravagancy in expenditures. It is in the spur of the moment that we got conscious of the sources of money we are using in our day to day life. This money could be from your marriage partner, family member or even a stranger. Take maximum caution as to why the money must come to you at the time they bring it in.

Renewing your financial discipline stretches to your own involvement in offering time to have money work for you. Gradually such great practices will pay off to see a better person with full respect accorded to money because you value its worth for a better living ahead.

CHAPTER SEVEN

Wait On Following People: Follow Your Heart

Be alone for wherever you want to go in life. I clearly understand the difficulties in the picture of always moving to the other side of the road without followers or friends. This is twofold in expressional terms; where it is a couple in an intimate relationship they are believed to be one and then individual persons outside intimate relationships. Rule out fear in what you are about to do and act the very direction of choice.

Every person you admire today for where they are today, did not start there. They must have gone through a situation you either have heard of or not known about. In a shorter period of time, you may never wish to have thought of making a step to go after them. This is often against the bad rail they used to get there or for things you desired in them that never were true in life.

We have time with us only when we have made our minds at taking on a journey well marked by who we are. I also want to be better and this goes without saying; people must be ambitious to go somewhere. Look upon the inner picture of who you are and go peddling to reach your destination. It will not be worked out in a day for your own information. Entirely this is when it is you peddling the bicycle.

You now know how to treat issues arising on your journey that seem against enabling us to reach our destinations. Someone that already has reached far close to their destination has had the tread marks of the tyres of the bicycle cross over several times on the muddy road they are believed to have used. Beyond this, the same tread marks are fading away for having ridden for quite a long distance.

Why would anyone want to follow these people? You will first lose sight on the severely crossed over tread marks on the road and start to hold the perplexity of other people's struggles. We ought to struggle our way on our road to tell the real need to sustain great things we later might possess. It takes well invested time to traverse a journey worth taking. Regrets will never exist on a journey you choose to take without following other people.

The self-blame game has a hiding place and you will not want to blame yourself for what you were not compelled to do. These are distinctively life agreements between an individual's mind and heart. To the best of my knowledge no person decides to keep on a journey for which they do not want to finish. From this guidance, people are close to the finish lines of their journeys because they have accepted to go through thick and thin of all the life principles.

How about if we dared to ask them the intent for seeing themselves far beyond the start? Society has not guided most people on keeping polite to self-simplicity and humility as far as wanting to know things they never knew. We-have gone to believe every attempt to reach the successful people as undesirable by the facts of the journey they themselves took. Few people are today considered rich and happy, for they decided to follow their hearts.

We shall still see fewer people go there given that we want to follow them. Let us be fully guided by the uniqueness in a new world we always wanted to see. I tell you to create the new world within you and have it shared to others.

This positions you for the world you create and want to see. This is how important it is to safe guard it from haters of practices therein. It will never be challenged by the lazy people and those that dream following us to the detail of competition. In a great reasoning sphere of competition we shall be fully in control of what goes on in the new world.

Greatness must start in us and then move out for other people to see. If anyone joked about the readiness of their work and brought it on market with being their first customers; they would live to tell how uncompetitive their products are. People will convince you of their products being better than yours and assure you of being a failure. They are right because they are not you and therefore deserve to push you out of business. It is all a recurring coverage of previous experience birthed out of individual careers, professions and skills.

Measure your capacity by your heart and go happy about it. It is relatively rare to disregard things you consider important. Who then shall have the courage to vindicate the wrongs in the journey you have started on? "It is not the right time to start on this", most professionals, people with relatively successful careers told me. I heard them shout and never listened to their cry.

Life would soon be lived and led by my instinct of hard work, persisting for who I want to become, trekking for what I love and risking for the future in sight. As you, getting set on that trail, where the race looks pretty much easier and flourishing is worth a step. Give it your time. It is only true that we accept to be discouraged; our decisions are paramount.

All the climbing lanes will truly be stations not to stop at but to take a deep breath and move on. The world is moving so you and I must move with it. If we do that, it shall never be us going for good things because other people have made the way. We are meant to start our own life journeys ahead of time. My eyes cannot imagine what young and old people around me are looking for. They should just start from nowhere to somewhere, work with passion to see a better day and never follow me.

I have faced multitudes of challenges that they never wanted to face and so they will not stand the tasks I will give out to them. The human mind is very strong to accommodate things you want to do. Rather it is a waste of time to go lamenting about God for not giving you blessings to reach where other people are. Look at what God does every time you make a prayer to Him. A just and merciful father He is; answering all prayers made to Him at that opportune time.

It is exemplified among three people who are of different ages but the same location, say Uganda. Jonan, Joan and Joker who stand with the same prayer intention seeking God to help them purchase good cars. They are at the same junction with other three roads where the three cars are stationed at the end of every road joined to that junction.

Jonan prays for Tata double cabin pick up car, Joan prays to purchase a Mercedes Benz trailer car and Joker prays to purchase a Toyota saloon car. All these prayers have coincidentally reached to God the same night of 1st January, 2023. God truly gives the cars to all these prayer makers and blesses them further. I want you to get in the situation of one of these people only for the car you would want to have in three years' time given you meant what you often prayed for.

In life we forget that God is one for every human being that knows they believe in Him excluding the atheist category of people. For that matter when we visit our respective prayer centres like churches, temples, shrines and mosques for prayer we are simply at the same junction all over the world. God sees over every other person like they are His own and the same because we have been created in His image. At the same time of prayer God grants our intentions and it is there that each one of us should start to trek.

The long distance on one of the roads we have chosen to take suggests how much you must work to see the respective cars prior to fully paying off for them.
After a while Jonan is still turning about the road junction whereas Joan directly starts to move to the direction of the Mercedes Benz Trailer car. Joker starts on her route leading her to the end point where the Toyota salon car is parked too. In a space of one year Joan gets to pay off for her car, Jonan is yet to start on taking their route and Joker is still trekking and has reached midway.

It is a green flag For Joan that all is well and God has answered their prayer in the event that Jonan starts to lament about God's unfairness and impartiality. "Why is my neighbour getting to have their car as early as this when it is more expensive than that I want to have?" Jonan returns to their prayer centre. Joker in two years also makes it to paying off for their Toyota saloon car. For one year now; Joan is using the car to trade over neighbouring countries and praising God wherever they go for prayers as Jonan laments over and over again.

Soon Joker will be driving to work and we all start to see light of where we have previously gone wrong. Every day I pray to God to keep blessing my talent as a philosophical writer which means I ought to get to my laptop and actually write. This involves waking up at 12:00am when billions of people over the world are turning on their bed amidst uncertainties that await them the next day.

You must invest in time to achieve your heart's desires beyond what people around you have done. Believe we are all capable of buying cars but how much effort do we invest in working to get the cars purchased. God wants you and me to pray and work to get that in our daily intentions. Short of work started by your effort, more people will keep following the few that have made it in their village and miss the point. I want to assure you that you will never get at the finish line together.

Let Them Whisper But Talk To Your Heart

On a daily basis you will most likely run into different people some being parents, elders in society, superiors at the work place, colleagues and friends. Under your continued silence over things you want to achieve in a given year; they might want to ask.

"What businesses are you involved in for this turning den of the world?" they will ask. With due respect open up to them what they must know of your work. It is not polite to think of telling them, it was never their business to be bothered.

Having narrated to them, only offer one piece of the ear to hear them out and largely accept things embedded in their utterances. True, they tell you what they need you to hear not solely what you want to listen to. By this gesture you have a little time to keep them disturbed by not saying a word or two to you. They are always set to tell us of the threats we must accept and the opportunities never to let go.

Threats will include nodding your head in agreement to what they have to say that merely means something to you. All this is when they are discouraging you for choosing to follow your heart. Whispers come softly and they go softly. For the better part of the day they are not grounded from the heart of people making them. You now take on dispelling the effects of listening to most whispers in your life. You may end up leading and living someone's life innocently.

It is time to walk away from people of the sort in your community and not to mention your family too. Achieve with your heart and mind guided by God not to be led by other people. As you may start to envision who to say no to on your way past them; have a self-talk to your own heart of what is most important in life.

On several instances you must convince your heart to have all the experience to start on what you perfectly want. Do not be carried away by a strange thought that delves in the mind of whether to listen to you or whispers from them. The human spirit is profoundly right to support following your heart for good endeavours. It is possible that the spirit will also whisper to you, just shun it and go for that talking to you. You may want to distinguish between the two spirits in us.

That meant to whisper is hidden in thoughts and exaggerated dreams that never fall in line with the effort one has put in to get there. On the contrary the spirit talking to your heart sees you act on things your heart has got you involved in. Grow to believe in yourself and speak out at this point for other people to know of your work. Strategically there is evidence of your work and nothing, whatsoever; can discourage you. Start going the talk with confidence that you are somewhere and extraordinarily, the spirits of whispers will die out.

The pace of every work will be recognised by other people and on a short notice you will learn of the great worth attained. The physical people to have earlier whispered at you will believe it was not the better part of the day to engage you. There is a transformative ability in each one of us. Disproving of what someone thinks about you and does to hurt you can end today. It is upon us to come out ready to transform our struggles for us to be clean before human sight.

To this note, you are not throwing yourself to birds of the air for cheap popularity and degrading fame. Come out of where you are, doing your work to save someone who wants to hurt others. It is in time of speaking out that wrong things will be keenly observed avoiding their reoccurrence. Every person at some level of growth has done certain things wrongly yet they previously knew everything was rightly put. Far from doing wrong today most of us have done the right things and still hesitate not to speak out.

You are sitting on a time bomb yourself thinking you are better than the rest. What will happen in the event that everyone around your homestead is a wrong element? Bit by bit your property will be lost to them, respect gone and fear will engulf the rest of your life. We can talk to our hearts too by changing from the worst situations we have left other people to keep in.

Human beings move from station to station awaiting a better carrier for their life. The property they have today is heavily in debt because you did not share with them things that matter in life. All this has happened in the darkened environment full of whispers related to impossibilities and unbearable risks. Carrying a different image is only for people that talk to themselves of their original thoughts, dreams and ideas. Did your business idea start in the elder's mind for them to tell us it is true but not achievable?

Nothing can be achieved tomorrow if you do not achieve something today. If you want to achieve with me and not follow me please adjust your pace accordingly. My whispers to you are telling you to come largely behind me and never get close to where I am today. Talk to your heart after an inspirational chat with me so that better things can be realised soon.

Through talking to your own heart you will discover the hidden abilities of self-transformation to accept going beyond my own movement. Adjusting your pace must entail more hours of work than you often invest to have reached where you are. It will not be easy by the way not until you feel the pain of stretching over the normal. Sooner or later it will be a memorable agenda to tell of how you are achieving above self and above the normal.

Most people have ideas that are never considered for implementation since time immemorial.
They have gone on to pile many excuses to justify not being able to reach the implementation state of their ideas. It is absurd for my ears in all the times I have met such people; young and old. "I have many ideas but none of them has been implemented upon for the last years I have lived", people state thus.

"Why don't you consider implementing at least one of them this year?" I always reply to them. Considering the good whispers to me even today, I just preclude them. Mark you these good whispers include me being blessed. However, they decline to say they were cursed by someone. In addition to self-defense they tell me how they have had no capital to make a startup and other resources.

This is very unfortunate; people hate talking to their hearts and they trust other people to entirely talk to their life. I see this as an uncalculated risk for one to consider worth taking. First it is about making you learn of the most precious resource in your life. Time is a resource you mustn't pay for and look for. It is what you give time that will produce more for you.

If you look at giving more time to seeing ideas in your mind and give no time to implementing one of them; It will be more ideas coming up and many more dying out. Ultimately, you will not implement any idea awaiting money inform of capital to start. No single human being started implementation of an idea with capital. Capital in form of money shall be created by the very time you offer for the idea to see light beyond the mind.

Go forward to realise where to get time starting today. Hint on where to get time, leave more room for your heart to accept what you cherish doing. The rest of the world cherishes what they do, not because it generates happiness but for fun. You have all to consider them wrong and go your way. Do not worry where you have started and the thick shrubs ahead.

You are entering a rain forest to be scared by the slippery paths where it is not about falling down. Standing up against is the business here. Also different species of wild animal and birds of the air will make whispers there but keep moving. It is for the fear to talk to their hearts and so they could not afford to listen to their heart beat while in the jungle. Life is not necessarily a hot cup of tea to take in the cold weather; never will it be close to that.

It is about making cold milk in the jungle get it hot and later on carefully enjoy its taste during the cold weather. Look around and if you rightly trace where the milk is developed, rear the animal in anticipation of milking it clean and packing it for a longer journey. As nutritious as milk is so is the ease for it to go bad if less care for it is availed. In the sight of the rain forests closer to your face; go in ready to have downpours during to the whispers therein or keep the milk in its container.

Very many people have never entered the jungle with the milk and I dare you to keep the resilience at the apex of the journey. You will forever prepare the milk if you harshly insist on talking to your heart about things you want to achieve. Experimenting on making hot tea in the jungle is one of the things that will work out definite.

Experiment To Find What Works

Through giving it a try in life you may notice from experiments, saving the entire race from a long awaited scourge. With a number of plights on the rise every day we live, solutions lie in our effort and God's power is always accompanying us. Due to immense fear people skip the expertise in their own hands and are falsely convinced by the witch craft operators.

They have positioned themselves to trap the lazy and weak hearted in meeting individual solutions.

All this stems from the worst intentions to lead a wealthy life for which we do not labour, have healthy relationships where we never stay with our family, rejection of ample time set for class work and infertility for respecting proper sexual conduct. Many issues could be aligned to help you understand the worst things in our own hands. Most of these issues arise because we are not ready to define time and respect time in what we set out to do.

Due to limited time situations, self-guided by the highest degree of impatience at the start; all seems well. Imagine people being hopeless to themselves and hopeful to other people strangely with less success stories than they already have. Why do you anticipate a witchcraft operator to offer riches to you when they are poor? I understand they so much want to be rich too. Do you think they hate themselves thus to give the treasure they do not have themselves?

Every day you choose to enter the shrine of any witchcraft operators as they commonly serve in Africa; you tell them, you are hopeless to yourself. With your God given and guided life you easily run out of solutions. The better medicine for what you go through already lies in your own put up laboratory. Have all the experiments done there by putting the brain to task as to why you still languish in poverty, have the worst and risky sexual behaviour and still insist on going against the directions of medical practitioners in hospital settings.

I urge you to try-out many things to cure the diseases in your own life. In this context every human being irrespective of race, colour, nationality and religion has a disease they know better than the world around them. I personally have a disease of forgetting people's names and faces. There is always a reason for the disease you are suffering from.

For my case I want to take time to know someone's name and face only if they are instrumental in impacting on society. This is open to both people impacting on society positively and those impacting on society negatively. At this point I want to know people to cling on so I add more value to them and in return I gain value from them. In a relative situation I will do better practices to meet people impacting negatively on society so that I could influence them to change. If they are not ready to change, I will have done my part and the other left for change to change them itself.

You are now looking at the situational analysis of my disease. Believing that I have a solution first is most pertinent here. The capacity building every other day triggers my occasional mingling with a variety of species of human beings from all back grounds thus identifying whose name must appear to me as memorable. This is a very powerful tool to me that heals my soul and enables me to cure of the disease. Truthfully without experimenting on this disease I may never treat the right disease or even find the right solution.

This clearly vindicates every human being to have had their own disease. You have one piece of information to take for you to get well again. The solution your friend arrived at yesterday is only to serve and treat their disease. They have had more specimen involved in the experiment and more chemicals to mix up. To this reference, they spent more time in the laboratory to try-out their possible solutions.

Following your heart re-echoes the spirit not to follow these people's way of preparing for the experiment. I see, you might have less time in the laboratory and use fewer specimen compared to other people only at following your heart. Under this guidance you are bound to have a fitting cure for your own disease hence the better solutions to your life problems respectively.

Witchcraft operators have experimented for the sake of practices well suiting to the faint hearted and lazy men and women in society. You have to prove your worth in instances where life seems shaken by a plight. A given situation comes to be part of your life in the sense of going over it. It is high time people stopped placing their hopelessness in the hands of wicked men and women. Instead view being patient as one of the solutions to your problems today.

Within the laboratory a lot can change; every day of your life you have a challenge. This challenge deserves to be approached different from the previous ones. It is sustainable and worthwhile to design a unique solution for every challenge in life. I intend to see off recurring challenges that happen as a result of use of similar approaches. All challenges share one aspect of the solution; ample time to enable one get to the bottom of the issue.

Away from ample time, you must apply more stringent measures to never see the challenge resurface. We over and over again happen to be agents of the problems we are facing today. It is possible to go hunting yourself unknowingly or with your full knowledge of what is happening. Why do most people run away from swallowing the bitter pill of their actions? To a greater extent these people fall prey of the game they master minded and get hurt in the process.

I want to assure you of the pain you go through after laying a trap and fall in it yourself. It looks like time to isolate your role in what you and other people are facing now. Shame is upon those that die of their own offence without turning on a new page of life. It is not today that the world is ending with you; subsequently it will be your actions ending. You have all the time to see the wrong actions fade and better actions take stage in changing the world.

Most of our wrong ends were entirely met because someone convinced us of reaching easily and faster. You have your own distance to cover and a different path to take all through. Time is not short if you want to have a reasonable stay in the seemingly good days of life. As people accord adequate time to work out on better solutions for what they go through, undoubtedly better people will be our neighbours. Anything to work better, one will have several times of failed attempts to attain it but keep hopeful by their involvement.

Do not wait to start failing on the final day of the competition. You have to start failing as early as the rehearsal sessions commence so you will learn of something new on the way to success. In the end we must be in alignment with what it takes to experiment of solutions that have for long been yearned among ourselves. The truth on my lips is for you to understand nonexistence of better solutions that come with ease. It is through knowing your involvement in disabling the solutions in life to taking a longer route in meeting long lasting solutions.

Use The Longer Route

Shortcuts to any destination have been known not to lead us to the safe routes. Stand warned of seeking easy life through abandoning stringent measures of the system in which you operate.

There are no free things on planet earth that call for systems to be broken and time to seem moving faster than it really should move. God made every person complete in whatever state you identify them to be. People have thought different to their completeness and opted to go half-baked by leaving out the most important stages of systems set to enable their work.

Sighting one who is in the security sector and wants to attain a given rank but does not go through the training accorded for such courses, they will have less to offer to their subordinates. Taking your own route calls for a longer period of time to understand how the system operates in your field of interest. It is a setup of principles, guidelines, rules and regulations that see you through thus the longer period of time.

Today we are poorly served in public spaces because someone occupying a certain office abandoned using the longer route. All we can possibly do is to blame the highest office in the land. Well this office has influence of things that happen in the country but the president himself never sits on interview panels for most jobs. You and I are to blame for not going through the right channels in times of seeking employment.

Institutions have been put on the falling ends of corruption; leaders have served to please their subjects due to the intent to avoid the longer route. Obviously the longer route is designed to accommodate both the young and old people. It should not be taken for granted that we wait till age breaks the human back to start admitting to the longer route. You need good health, longer working space and courage to keep on the longer route.

Amidst temptations to quit off the longer route, there is love for the projected view of the final destination. The trajectory sense of this carries with it passion for what people see themselves doing. Be mindful of what you are doing to elicit passionate encounters for self-worth. Do we deserve the good ahead of the trek? With a clear image portrayed by big spenders in society, they always are not the sole owners of the money. You will most likely spend recklessly of the things you have not struggled to accomplish.

While on a shorter route it is about getting to the end but not realising how to get to the end. Why do people choose to answer the when question wrongly and not to dare answer the how question to where they want to reach? Most people have of recent learnt of the role models in their lives. These people are influential in society and can easily enable a preconceived mind of their most unknown followers. A Ugandan happens to have a footballer in the European league as their role model.

Soon the Ugandan wants to get close to the life their role model who goes on to lead in Europe. This Ugandan seems unfortunate to have never physically met their role model in life. Believably, they would share a lot of stories to answer some of these questions. Nonetheless, even people who have their role models in Uganda; given that we have previously run into these people life seems a lie. People are so much concerned about when to reach these role models but they are not bothered for when their role models started to do what they are soon accomplishing.

Given that we admire people for what they do, it would be different for us imaging to reach where they are by use of short cuts. It is now hate for oneself and love for them. It is dangerous and hurting to ourselves in the long run as time shades light on the shorter route we used yesterday. We are living in fear of losing the status earlier earned wrongfully even when we knew there is a right way possible.

People have had to run out of your way thinking they could be hurt too. At a specific point in time when both the wrongly placed people and the rightly placed people are in fear of the possible future, the best will be to resign your position. Giving way for the truth to get delved into does not exonerate us of our wrongs that we went through to get to where we are today. It comes to realising that you have been the driving force of a failed system.

Shall we say productivity never could come our way due to your personal interests further than public interests? Well, time demands we place the right people for the right jobs as long as development should be sustained. At an individual's level, there are demands of your heart that are never met because you think it is not the right moment for them. More demands to your heart will turn out to contradict the mind.

The heart will open up for the most right procedures where other people will say your system is bureaucratic. The heart contains procedurally made attempts to see a successful individual than the mind will. The mind is directed to interpret what is before our life thus availing multiple answers unthought-of. If people go patient they will easily see the mind communicate to the heart for a better steadfastness.

Do not confront the heart to considering all the decisions made swiftly by the mind. Take time and get a deep thought, it will not be about taking less time for a longer journey. In the actual part of life, you will walk there and see more difficult practices which will shape a better person in you. Providing better insights for what we are getting into is crucial and further additional knowledge resonates with preparedness for the future.

All over life opens up for opportunities that we never expected but with the degree of readiness attained, it sounds okay to move on. The hope of the journey is the most precious gift there is to wire the brain in belief of what the heart went in for. It is not a stone throw away match but a networked system of life with reliable people around us. The memories of men and women that saw you grow appear in smiles of every day's achievement.

"Great that you did not play about with your heart and now in our old age we see you happy", they will say.
It is arise in the habits of our existence that stand visible to every person on the surface of our work. The great habits are floating and no object can afford to get immersed thereafter. People around you will not dare look for the bad habits in us at sight of a lifelong lived and led by the heart.

Look around your community today for people with good habits and those with bad habits. The difference is hidden in the distance covered within the routes each one of them took. It is evident enough that people we see today with bad habits in their mid-40s took a short route to where they are. It is also true that people with good habits in their mid-20s accepted a longer route. This is to tell you that your habits will never get altered if you don't give adequate time to travel the longer route as far as being disciplined.

It is greatly a thought of where your young ones are with their habits today. Much realistically young people having read this book, can groom their habits by taking the longer route that has manifestations of pain and joy. Whenever a problem strikes it irritates men and women that used the shorter route to where they are today. The expression therein goes as far as not feeling the possibility of solutions put up by them. Living alone when in troublesome situations should have changed the earlier expression to perhaps do something different alone.

We have unresponsively performed with every state of mind basing on the fact that the right people shielded us even when they knew we were wrong elements. They see us walk the wrong way but still tell us it is okay. There is no person you tend to waste of their time but your own time. Simply readjust the origins of what you are doing and seek pardon before facing a rough edge of impeachment or resign with shame all over.

In a bid to run away from greater embarrassments, we deserve to look at where we are today and start there. There is absolutely nothing much to do with the past but something to change for today. Make the reflection of every action you play a part that the longer route is appreciated in the good things. Choose to keep silent about the wrong you did yesterday and pave for the better people that shielded you for a better person.

If you insist on reaffirming your position to have always taken the shorter route for all your destinations, it will not make sense to the world. "Enough is enough" they will say. All will be irreversible to see the little good practices as time rudely might put it. The play field was levelled for all players but some of them chose to see it slanting against their role but for their selfish gains.

Did you know that a young person can offer pieces of advice to their elders? If it is true for you, the young person will have met a new pit dug by the hunters as they dared to trap a beast last evening. If you do not pay heed, you will smartly walk out to the hunting ground and fall into the very pit the young person alarmed you of. In the event that you survive the sharp placed spears in that pit; you will instead develop fear for every young person in the community.

Imagine you hardly respected a given category of people but you now fear the entire race. Soon they will learn of you to be a coward and tell you what you never wanted to hear. You then will turn out to listen to the wrong elements sent by the enemies of your family and believe them as against the past. Being an elder in the community should be a point to draw us closer to the young persons. This gives a reflection of the intent to gather information that we could not make clearly heard to ourselves from the neighbourhood.

Tell yourself of what is important before you go wrong by allowing to talk to your heart through which your conscience will attain courage. Within this setting of a community, both young and old people have a part to play in doing right. Humanity stands an oath of building a better world on deep rooted promises. We should promise ourselves of better plans every year, more love for people around us and acts that positively impact on society. The longer routes will be the way to go for young people especially girls from deceptive boys and men.

Old women and men will work for their food and live to enjoy themselves with life threats from fellow human beings. You and I ought to promise the society in which we have grown and live full of the determination to take a better route in whatever we do; for unfulfilled promises we shall be inexcusable as one runs out of time.

CHAPTER EIGHT
Unfulfilled Promises Are Inexcusable

People who are forgetful in life have time to defend their stand for making it possible to forget. "I was busy yesterday and so could not make it there as earlier promised" often we may say. On a different note some other people will simply put it, "I just forgot about going there". All of us have ever forgotten about something and still will forget today. Who are you and me starting to live with, that they will often be set to remind us of our supposed to-do activities?

Even at times that we go artificial to involve the alarm clock in reminding us of what to do; it may not make sense any more. "You cannot defeat nature", said Mr. Ashaba. L. Following some pupils dozing off during his Mathematics lesson sessions in the day back in primary seven; this teacher would make the above statement and laugh it off. He went on to explain to the entire class back in 2007 at St. Mukasa Preparatory Seminary – Mushanga that we all must do our work at the right time, with the right people, in the right place and for the right reason.

I must be honest that I then heard him speak but never took interest in such wise words from him. I do not mean to say I was the pupil always dozing off. I had no room to fail this test of time because I then invested less time for academics. Often I was driven by a spirit of talent realization and skills development way different from what the academic syllabus had. In a greater understanding the pupils would spend the whole day occupied in class and again read under blanket cover in the night.

Believably as candidates the year they anticipated to seat Primary Leaving Examinations (PLE); in the evening hours of the same year. The next day they attended class, most of this type of pupils dozed off in class. This would soon explain that no human being can defeat nature. True, to date you and I cannot defeat nature because we make empty promises to ourselves.

What shall it look like that you choose to make empty promises to other people? You shall not be safe either. At this level it is a crime that you may commit for your own information. People will no longer want to associate with us because it has been proven beyond doubt that we are liars. Making a promising statement to an individual or a group of people is not simply to please them. You are saying you will respect time and these people for the success of an agreed plan or activity therein.

It is implied that failing to meet our promises cannot be justified by being forgetful either. You have to do away with excuses all the time it is starting from the mention of something. It is all for us but about honesty and sincerity in the life we lead. It may cost us nothing having lived a life of honesty but will cost us everything living a life of dishonesty. There is a negative debt created in our life that every time we see or hear their voice especially for people we made dishonest promises to, it is never a desirable moment in life.

We derail ourselves of what should be done in a given time due to dishonesty. Take time to recall the day allocated to a young person for a visit they were to pay to you. It was so that they picked up the gift you offered to them upon their birthday party.

Well, signs are in the air that you wanted to be recognised for having made a reasonable contribution of a cow to the eight year old boy. Trust me even when the family of this boy's origin has no cattle, the boy knows of what a cow looks like. It is rather not a toy cow with less than 500 grams. Since you are not true to yourself, you will easily forget the day of the visit but the family of the young person in context will perhaps make a phone call. "This young person has often wanted to pay a visit to you and they will be there shortly" the call will contain more to such words.

To your surprise, the young person will assert; I have come along with my daddy to pick up the gift you offered on my birthday party, a cow by the way. Yes, I recall and well my son the cows are far away to the other grazing field. Do you mind if I take it upon myself to call you on a day better set ahead of time. "I know the cows will be grazing around the homestead and by the way they will have fattened more", you will add.

Silence will first prevail in the entire room and something crazy may happen. "Daddy told me this man was a liar and dishonest for that matter" the young person goes. I want to tell you that it is incumbent upon ourselves to make good labels to our identity or not. The world will know you and me for who we are. It is not again where we come from that they will see dishonesty.

It is now clear that you cannot give what does not come deep from your heart. The actions of the sort, whatsoever; are inexcusable that both the old and the young generations truly know of you as a dishonest man or woman. Cast your eyes back in the days when you went to school with no school fees but the head teacher allowed you to start off the first term for that academic year. Coupled with your individual discipline and the bread winners' honestly, the head teacher knew there was not enough money to cover school fees and school dues.

Also it is true that your classmates were never from a poor setting or a well off family like yours. Today not all of us are successful in life. The disparities that described our income levels back home cannot define us anymore. The promises made to oneself would be a bright future basing on what parents held in their possession. Gone are the days and now is the time to make promises based on what we own beyond other people. Promises to make to ourselves are promises to fulfil by ourselves.

Every promise in life sets us to work to meet these promises, to walk without self-denial of the days ahead. The weighing scale should reflect promises made to ourselves heavier than promises made to other people. You should love yourself first to know how to love other people. The world anticipates us of a life that yields good fruits. This year promise yourself to achieve the goal set ahead of the twelve months in a year, go for what is constructive to seeing you the person you always wanted to be.

You must labour more than you have previously done to harvest more at the end of the season. We have a lot to plant given that we promise to ourselves that all is possible. It is possible to go where other people in your family have not gone.

You are not special from them but you have made a special promise to yourself. Make assurances to desist from unworthy and unyielding practices.

Fulfill what you set out to do so that you build a foundation to last longer than your life on earth. The works of our hands have more strength rooted in things we do without people telling us to. There are multitudes of things you cherish and want to accomplish. Keep them on the list of things to perfect before what other people want you to accomplish. You must give yourself a pat on the back for what you managed to put to the end.

The blame that comes your way is not emanating from your own promises at least. Do not be blamed for who you are not. Beware of what you decide to do without people telling you to be part of them. It is entirely a promise you make to yourself now. Very few people will be in the know not until the fruits of such kind of self-promised to-do work are seen.

It is very risky to do since no one will blame you for what you are doing that they don't know. However; it turns out to be more dangerous to your reputation in instances where you have the work in there, unaccomplished.
Most people around us are readily set for mockery of things we started ourselves but could never finish. Yet these are in most cases great innovations and extraordinary pieces of work. If you have always done only things other people have told you to do, it might seem a nightmare experienced during the day.

Most importantly you know less about yourself to continue doing the other person's wishes. Well, keep doing that and go an extra mile to promise yourself something above the promises made to them. You went to school when you had no knowledge of what would be done there. Day after day you learnt of the best practices the school would indulge a pupil in. Today you should have decided to be where you are as a student or someone in the working class.

Presumably, make your own school where you make an honest being at least for your own endeavours in life. Know what you are capable of since you know the time you spend at work and the time you spend in bed. To a greater extent you know how lazy you may have been before. There is no sense in making an accomplice of your of own promises.

Let go of the partners therein that could be your friend, a pampering parent and comfort zones elsewhere. It is wise to ask individuals that care about you of what is becoming of them. "What is your goal for keeping asleep all night?" ask questions of the sort to know if they are set on personal promises that make a positive response. No wonder, it is the reason someone tells you to do good when they have done none.

They want you to promise the whole world of readiness to perform against their own promises. We live for none other than who we want to be. How then shall you get rid of these accomplices and still call them workmates? I had many accomplices back in 2004 when I was 12 years old. What would make me realize the boat in which we were sailing was carrying people without promises to themselves?

The boat was starting to absorb water through a small leak but all seemed okay with the crew aboard the boat. Whenever, bad words were to be heard from my class it was just a count of about seven of us. Strange! My life was losing shape yet I would soon have a way out. I grew stubborn not to walk alongside the other crew members. Setting me aside offered a great deal of the rotten appeals we always portrayed among the school community.

You have to do yourself a favour or else no one will favour you among your accomplices. You know how they have abetted crime around your family home telling you that you have to keep home and leave work, abandon friends making you say no to your intimate partner for not doing what their wives or husbands do and parents seeing you off to school with drugs like marijuana. For all we do, it is always the right thing at times; changing a life of this standard of beliefs and understanding starts with you.

Centrally, you will have to mind your own business to get these promises fulfilled. There are a lot of demands arising from your family home, workplace, friends and the aging parents. Please keep doing enough to meet these demands as part of the promises made to them. Uniquely, combine your own efforts to start minding your own business too. Tell us of things you can offer from your store of knowledge that can save the world.

It is not about your profession any more, it is about where you invest your money. What business do you have today? What makes you think it is even business when you are foreseeing your children not going to school due to lack of school fees?

In other words it is time to build your life for the world to be better than that before you were born. With knowledge in the professions of Human Resource Management and Peace and Conflict Studies. I made a promise to my parents too for the former profession and I am making a promise to myself for the latter. It is crucial that I have not yet shocked you. Conflict management skills made me start-up a nonprofit making organization. It was not taxable because the investment was made to change people's lives.

In the promise I made to myself was to control it. On the other hand my late father called me an investor having seen this organisation's strength. There is a lot of sense in his position. What do you invest in for you to be referred to as an investor? Hope you are not investing in liabilities for one to be referred to as an investor.

With the power of writing too, it is yet a bigger promise I have made to myself with three books at 31 years of age. This is not yet business by the way, rather the way to business and being referred to as a rich man. The business is what lies in my position to own intellectual property on my asset column. What do you consider business at your current age?

I still have the courage to promise myself survival without work for some time. You will need to be rich someday if not today. Work about it so that you change the world in which you were born into. I see you aging and not tiring from promising more great things to yourself. You can do things you promise yourself as long as you live today.

The only deadly spot in life is living to the promises we make to other people and fail to see promises made to our hearts come true. When will you live your own life my brothers and sisters in the reading world? Stop running about the deadly spots in your life, you just have run enough and survived. It is not good to tempt the bad road users to knock you before you realise people around you are in the Intensive Care Unit. God forbid that this never happens to you as long as you start to live your life.

Start to mind your business. You ought to make gains so that we are able to say it was because s/he served us with the cake that had better ingredients. Then the wise will have better ingredients come because you have reinvested the gains there thus being better than other people. Your main intention for setting out on promises is to push yourself against life that often pushes people away.

You must believe you will push about with life in times of inflation, poverty in the other corner of the world, disease in the other part of the town and unfaithfulness in other intimate relationships. Promises are not scaring you away from progress. Your promise is devising better means of getting to the sea shore having noticed the number of accomplices aboard the same boat. Making up your mind to a better life gives you room to abide by the promises we often make on party and burial ceremonies. It is far reaching to the promises largely to be made to ourselves.

It is better for promises made to oneself to be set as a priority and stick to those made to other people, knowing they will not excuse us at the end.

Set Priorities And Stick To Them

Have a number of options availed to you and set on the table so you go with those you love to start on. Why would most people want to start on something they will not finish? Even on the days a lion sets out to hunt, they will not hunt down a crocodile in deep waters because they must eat. We mustn't do something because there is nothing to start on. Setting priorities means looking out of the current options to circle on things one is ready to take on.

If you are this person that does what is set before them and takes every other cup of tea that is served to them; you must check up soon. The world keeps us in the middle of events and very heavy winds move around us. The winds identify easily people who can travel with them wherever they go. These are men and women without clear priorities in life.

How do you get to know that there are options among which priorities can be set? Many things are already known to you and people have also often told you on other things you are capable of doing. At this point options are already piling up and it is definitely difficult to work on all of them satisfactorily. Time makes it impossible to chase a number of these options. You now have to pick on those you love most and believe you can take them on amidst all challenges.

In a broader perspective you stand prepared for any hindrances on the way of executing the activities later set as priorities. The measure of a post success of any priority is a plan which must be operational based on a given timeline. It is a boundary one will try not to go beyond amidst luring situations to wait till there is a better moment.

We may always be deceived that there is a better moment to hit the targets there in other than now. The timelines also enable people to stick to their priorities in respect to making one or two accomplishments. Who else would delay us from meeting and sticking to our set priorities apart from those we give ear to? As you work, keep in mind that you are in the middle of destructing features like friends as limited to enemies. Be bold in the eyes of everyone to mention of a change in schedule either for personal or group based reasons.

These people are innocently coming in to keep the casual business going on between you and them. You are just the wrong person today not being open to things that carry more weight in relation to the day's or year's priorities. Gradually you will enjoy the liberty of speaking out on the new position taking course. With positivity among our individual priorities the world around us starts to change for us.

The basement for most of these priorities in the end will gain support from the community itself. People are so pleased with continuing on things already in motion; they do not want to start and fail. They will be ready to grab the initiatives of your own time shaped by your hands. It is not necessarily support because you have failed where you are but an eye opener to reveal a lot about the work going on. In every good work that makes us more recognisable than before, people want to fall on both sides of the coin.

They do not want to take chances of which side of the coin will appear on top at making a toss to identify community members ready to take on from where you are. This on the other hand exposes to the entire world of what lazy people cherish most, claiming they could not see something fall and keep quiet.

We forget that the silence always put forward living a life of no priorities is louder than anything else. We have never promised ourselves of doing better to that measure.

It is true that there are some people set to have their eyes opened by what we have done in society. You and I should not worry then, rather concentrate on our priorities today; it will stand out as an inspiration for the rest of the community to receive a wakeup call. Are you not concerned that more developments are not visible in your home country because you have done nothing to inspire them? You already are doing some good piece of music, innovation, stretch mark in the business sector and humanitarian sector; just keep it on. We retire before change is seen in life.

The government in Uganda allows people to retire at sixty years of age from public service. If you have fallen a culprit of old age in this capacity, you mustn't be tired to change the situation in the community. How come you managed to accomplish and retire from public service before all work was sorted? This is vindicated by the new advertisement posts run in print media close to your retirement seeking competent people to replace you.

To the worst of it for centuries this has sounded the norm of doing things. We are happily living in our imperfections ahead of time. "I retired last month but the right person was around two months to my retirement", retirees will say. Look, you have not done enough there and other people coming in mean it all. The government is not open to tell you: "we wanted to exploit you and it is simply enough of it". In a profound analogy of who the government perceives you to have been and what you were to yourself, these are two different people.

One is working for the promises they made to the government and the other is not yet working for their own promises. In a clearer sense, the government was set to make you understand their promises and take them to be your priorities in life. A timeline was set before you, on a plan that you shall work till the age of sixty. I vowed never to work for the government in the short run to this capacity to deny their own citizens of freedom to set their own priorities.

How many people apply to join government agencies every year? They are as many as the number of lazy people the world has ever seen. People who have no time to think and do things for themselves and their people in society are well located in governments. People hardly think of making promises visible to themselves thereafter as far as setting priorities. I do not mean to demean the government and tell government employees to quit.

Adjust to paying more attention to your own priorities alongside the government set priorities. How do you articulate the priorities of the government without the capacity to set your own working? This is perhaps a bigger night mare met during broad day light. Again it is not time to procrastinate on official duty because it is harder to join me. Join working to meet government provision for early retirement and not forced retirement.

In a greater understanding keep within the confines of the law and reason yourself out to be a better person than keeping to fulfil priorities of other people. You can as well hold yourself accountable to what will yield better than your current source of earnings. Look at things that will reorganise your sense of priorities from liabilities to assets of life. How will you make a renowned contribution to your family and community at large? Stick to priorities that gain beyond the others, for it must be worth the time invested and sweat coming out of the body.

There in every human being is urged to go where they are today but note the discernment of where they are and where they ought to be. The ball is still rolling in your courtyard, play it right. Start gazing at players better than others so you can play alongside them to beat the opponent's side. I want you to know that it will not be easy to spontaneously stop what you are doing and start on something else. Also set a priority on when to quit or put to halt what you must leave for another bigger gain.

It is wise in such a scenario to have a priority lead to another priority because you do not have to lose it all at the end of the day. There is nothing for what you do not have today to underrate yourself. You just are not yet there and something beyond a calculated risk should be avoidable. It is yet another moment not to frustrate you over the good that will end wrongly worked upon.

I will further consider it a worthless option among your priorities to consult your superiors at the place of work. It will most likely be a regrettable incident. "Why do you suggest that I am not aware of what I am doing here?" the superior will put it. The wise will know that this will never be part of the agenda in the board rooms. If you are the topmost person in that office you will also fear for your ears.

The subordinates will not daydream to raise such an issue under any other business of the meetings. It was only me to tell you that time demands you set your own priorities alongside serving to meet my priorities as your boss. The only way to do better than your superiors and your past is to engage in positive talking actions. There should seem way where there is no way for your life to impact on others. Hold humility and simplicity to make people understand that you have more to do to make your life more suiting to serve other people and their priorities.

Ultimately this will not be accommodative to discussion. Choose to set the first priority to lead you to another priority than offer bigger gains for the rest of the world to benefit in return.

What Is Not Discussed: Engage In Positive Talking Actions

Did you know that acting your way to good deeds is positive and being time conscious? Keep in the boxing match even when you are outside the ring and you will still be liable to every other punch you throw at someone. I want you to still be safe even when it is a fight you are involved in. It is simply that you will not be given ear and no one should understand you for your own life. It is about us there and for us or not about you.

You had better realise what you missed in life and go for it. It could be your family that is facing the dark corner of such a scenario. This would further suggest that you are no more yourself at work but a partial picture that must be completed in the little actions one would carry on. Broadly, the organisation with which you are working gets disturbed at seeing your own new born baby and further highlights more hours of work than the normal.

All they will try to tell their employees is to spend more time for work than family; for maximum productivity. You just have to jump out of this and see yourself different from all other employees. The more time accorded to your family indirectly serves to provide room for a going concern for the organisation or business for that matter. It happens that a relationship between the family home and the workplace is gradually created. Through this gesture within the family setting adept minds of the family members make a supportive vehicle to your work station.

There is a right to feel we are part of these other family members and they cannot be detached from us. Fear for losing what pushed you to where you are is a normal encounter in your life. It is good to hold back to such things in whatever we do. I want to remind you that if we say we do not know where we are coming from then we do not know where we are going. Is it any more important to deceive yourself of the origins that matter like family for work?

What happens in the incident that the job is no more? Which people to turn to is uncertain but you now know this. Sustainable achievements are not easily attained for the reason of deriving satisfaction. Your achievement is likely to be the new job that appears to be more demanding than the family which is a sustainable milestone. We do not reach such a mark to look for money to support family.

The good job you have always yearned to attain is supposed to help you create quality time for the family. There is a quality status people never attain because they think the latter needs the former to exist. You may soon learn of the gap between general development and family. Often there are a number of children and suggesting there are those elder to the young ones. The worst mistake that is regrettable on a later time is parents believing solely with the mind put forward by the elder children abandoning the younger ones' suggestions.

Why would you trust to go with people where they have told you they cannot go? You merely do not know the capacity of someone based on their opinion. You must learn to be a neutral listener and a wholesome actor. Age difference is not the capacity embedded in us but a sign of who was born faster than the other. In the event that the younger children want to start up something totally different from the previous people that ever were, in the family right from the clan level; it seizes to be a point of discussion.

The elder children strangely get consulted by the parents if something of the sort can work out right. On a short notice the whole family would soon turn against the younger children with labels. He is so disobedient and we all know, she does not listen, await her future; they will fail and so much more labels by far to equate you to people you do not know. The most successful people today are those that have been stopped from making their set of issues ready for discussion.

These younger children will start to see the difference between them and their elder brothers or sister beyond age difference. The younger ones will always choose to take the paths that have been marred by criticism and insults. This situation is really interesting and meant to sharpen the brain to stout heartedly go for what you believe is right for you. They no longer thirst for discussions over their ideas but they are already quenching the thirst of engaging in positive actions. They will not step on anyone's toes but still go where other people never thought they would go.

They avail quality time for what they want to do and soon a brand new product exists for others to follow the earlier rejected persons. The work station will always keep people in a balance and appear to be the boss of your life. Wait a bit, is it worth your life or you should soon think of making a clear step backwards. It will make more sense to turn our backs from people who do not want to engage for discussion over things they consider more important over others. Again take up what is necessary for any jobs because your family ought to have quality with the job you have.

Your family should not be dependent on any job. The promise made to oneself would be to consider sticking to serving the family and get served for the job. It is very tricky on how one would experience the two distinctive capacities in their life.

Simply stop working overtime for more money because it will never be enough. The would-be overtime now should be invested for family. You will never think of rubbing shoulders with superiors at the workplace in absolute rejection to work overtime in order to earn more allowances.

Disregard procrastination of duties at the work station to create an environment that accommodates people doing the right thing at the right time. Your desk stands to be free of piles of documents to look at and keep to be attended to later. This would deprave you of job security and subsequently steal your mind off your own made priorities.

These demonstrations of talking with positive actions are rarely a choice of many people. It is always a battle withheld in our own minds. You ultimately are a victim of love for what you always wanted and now proving to be the living hell. It is not easy any more to think independence is crucial and is your right for whatever you want in life.

Did you know that everyone wants us to tell them what is making us uncomfortable before they know it is indeed discomforting? Stop using your words to tell someone wasting your time that it is hurting you every day. Carry the positive actions of saying no to what is against their will that is right under your principles and governing priorities. If you hope to see them stop engaging you for all you shall call a wasteful moment of the day, you will still live never to believe they wasted your time. You will not reject them for what they want out of you compelling a trigger of self-hate for the ever better priorities meant to support promises made to your life.

CHAPTER NINE

Get Involved With Someone You Love

Whoever is a human being deserves to hear if they really have the sense of hearing. Love will continue to hold a lot of sense for many and still lose sense against many people. You may be deceived that love will ever become a game to take chances on who should win today and who should lose on the other occasion. It is you alone trying to invent a game that shall only survive against you.

Who would set a trap to fall in themselves? Human beings will certainly set one to trap animals. Similarly, wrong people will be the ones to set traps against other people. No one truly wants to lose themselves off the rules of this game they wrongly perceived was the case. Many young and old people have chosen to hate themselves by loving the wrong people.

Why do you expect more than you can afford to hold? There are crystal clear issues to avoid for people who think they must love today. Do not put yourself to test by loving someone else's wife or husband, boyfriend or girlfriend if you really know about their relationship. Do not dare to sleep in bed intimately with people you do not love. You mustn't test your capacity to love on other people rather test on yourself to see how much you would want to be treated in love. Base on that to love your match. This is a warning especially to young people.

Every day of human existence you will meet beautiful and handsome people. Be as careful as possible not to waste your time with people that are not your match. The area local council chairperson may have less to share with the minister at a national level on profound issues of national governance.

It is all up to you to start dreaming in broad day light thinking there is a lot of sharing to take place than one party just hearing out the other. In any kind of intimate relationships, the people ought to share a lot in understanding and on common grounds. These days most young girls and women get involved with young boys and men having realised it was accidental to get pregnant. Coincidentally this is how most people have seemingly had these people get involved. It is already evident that this relationship is not founded on love.

Anyone would continue to get confused over what it is that is not love at the point people have a child together. They simply did not prepare on how they best would love each other. On the same note, one of the parties did not have consent to having sex with their now partner. The prevailing silence is for some structural reasons meaning that it is not easy for the wrong elements to be brought to book. Through most people there is a thought that they have a game to engage in, making possible tests with their own life.

Hate for yourself is unveiled even when you cannot tell. It is on plan to use their life to attain sexual pleasures and go from one person to another. Why are people continuing to fall prey of the game one thought would yield great results? First look at what you have and start to imagine what you want. Who you are and things you can do matter to the extent of predetermining who you deserve as a marriage partner tomorrow.

This is where the tactic resides, simply on working out our own way before we chase on someone. You must discover a part of yourself and base on that to look for a partner matching to that you really are. You will obviously invest more time in building yourself than looking through the window to see who intends to pass by the hotel room. There must be a list upon which a plan is spelt out for who you are.

Key to this is the value hidden in character, talents, gifts, level of education, specialty in life careers, profession if any, personality, health, God guided being, individual weaknesses, individual strengths, time for oneself and love for oneself. These are a few issues to be considered pertinent in building your own soul, heart, mind and body. Keep in mind that you just have done a very important part of your relationship with a silent marriage partner. I tell you these people are somewhere in some defined part of the world doing the same. You ought to be linked up by things you do after waking up in the morning, in the afternoon and in the evening hours beyond working time.

People have met matching partners undoubtedly, in the bar, on line dating sites, church, mosque, temples, school, and on streets. You have a number of chances to determine where to meet your marriage partner. You also have a million chances to play the game you will ultimately lose.

The assumption is seeing someone meet their love in a bar. From this time on you proudly should believe a couple that drinks different kinds of alcohol. It is easier to even realise things you share in common without necessarily having to have a vacation for one to open up the kind of drinks they take. However; it is not drinks with alcoholic content that make of a problem.

There is no room also to say it is bad for women to consume drinks with alcoholic content. You must keep reminding yourself of where you met these people and what they were doing as you drew closer to them. In other words you may both be drunkards at some time in the day. Going on to believe it is a positive match though other people are now nodding their heads in disagreement asking why it has to be a bar as a meeting place for a partner. Concentrate on the actions of one of the parties thereafter.

You definitely have no room to change your partner for them to stop drinking alcohol. Having realised the whole family is yet to be labelled that of drunken master and drunken mistress; one will choose to take a different direction as far as taking drinks that have alcoholic contents in them. For anything to go as positive change it starts with us before it can go to other people. With a change in behaviour the other partner feels it is real that change comes before mankind. The time you used to visit a given bar will still be respected and one party will put this clear; "I have stopped drinking such and I am okay with it".

This will not take a longer period of time before this unchanged person gets influenced by the other person's conduct. They will opt for positive change too and with reasons backing up their actions; it will no longer be people drinking in bars because of love for oneself. There will not be crossed wires since the couple is founded on certain matching principles. I want to remind you that this is because of a common meeting place which is a bar.

Consider what will happen if these people often met in a prayer house. They will absolutely invest more time in building the relationship given that they carried good intentions than trying to find out why they initially loved their current partners. Love is not met on the wedding day like it is not met in engaging in sexual affairs with multiple sexual partners. You are delving where you do not own a heart and where you will soon pay a heavy price for your derailed actions. It is far much different from requited love to cherish worthless love.

This is so for reasons that include both parties looking at one side of the coin; how to benefit from the other for just a while.

Well, you will have no price attached to your life by gaining sexual pleasures, petty money, and petty materials and ultimately lose yourself from enjoying the dirty sweat. It is possible to jump on to another road by the way but the truth holds that you want better people there. Why don't you want to meet people that carry the same behaviour like the past men and boys or women and girls you have had?

We must go working for the good in other people that we anticipate on a path of love to the extent of resembling it. Therefore from the word go, respect yourself, love yourself, value yourself and attribute your achievements to God. You will not have to waste your time to love someone for an intended event. Love them for who you are. I recall meeting multiple beautiful girls all my past days in life and not dared to get involved with them.

They might think it was worth considering having them for a relationship but not now. It will not be until we notice something more that has to be done in our life that indeed we shall be suiting for a perfect match. There is always a perfect match in life to say love is not accidental and the consequences of love are not meant to chase us out of happiness. There is a rude possibility too, where you are investing time in a requited love relationship. I also faced the same in my early 20's and while at University.

Did you ever love people that did not love you back? It is hot and real that you will fall from a frying pan to fire every day you wake up in this relationship. I knew it was for us to love and strangely it was for them to love other people. There are always red flags in such environs of love but also a beep up call that something is resurrecting to life.
People have often disregarded the red flags that include a lapse in communication, financial over dependence, frown expressions when you mention it that you love these people and hesitation to see effective communication take centre stage in a relationship.

More to the red flags, time will seem inexistent for a relationship and more time for excuses in life. Like I always got mindful of who I am and what I often did where she was not, it was time to clearly get mindful of where I was going and how much time I was wasting close to everyday. Since these people did not love back, I wasted time thinking about them, meditating and working out about our future alone and making frequent phone calls and text messages.

What would be the reason to keep quiet over digging down a pit I would soon fall into and lose a leg of love? I had one thing to do and not to think about. Make an end to the relationship by speaking out against it and going on to build myself for a better partner in future. You may be in great trouble beyond what I went through and you are dying faster in love. Loving people that do not value themselves and taint your image by things they do. If they cannot be influenced by your own life, they are simply not a match and act towards leaving them there.

The bitter truth is that I was hurt even when I thought I would keep myself firm and simply move on. Sooner than later I understood that it was worth it not because it was my fault. It was their fault to drag me in the filthy game and I was right to get rid of the nasty experiences therein for a safer ground. You must get hurt else you indulge into unworthy practices to tend to rub these off your mind by drinking off your head and postponement of pain. Ultimately, it all seemed easier to go over.

I accepted to face this experience for three years and it is a long time that you should not go through having known some of the red flags therein. Being a boy or a man and you are facing this today means that there are more girls and women facing the bitter taste of this pill too; requited love. It happens to everyone that appears in their trap fenced with love regardless of gender, sex, colour, race, religion and nationality. Open up your own way to get involved with someone you love by working out on yourself first.

How did I keep on track without wasting more time? I always was doing the right things with myself. This meant being faithful and not opening up my body and heart to them through sexual encounters, kept working hard on my dreams, talents and God given gifts. Through this I enabled a self-initiated recovery process. You will need to find yourself on a healthy and safe road for you to keep driving on to the real destination. It is only based on what you have been doing to yourself where these people never reached that you get easier back on the road.

The world over seems like a roaring lion that has not met their prey for the last three weeks. Do not dare the world to swallow you because of how you are treated by someone who will soon be labelled a wrong person. How should everyone look out on wrong people in relationships that are not their matching love? Let us use epitomised characters on social media. If you love Jane or Peter and you are in the know of their social media platforms, believably; not stalking this time watch out for three things:
1)   Who they describe themselves as?
2)   What posts do they make?
3)   What you share in common as far as values are concerned?

Why does someone you love describe themselves different from the people you know? They want to attract a different world outside where you are, simply to put it; you are backward to them. You most likely are not their match and they know this but there is something they want to snatch from your hands. These people do not want to grab anything from your heart. Close to this they will never post what they tell you they value so much because they do not want you to discover their passion in what they do best.

In a blink of an eye you will notice that these people have values portrayed all different from you. There are no grounds of compatibility to support a fast developing relationship and all in bright colours is degeneration of a milestone achieved a few days ago. To this point they are not concerned whether something better can be done to reconcile the differences that they still will not value.

Value the differences in your relationship by understanding what social media means and how to better use it. I will go for one social media platform like Facebook. It is not about the number of friends you have on Facebook but the quality of friends you have. They will like your posts, share them and to a greater extent tell a lot about you by what they do there. With Neils Abel when the Abelian expression originated; the mathematical expressions are interchangeable for any result.

It is fascinating to take you through this. Did you ever allow the person you say you love to take up your position when you are not around? If you subsequently cannot allow this man or woman to know your financial position, you will not allow them to have your ATM card for the bank. You definitely share less in common and they are crucially not your match to share such details with. There is a lot of fear in the relationship to the extent of fearing for your bank account to the worst fearing for your credit card which is a liability.

Social Media
S- Sensible   M – Mindful
O – Operations   E – Encounters
C – Considered   D- Discovered
I – Informative   I – In
A – At   A – Abelian
L - Linking

In a nut shell, the people you make friends with on Facebook as an example of social media platforms should be people that matter to you and that will enable you reach to your destination. Very important is what you inform each other about, the link between you and their minds to discovering if these people can be trusted for who you are. With this I am not scared of having friends on Facebook that are just enough to enable me reach my destination.
Why does someone have five thousand (5000) friends on Facebook and they are not self-employed or even employed by other people for the last years of their life.

Of what importance are they and by the way what you share in common with these purported friends is important to note. It is easier to accumulate the big numbers of friends on Facebook than it is to retain the few friends there. It is not a one day's event to build yourself and attract people that move to share who you are. In the same reason of mind you are not an angel to build yourself in a day and attract thousands of friends. It is more complex to build yourself thus attracting one person.

Good Love Making Takes Time Too

Everything good is not good indeed without understanding how it comes into being. It means you will have to accord enough time to love for us to understand when, how, why and where it happens.

The understanding is versed with actions of love rather than assumptions of the wishful love in the air. People have always wished something good like this happens in their life, it is not about sitting back on a wait for it; even miracles involve multiple actions from either side.

During a campaign to end early marriages in Kamwengye District in South Western Uganda, it was around March, 2018 when the Municipal Council Education Team swung into action closing unlicensed schools. In the event of ensuring quality education with a team led by the Municipal Education Officer; they learnt of high rates of school dropouts in the area. Community members quickly convened a meeting where they unearthed the truth with the then most recent evidence.

"There is a girl who has dropped out of school at seventeen (17) years of age for marriage, the wedding party is on the way this Saturday", said the indigenous people. All leaders had often wanted to be there to stop such occurrences than watch on such a young girl lose their education to early marriages steered by high rates of school girls dropping out of school. Crucially, they had not dropped out of school due to lack of money for school fees but due to early marriages in the area.

The Education team moved on compass direction to the home of the young girl ready to epitomise saving the girl's future hidden in education. "You will not be married off like earlier planned with a number of reasons here" the team said. This girl instantly had a frown expression with a loud burst into tears claiming these people were doing wrong. The family of the bride groom had nothing to say simply because they knew one deserved to be in the prison cells for supporting early marriages in the area.

All this was because this young girl did not understand the concept of love that it would be worth it to accord enough time for good love to surface. Actions must be visible on this path to enlighten us where love is. It will often start with an individual to see love fly over to other people. The individual person intending to love someone will spell out the qualities they want in people yet to be loved. People will expect a lot of these qualities in other people and strangely mindless of their own qualities.

Why are people tempted to think the person in the light of love might be taken away by other people? Within ourselves we notice a gap in reference to have worked to meet other people's qualities they would want in us. This expression is often hidden in fear of losing someone you just physically said to yesterday or even saw on street last week. It should never be in a rush to love someone.

In a number of instances when love is quick to find and get acted upon with people engaged together there will be less sacrifice from either partner. For all that flourishes in love takes time to be what we see it to be today. Make yourself ready for someone you want to love tomorrow by minding more of what qualities live in you. If you are a God fearing person, it will not be coincidental to look out for such a quality in other people. You will offer a lot of time in sacrificing to make self-discoveries of that you are and what your heart cherishes most.

From this point of view it will not be the first day you see someone beautiful that they will fall in love with you. The actions to crown up the love in the picture are meant to continue unfolding every other day. There is a visionary endeavour of making a lasting relationship: a one day event of expression of love. If it is about understanding love, it should solely be about a love relationship that will definitely stand the test of time.

In anticipation of a long life together it should be possible to make the first sacrifice of time offered to the people you love. In the biblical expression of sacrifice for love; Laban had two daughters one Leah and the other Rachel.
The former was elder to the latter though all were beautiful girls. On a specific day Leah went herding the sheep as Rachel went fetching water at the well. In a short distance, there was a young man known to be Jacob.

Jacob fell in love with Rachel at first sight and moved on to help her fetch water from the well. Someone that saw them would soon rush home to tell Laban the father to Rachel and Leah of the love at the well. Later Jacob moved with Rebecca home to meet Laban. We already are seeing actions of love at the well between the two people. This is purely platonic which makes it more distinctive of love sought in a longer time.

Having reached home, Laban asked Jacob what he wanted and Jacob had this to say, "I love Rachel your daughter". Jacob right from the well was ready for anything for him to love this girl as his dream wife. It was a dream come true event and more events ahead. Laban was very clear; you have to take seven (7) years working for me to take Rachel as wife. Jacob sacrificed his time to labour for seven years in a bid to get married to Rachel. It is beyond the love that is at first sight today.

Love at first sight does not mean taking away this girl the day you have seen them for a wife or even to the least a girlfriend. This will be short lived because it involved no sacrifice of time itself. On the wedding day, Laban dressed the bride and she spent a night with Jacob. It was only to realise Laban had offered the elder daughter Leah to Jacob for marriage and for the night. They could have had a sexual encounter during the night but this was not enough to stop the visibility of the sacrifice Jacob had offered to take.

He then went sounding to Laban in the morning after the wedding night, "You married off Leah instead of Rachel." Laban said this means you will have to work more seven years to take Rachel. It was easy for this relationship to last basing on the time it was given to grow and manifest in the lives of the two; Jacob and Rachel. People who will not love for a longer time can easily leave you for other people even when they accidentally met them.

At the end of the day Jacob was married off to Rachel after fourteen (14) years of labour at her father's home Genesis 16: 29 – 32. Love grew everyday they met each other and worked around the clock to meet. The couple drew a curtain of trust and through the window it was a beam of light painted with trust for one another. The biggest gift you can offer for people you love is time to be patient to discover who they are with you. What do they love about you if that is what you are?

It is rather time to shape each other for one's actions directed towards loving their partner. Consider if you wanted to love, what character would you want to see in other people that you have today. There are imperfections among ourselves, though it still goes evident that we never seek these imperfections in people we want to love. In the same capacity on the side of going against imperfections, go for good things you have within you.

How many people are ready to build on love and experience love? We should spend more time building love than developing the feeling to love. It is the foundation that is most important for a lasting relationship. Most relationships have fallen and never to resurrect because of lack of trust among the people seemingly in love. You might forget about where this starts before you see it ending. Many people have failed to keep a distance in tending to make love a great issue.

It is very difficult for platonic love to be manifested among many relationships that involve both young and old people. Sex will never be an affirmation of love whereas love will bring about a greater measure of intimacy in a relationship. This is where most people have lost it to unending conflicts in a relationship. It is more to boys and men demanding to sexually engage their counterparts.

You are not seeking trust by demanding for sex and the other giving in either. You often have chosen to shake the trust in this young relationship. Trust is built on patience and it is only people that are willing to be patient with us today that will walk us through any hard times ahead. Be careful of what you are seeking for in the early days of your relationship with people you love. Go for long term seeking approaches than the short term events.

Your life is a long term event and you will have to look at the time you most likely will spend with the people you love. It is for the rest of your life, say your current age plus sixty (60) years. This shall be only for the people that truly take time to love because God will bless them with more years to live on earth. It is a life decision for the people you take on as wife or husband in a few days to come.

If you pretend to be busy to find out of their family background, shock will overwhelm you to see yourself walk with a thief when they are your angel. You can also walk with them to invest time in making a better love agenda and soon walk with humility reflected from someone's heart.

There is always hope in things you struggle to put up than those you easily arrive at. We all want to be happy of where we came from to appreciate things we have done to bring us this far. Keeping the rest of your life to be with someone, calls for more colours to make a better painting of you with them.

More time to mix up these multiple colours and make a unique appearance of both of you into one being. You will ultimately need to thank yourself for going with the right people. It means you will live a healthier life, play about unceasingly and make money carefully. You both value the journey you started at some point and truth be told; you both did not know when to get there. It is only a belief when we are working hard to attain our vision.

The visionary muscle will only keep stretching for a higher table upon which the love will be shared. The small golden things today can blind fold you of the real gold you always wanted to have. It is similarly true that people can choose to make us their own for a day and drop us off their mind tomorrow. More to being heartbroken and misled in your current relationship can make love seem empty. It is the people we meet that are empty of the love in pursuit of our likeness.

They have no time to offer back for the little we give to them. You are well placed to expect the equal measure of what you give and it is only trust that can fill the remaining gap of expectations. It amounts to express that they could not make it because they were alone. People will not be complete because you came into their life but they will feel enough for who they are.

Love demands every human being to see the capacity in them; a capability of others in that relationship. Your boyfriend or husband can cook, wash utensils, make the bed and clean up the children. It is not meant for you alone and it is not only one side to feel free of discomfort. The biggest worry should be if the people you love have room to exercise what you are. If you do not see them as your mirror, look at what you did not point at in making the foundation in this relationship; share the love equally in respect to gender.

Appreciate Gender Equality

It should no longer be a question of who must do kitchen work in this era. Most families still stay in a building not called after a home due to gender disparities. Your role is not going to be defined by different sexes if we must call the building in which you are in a home or family home.

I want to put this right; you are not a man because you are watching your wife do all the in-house chores as you read newspapers or take drinks with alcoholic contents.

In this capacity we are all equal before time as it continues to demand the direction best suiting to leave poverty for posterity, leave violence for peace and shun sexism for love. Your hand must be laid on something that produces more great yields for the family home as compared to keeping away from it. We all have assets in our hands, courage in our strength and hope in our unison to build family homes.

Every day is casting a reflection of the position you and I want to take in society for our families as men, women and children in these homes. If you want to prove your position today, just sit back in and wait for work to be done on your behalf. Believably, you have a wife not a kitchen attendant anymore, you have a husband and not a sexist and you have children not guests.

It is time to do what we know already and learn things we never knew yesterday. This is yet to involve unlearning the fallen way of doing and believing. Holding a duster to drop all the dust on your jacket will not stop more dust to get there. There is a bigger solution to this which is lasting. As the owner of the jacket you may merely know how to clean up the jacket and you never know how to build it up. Make your wife, husband and children part of the building team to see the well-designed jacket at this epoch.

This is a sense of shifting from directions to being fools of circumstances in order to learn and go places for our homes. People involvement in what we do is crucial. It is not Television, newspaper reading, nagging in a sofa set and browser attendants that make the involvement to produce what is of phone application operators.

Before I can highlight what is bringing down a family home into a mere building, look at things you do to be called boy or girl and man or woman.

Similarly, open your eyes to see what you do as husband, wife and children. If you are still poor and not rich, rich and not richer think of doing things different with a highlight of a building distinguished from a home today.
I will start by narrating to you a true life situation upon which people have decided to keep living in buildings. The morning sets in at 12:00am commonly referred to as midnight. A man wearing the face of a husband is the biggest struggler to make life come true with fancy anticipations that are not worked for.

At midnight this man is not yet home where it will automatically get to be a building as they arrive. Your life too is working along the speed of the second hand of the wall clock. Your life is simply like other human beings and you are not immortal by making a sad situation for other people you pretend to love. People are indeed wrong by what they do to get there. Who is this man attending to you where their wife and children are not?

This man is an associate to colleagues and friends that do the same things for their homes where they get to and vindicate them of mere buildings. The children share more time with their mother prior to midnight that through preparing meals and eating the meals they were together. One day it will be a different story where an inquisitive child goes; "Where is our father every time we are home to the time of eating up a meal".

This child did not sit back to the time of enjoying a meal. There is quite a big difference with this language. The things you choose to eat will quickly get accomplished without questions and answers and things you enjoy will not easily get done on the dining table.

At a very close interval with time the children sleep off in sofa sets waiting for their daddy to return home even when they forget he is coming to make it a building.

This happens at only a tender age and later they simply recognise a man and not a father so they will no longer wait in the living room but go sleeping to their bedrooms. As these events unfold, the wife is wiping off their faces unending tears and they have had the bed time a sore situation of the running tears from their eyes. They will cry every night that no one will know they do so; the emotional grief they go through is more than losing a friend.

You lose at once but here you must be reminded of what is going on where you are being subdued to a losing battle before your children everyday with no answers. The God that never sleeps will soon rescue you from the perplexity of your ever unanswered questions. At 6:00am in the morning the long awaited man appears pushing the door to the building. They are no longer calling you with joy but with predesigned minds of wrong friends in his life.

Wrong friends are emphasised in the event that they keep him out there till 6:00am in the morning. Quickly she rubs off her tears and puts shape away from a frown face to a seemingly happy wife only to open the door. "Good morning sweet heart" she says, it has been long overdue that our children never prepare a meal and share the same meal with us. Please come in and stop keeping me unable to answer questions that are really overwhelming for these children. It does not stop here because I am also trying to answer related questions to my heart though there are no answers.

You are already seeing the time gap from 6:00pm in the evening of one day to 6:00am in the morning of another day. Twelve hours are all lost in the life of a home and there are a lot of struggles in the fore sight of the entire family. Through this they continue to keep the watch of a failing home to suit a building. What would make of a family home in this case? Time for the family home that calls for shared joy and shared sorrow where it arises in part for the home. Time to guide children and offer a sense of direction where a man will be seen working alongside the woman to make a husband and wife for the children.

Right from the kitchen to the washing parlour and to the living room the husband, wife and children start to value family. It is upon you and me to make of homes or buildings by what we choose to live life like. Gender equality opens up the doors of a family home and gender disparities open up the doors to a big building. We have to interpret this rightly for us to have time make sense with what we want at the end of the day.

Why does your partner make things happen as you keenly watch things happen? It is shifting from enough of entertaining the eyes to enough of making a better home. In this age it is prudent of us as men to enter the kitchen with women and share the kitchen work there. The definition of this is painted to the wall of washing utensils as the women are powering the cooker or a stove to prepare a meal. It is also time to carry our babies on street as we go shopping from one hall to another and the women are walking alongside us.

I want to say that men have entirely depended on women to attain the material wealth they have today. Even when this happens they still do not see it in its true sense. They see it all by themselves and think women are not recognisable.

Time is genuine to the extent that it has done it all to recognise women from the back doors to the board rooms and influential positions in the world. Hillary Clinton while they still served as the Secretary of State for the United States of America; time was recognising them. Time still went on to recognise them as the first female contestant for Office of President of The United States of America in 2017. I want to imagine what it meant 2016 years ago and the period before Christ to say The United States of America is the laboratory of Democracy. Does this mean any sense for the last estimate of 2000 years?

If you choose to keep your wife imprisoned in the kitchen back home, you will soon not have food prepared by them. It will be simple and you will easily have these women go to the podium seeking votes as President of your country, so will be the time to awaken your own conscience from being dead asleep. In light of a home, there are more things that are demanded of us as men and women. Respect for each other and trust that we all can do to the better part of a home means it all to love.

In a home there is the planting season and harvesting season happening at the same time. The love you share between you and your partner carries a great deal of a home for any failing state. We can reconcile personal crippled agendas to suit service for the entire team.

We work to make the team happy and shine all over. It is not for individuals to shine in a home; they shine and make it of a building soonest. Appreciating gender equality is a tool meant to save time in itself. There are a lot of things to achieve for our family homes because we have love for the wife, husband and children. Work is divided among family members by their presence and health. This makes it sound clearer as far as who is to perform work at home.

Men have often gone saying we are strong people. Well, physical strength is good but how much has it been shared to other people around and pre-eminently people we love. Your physical strength has only one position to cover. The good out of your physical strength should be the prime cause for its recognition among your family members. Why don't men exercise their physical strength with seemingly bulky activities in the home?

You can start to be one carrying the baby as you head for prayers to the church, carry items purchased from the shopping malls, clean up the baby and dress them every day and sit the washing parlour to clean white all the clothes of the family. It is so absurd of things we copy from colleagues, neighbouring villages, developing countries and developed countries.

A friend of mine one Dr. Specioza Twinamasiko shared with me the concept of men being considered a stronger sex than women in Sweden. I was there to add on what is happening in Uganda in relation to seeing women as a weaker sex than their male counterparts. I wanted to know why boys and men are not living to what they think they are.

Dr. Specioza is a Ugandan woman who has grown and lived in Uganda for all her youthful life. On arrival in Sweden she notices the actual paths the government of Sweden and the men in Sweden have taken. On street and in the home a man genuinely expresses their physical strength to tell of the difference making them a stronger sex than women. In this regard, men wash the babies, dress them up and carry them around for wherever the couple intends to go. Furthermore and more reasonably, the men carry bulky items during shopping in supermarkets to vindicate of the physical strength more than it is to the women.

Did you know that Women do not cook in Sweden? This does not mean that there are machines or computers that cook where women are in control. It is the men in the Kitchen that cook which is not about cultural diversities but about the truth in managing time. The truth makes us believe that time is well spent based upon cooperation of what must be done on a specific day. You will be reminded that this is better done with your match in love.

In Uganda it is the contrary and women are diligently suffering with redundant men wearing tags of husband. With the history Dr. Specioza had on her mind at societal understanding and not in her own family home; she was perplexed over the change of guards in Sweden. She further narrated going out with the host Swedish family to a supermarket. It was the man in that family that held the baby in the carrier bag at their chest and holding other two bags full of items purchased in the supermarket.

Sooner than later she grew sympathetic to the man who carried all these as their wife matched calmly alongside them. In attempt to save the situation she was first told by the man, "no and no I must do this lest I will be arrested here". Secondly it was the wife's turn to speak; "you should never attempt to help out my husband". This was not to punish the husband in this family home. They were sweating because they are stronger than their wife, rightly so.

Similarly machines are employed on a farm and in a factory because they are stronger than human beings. This is the reason we must go for our positions to see work done faster, save time and grow happier and richer than yesterday. By far gender equality is doing better with someone you closely associate with in a bid to save a time and make more money. Why do we have to copy the good people and ultimately have the worst practices in life?

You can take keen interest in seeing how married people are using social media in most parts of your community. Specifically with Uganda, most people have had marriages break down because Facebook and WhatsApp have consumed all their time. Social media has a lot of wives, husbands and children.

The founder of Facebook Mark Zuckerberg per se does not spend all his time there and still makes more friends and millions of dollars a year. Chamath Palihapitiya, a former Facebook Executive once in charge of User Growth has been quoted saying, "We know people are unpredictable and so we psychologically manipulate you and quickly give back". He added, "Failing fast is the right path to exploiting psychology of mass populations of people; if we feed the beast, that beast will destroy us".

Chamath is now the Social Capital Founder. Similarly, Sean Parker who was the Former Facebook President said, "God knows what it has done to our children's brains; If the thought process that went into building these applications like Facebook, was how to consume as much as your time and conscious attention." The initial goal was to get people hurt. These were once Facebook Executives and now exposing the wrath social media has created for the youth and bad users. Mark has truly showed that he is business oriented and we could also use these platforms to market our business ideas and actual businesses.

Having seen people you admire and want to be like do something, start to be mindful of your actions and what it means. Uganda is a developing country but does not take the good admiring position of Sweden, a developed country and turns everything to the worst side of life. You ought to control your heart to do better than people you admire around you.

Only Control Your Heart and Actions

We all must have run out of time in stopping people from going where they have to be at the end of the day. It is rather the opportune time to enable them access where they must be. Your wife wants to go somewhere beyond your bedroom and the living room that you let go of their hand from the confines of the kitchen. Likewise every man you know and refer to as husband wants to delve more into the work done in the kitchen and the entire home.

Let go of your children, they want to play about with you every day and call daddy and mummy. This may sound a simple situation to arrive at but watch the space and see how it must happen. Stop controlling human beings far beyond husband, wife and children in a home. These are parents you are called to love, partners you are must love and children you certainly shall love.

You are not in control of anything in life apart from your heart. Purposely having controlled your heart you get to control your actions and not people. We are painting the picture of love together and living a life worth living universally. Is it relevant to control your actions when you cannot control people you love? There is a signal of achieving beyond human made limits. People are opened to think everything is possible and we can go where we want to reach without hindrances set by fellow human beings.

Two people from two different backgrounds of school life, religious perceptions and culture upbringing styles want to make a couple in the near future. Life for them must be perceived to have been a squared box but live to have it roll easily. In other words the control points from seeing a rolling object would be the edges of the box. It is dangerous to change our differences by closing one eye to the reality of these differences.

Well, as a couple you will obey the rules of oneness and move on. There is always a strategic consideration of understanding the people we live with in respect to what they do better, like and consider threats in life. Before I can meet someone to live with as a wife, I already have things I believe I can do better, like and one positive threat.

I can better be a writer, I like to love myself for other people and there is only one threat though a positive one; someone younger than me by a day. They can choose to be better than me tomorrow and have all my life records fade. In a greater capacity I want to recognise the differences between me and other people as a positive. It is much beneficial and yielding to say, I then can understand them better and work to influence the world to a better stage that is free of violence.

Appreciating the differences among people brings a common ground of positive difference in skills, talents, education backgrounds and financial literacy for the rich, careers, professions, personalities, likes, hobbies and strength. In this, there is a broader view of what must be used, borrowed or bought from other people that we do not have in our control. How can we better coexist without acknowledging that someone is better at something and so we need them for that?

If you will understand me from the other angle due to the difference in my personality with yours, save a minute and appreciate the weaknesses of your partner alongside your own weaknesses. Should the rest of the world leave you abandoned in your weaknesses? It will be my fault not to have mentioned it to the world; love sees the positivity in the differences surrounding us. The difference between you and the person you love is the strength in them which should be a bonding factor.

The involvement taken at loving the right person exposes our unique differences and makes us stronger than when we lived alone. This probably made us unmatched to the rest of the world yesterday. Someone is now in love with us to see us connect to the world away from imaginations. Gradually the differences between you and your partner will conform to the figure of a circle thus making love gets to the centre.

The circle makes the best family home and the distance of love to every other member of the family will be equal. It is based on this fact that your actions reflect how your heart perceives loving people unconditionally. You therefore should focus on what you do to other people especially your girlfriend, wife, boyfriend or husband. Hopeful gestures to demonstrate love may have to create openness of courage among what you are set to do.

We all need support to be better than who we are. The heart in people who choose to love their partner is flexible to taking on better actions in life. As people go on to control their own hearts they develop a foresight of what must keep a peaceful and development centred life. We all want to see prosperous families but we have forgotten about these that outpour as a result of love. Peace and development are inseparable where love is working for us all.

Through time there is discovering the abilities of a joint family through unveiling a proper networking system. With this network, hope is envisaged because there will be no gap where one of the family members is sick, away for a work related trip or even when one is delayed somewhere.
It is about being equipped with courage to do all sort of work and be an all-round person. Very few people can do multitask; they fail to perform given more work since they could not engage themselves to fit in other people's shoes.

Empathy is a pillar through which we realise what people demand of us to pay attention to; a feeling that we must coexist. What do you feel for someone you love? You should have room to protrude through the inner being of people you stay with through your actions. In guidance of our actions a lot more is seen on a smiling face. It is not to be taken for granted anymore when someone you love smiles at you. It is deep from their hearts depending on what the past held for you and the people in the light of love.

Make your first strength in life; a smile to your intimate partner. It only costs the first actions of your life hence in today's understanding of the past. Every past moment behind us are not trash because they are partly the foundation for the smiles you see today. Build on other people's smiles as their strength and see your own weaknesses for a positive change. The strength of your love life, intimate partner too means your joy.

If you did not smile back at them it is someone's weakness. This may not be your own weakness if they are putting on a pretending smile all over their face. It should be a genuine smile for the greater cause of the past which might make of the events of yesterday. There it is your weakness for that matter. This is a call for your full acceptance to taking a recovery pill to reveal where your strength lies.

Your strength is evident in your partner that they continue to smile genuinely. Consider this being your solid foundation for a better family home. It is a gift of unending love with people you got involved with because you love each other. A lot of strength will soon cross cut to your side as long as you get your weaknesses revealed to them. Every human being is not a perfect match for the other but we have a leaning wall only in God and people that retrospectively love us.

CHAPTER TEN
Discovering Personal Weaknesses Reveals Your Strength

Millions of people have lived some other person's life, a deceptive life. How can you live on a set of lies made to you and by yourself? I have manageably been lucky to have set lying myself aside and concentrated on knowing the presumably ugly face of my life. We all have our dark side of life that would be a land mark for how we get to be different from other people. It is not doing justice to yourself choosing to run away from the dark corners of your life.

The impressive part of a dark corner is the belief that there is also the centre of our life where light is. With this source of light you will be safer; God is the provider. Keep in mind the biblical approach of creation in the book of Genesis. The world we are in has light and darkness represented by day and night respectively. Scientifically it is more than two 'planets'; of heaven and earth.

God went on to create darkness in Genesis Chapter 1 Verse 2. He saw this get to the face of the deep and created light in the third verse of Chapter 1. Sooner than later He realised the need to separate darkness from light and it is how night and day got defined to date in the biblical context.

God is hope of change in time; for He is the only power therein to see night come and go; see day come and go. By His Work we live and therefore must attribute all we attain within this time on earth to Him.

His joy is seeing the weak become strong since we are His own likeness. It is true, "the joy of the Lord is my strength". He derives joy from things we do that He wants to see us do that glorify His name. You may have never thought about where your strength comes from. Your strength comes from your weak part of life. If only you knew this yesterday then you would be stronger today.

In the earlier quoted biblical context God was aware of our sustainable mandate to life successes and the strength in them. It was the reason He created darkness first when He would also have chosen to create light first. This is on purpose that people be positioned to believe the struggles of life, the pain, sorrows, injustices, shame against us, inequities, inequalities and pride to mention but a few crippling things in life.

You and I are created in His image not to remain in these inequalities and injustices but to wake up and find way to light. Equality and justice constitute light that we ought to stop gazing at and only keep our eyes wide and open. It is not a portion of the cake to eat in the dark but worth a journey to trek. You must be a witness to your own discoveries of the dark corners of your life. It is not your parents, wife, girlfriend, boyfriend, husband, children or superiors at the workplace to face these discoveries fast.

Your own effort should be recognised wherever you go. People will see you on a struggling lane and imagine, they are moving from this corner of darkness to the other or they are steadily trekking to the centre where light is eminent. It is up to you to decide to keep moving from one corner of the dark to another or experience the centre where light lives.

Indeed nothing is impossible with God; in a space of 24 hours people can have a drastic of change in life and better build up for the future. You simply have to believe that as human beings we are weak today and should seek strength for tomorrow. Time grants this allowance for all mankind and often other people fight hard to keep handcuffed by their life struggles thinking all is impossible.

Even when I did not know God's love, He indeed loved me. All through my life I came to find out that I was a weak pupil and funny enough transcended into a weak student in academic classes. I was true to myself and did not waste time lying to myself. Many people that thought they were polite with articulation of language called me an average pupil and later an average student. It was understood that I knew how deep the darkness had gone in my academic life; often academically challenged.

In my early days of school I was commuting from school to home. Every other day my mother lived to pull my ears concerning the illegible hand writing, failure to write down my name and hardships in expressing myself in the language of the English man as a pupil. These and more characterised the weakness met as a pupil; primarily my mother would mean I was never created to give up by her gestures.

It was from that point that I wanted to do things where everyone around me would see a difference from the quiet pupil in class. The football pitch was partly a new avenue for my strength because I had room to be there as a better footballer. From this point I would soon ask my father to purchase me a pair of playing boots. Subsequently this was not enough that going back to the class environment inferiority complex in light of academics covered the entire classroom for me.

I took time in doing simple things when other pupils went for the hard ones. These included for me drafting letters starting with addresses, dates and stopped at trying to make an acknowledgement of authoring the letter. This meant that I barely had any content of the letter for the start. This was enough to prove a weak pupil in comparison to others.

In a reasonable space of time the average pupils had words that could constitute the body of the letters in all kinds of simplicity. Gradually writing became my strength too and I have authored three books today. If I insisted on struggling to be the best pupil I would never have been the best indeed. Notwithstanding, I would soon be a better pupil since the academic giants consulted me whenever they wanted to write letters to friends and family. The weaknesses in my early childhood gave birth to the strength of my life.

For those days of my life I was made to trek from a dark corner to the centre where light existed. Turn to people around you and ask them of one thing, their weaknesses and strengths if any. You opt to dispel polarity in what human beings set out to do every day of their life. It is more of supporting ourselves to get in the light by seeing the weaknesses or dark edges of other people. The differences in our work should attract us together like it is the power of the South Pole and North Pole of the magnet.

Life is not about independence in society, it is about living a life that is dependent on other people. They can better put us right and use their good experiences to shade light on our faces. From the point I showed every one that I had my strength beyond being an academic giant, I was often shielded in class. To the ground I went in humility which would later expose me to attracting guidance from my fellow classmates. Likewise I would stand to shield the strong people in class in positions where they learnt of their weaknesses such as on the playing field. In trajectory of what we ought to prepare for; like darkness and light coexist so are human weaknesses and strengths.

There is power of success in the weakness you know and work on to change your capacity of keeping weak. It makes absolutely no sense to keep in our weaknesses thinking there is no way out. Going over an individual's weakness is even prettier than searching for perfectionists in ourselves. The secret about individual weaknesses is becoming an open minded person that allows both critics and supporters. Within this we are obviously going to stop the struggle to be perfectionists.

It all goes to accepting ourselves for who we are and work from that point. It gives you a measure of what you could afford to offer but did not accomplish the words you could have said but insisted on silence and self-centeredness. You and I cannot leave in solitude of the world around us and believe it is okay. There must be a problem in such occasions where someone chooses to live a life that is self centred. These people are not necessarily selfish rather self-seeking to the extent of seeing themselves for their own existence.

Then you will have no weakness to look out for in your entire life and it is again okay to pretend there are no environs around us. Every fault line in every individual's life is dependent on who they know to be doing better than them in that field of work. It is only your weakness because someone else is doing much better. Short of this, people would have all as strength and therefore appear as mighty beings. Offer yourself present to crowds where people of different abilities coexist to create a complete cycle of societal success.

In your silence the society is crippling in many weaknesses and the awakening part of your life supports the chain of strength to fulfil societal obligations. Everything around us is for us to use for a better world. The small things must grow at some point of our life. Time does not allow small things to get smaller.

In a scenario where something good is small and they become bad tomorrow, they will have gone bigger but got reflected in a bad image. Many people today have run away from the small beginnings of their businesses without appreciating what they have as a second person. For the survival of any business there are two people; the business attendant and the business as a separate being.

With the humble beginning of the business it stands different from the business attendant. For all the businesses that collapse, people may have not taken into account the strength in the humble beginnings but bless their own weaknesses to fail the entire business. At times and with this example of the business and the business attendant, people want to live in solitude and continue the blame game. "It was a bad business that I had indulged in with few customers" they always say.

They have forgotten the concept of success to be man relying on man. Your strength shall always be dependent upon my success. We can now learn that it is not a vacuum people live in and so they are right for their weaknesses and strength. Multitudes concentrate on the weak points of life to self-isolate for the worst inner most critics of themselves. Why do you bring yourself down the mountain?

No one will tell you it is humility to keep strangling yourself for thinking it is your fault all the time. Acknowledge the smallest of good deeds in your life. Pick on a different consideration for your weakness to be room to exhibit the strength of your other life. We all are good at something and good for something only if we decide to participate in the exhibition set for the town tomorrow. As you prepare for the exhibition, only mind of what you have and no other people.

It is of your own innovation and other people have set up their apparatus to make it come true.
I am telling you to internalise the weak marks of the innovation so they will be sorted sighting more supporters ahead. It is all about the idea of seeing your weakness for strength and their strength having come from your weakness. They have made up their mind to get more productive and prove to every other person of the strength in the exhibition. I know that it is a matter of time as long as you accept yourself for who you are.

Essentially, we are novel due to the capacity gaps between individual weaknesses and societal strength. Well, it is harder to believe that the success of our society does not guarantee personal successes. On the other hand personal successes can guarantee societal successes for the civilised world. Work to meet the needs of the society and it will soon pay back in a stronger currency. Go beyond self-centeredness and you will receive a banquet of flowers for a mighty welcome.

Seeking to guide people out of their dark corners of life makes of us a lit up city with lights illuminating for all people indiscriminative of race, sex, gender, colour, nationality and religion. It is wise of us to save time in such a manner for us from the probable future incidents of regrets for celebrating success amidst societal failings. Given that we stand in unison for the discoveries of human weakness on an individual's perspective, there will be a safer world ahead of us. The challenged will become stronger on a different piece of work to see a trigger in all spheres of the world.

There will be fewer numbers of road accidents, a drastic reduction in diseases, higher income levels, high literacy rates and lower death counts. The world will not be over crowded if it is what has denied us of the opportunity to know of individual weaknesses.

It is immeasurably absurd that young and old, all humanity rushes to see the weaknesses shaping the world and fail to look at their own weaknesses. Everything good or bad must start in us and with us. The degeneration of the world; its systems, climate change, public health, domestic violence, terrorism and control of super power states over Africa and Asia are all because an individual is contributing with finances and man power in one way or another.

Time keeps alternating with nuclear threats, air strikes and the health system bombardment with manufactured virus from one race against another. Today these are vast world weaknesses which keep the headlines of every International and local television. Where are individual weaknesses highlighted for us to get to the origin of this matter? The smallest of the polarised situation you create as a superior at home, workplace, market place and on the walk ways makes this explosion true.

There is a lot to be considered for our individual weaknesses that further pushes people and at times drags other people from the centre of light to the dark corners of life. It is not until you measure up as a superior of your own life that these worldly centred weak grounds can get to positive strength of the world. Even for the positivity to be felt, the strength therein shall be for the people and by the people themselves. Let your superiority move ahead of time from your office and homes that are not home to the inhabitants anymore.

A vivid scenario on how Individual weaknesses have marred the world and supported worldly weaknesses; Superiors in higher institutions of learning a case in point Universities are key to this. A male lecturer married to someone with children engages a student for an ugly intimate relationship.
This is on the back drop that she must submit for sexual assault and subsequently sexual harassment, shame, worthlessness, loss of self-esteem and loss of confidence in their future.

The perpetrators of such acts may hold doctorate degrees and honours degree at both masters level and under graduate level. It is simply loss of morals right from the upbringing of these said to be best students that were retained for mentorship of the current students. The future of the young, beautiful and energetic female students throughout many universities and other learning institutions has been hailed down. This goes on to happen in the name of marks for tests and examinations in some countries in Africa. Is sexual harassment part of the procedure to award marks to female students?

The loud chorus of disapproval ought to start in our hearts as individual persons because deep within; the truth lies unveiled. Without coming to terms with our own weaknesses the trigger is instantly pulled against the future due to our insidious actions. Through this, HIV/AIDS shall keep the song of the day, girl child school dropouts will keep in question and terrorism shall live on the minds of every other generation.

Why wouldn't such a female student who has sexually lost to a lecturer easily give in to a terrorist organisation like the alshabab militants in Somalia? It is true that the conduct of such a girl will not be a worthwhile solution to consider. They will gain strength in winning a battle by doing anything possible to make every man in their presence perish. It will not be bad to them to dress in a suicide belt and move into an area crowded with men. The eruptions in politics have often been steered by individual weakness though a blind eye is turned to them.

The world will forever have a shape desired by human actions both in the private and in the public domain. We can start to discover who we are by fault lines and find the possible remedies to them. Your superiority should no longer be seen in perpetrating acts of domestic violence, terrorism, sexual assaults and controls implanted on people. Let us have pride drawn from being superior to the past weaknesses thus individual strength. It certainly varies with going over the weak point of life for a much recognisable and appreciated life.

Keep in mind you should never walk alone in pursuit for a stronger you and the strength of the rest of the world. The entire human race is practically going in support for a better world where successes are the order of the day, where light means it all.

Scientists continue to spend sleepless nights making advancements for the possibility to have human life exist on other planets other than the earth. All these practices are a clear manifestation of going out of our weaknesses to making other people see their strength. If scientists do not aim thus, it makes life less purposeful.

Scientists are superiors to their world of inventions; artists are going for their world of innovations and creativity today as well. Is this the kind of the world your own relationship is getting to for strength? If it was not for individual weaknesses, there would be no creativity, innovations and inventions. This being the strength of a scientist and an artist, it provides all avenues for who is to give guidance to us. Not every person will guide you to meet your strength.

Be true to knowing that these people are; your mentors depend on your strength to guide and make us accountable. People should hence forth be keen to notice whether their mentors recognised them for individual weaknesses or strength.

I insist on opening this up to you, if they came on your journey because you had failed something; they are mentors in themselves meeting a wrong person. They will simply guide you on the best practices of success from your failure; trying to awaken you is not enough. Your own discovery of a successful point matters.

Mentors That Keep Us Accountable

They that suit being a mentor for someone who is the right person will not demand for more pieces of good work. To a greater extent they are believed to have done their part and now assure you of a better future, "Wait and see what will become of you in five years' time" a mentor will say.

Every time you meet them, they have fewer words to tell you because you most likely will only want to come before them as you achieve more in life.

The presence of a successful person is not meant to be an everyday encounter. You only should think of meeting someone for any engagement if you have better things to share from your store of success. Often people feel they must be popular for their mere presence. What do you add into someone's life every other day of encounter? Do people detest meeting with you and you also did not know the backdrop of their conduct? You simply mean the same if you did not meet them that day.

Your words should be out of songs they cannot mimic or sing; it should never be an anticipation of what you must say to them. This does not mean to say the world demanding more of us every day we wake up alive. It simply should be our way of life to make a difference for whoever we run into by the break of the day. You must make a difference in their life every time you meet them. This is applicable for all sorts of relationships; school relationships, family relationships and workplace relationships.

You will not think of wasting your time for the occasions you are not in their vicinity. All people will do away from their mentors and the rest of the word is to build on their own goodness. There is a good aspect of our humanity which needs to be worked upon.

We must safe guard the relationship we have with the people that mentored us for who we are. It is not by remunerating those mentors in question. It is largely by developing yourself much different from the last time they met with you.

Tell them how far your project has taken your life. Is there any other new project or innovation you have come up with of recent?

Open this to them too. They also want to learn from us at the point we continue to do better than they saw us. They must be missing something that you are not easily traceable. You should only get bothered if you are easily traceable.

It must be your pieces of work and the results therein that should easily be traceable for all persons. We are not important for the past; most especially if one wants to live a better life that is based on offering accountability for oneself. Why would you wait for an external person to audit your life and go on to say you went wrong the other day? Please take it upon yourself to be the first auditor of your own life. It is about having time for yourself before you give time to other people in your life.

It matters a lot when you decide to look at your life and imagine where you are heading. People will all have where they are heading to. Unlike what it was in the past where the entire village was concerned of your destination, today you must keep going and do not wait for a question. Where are you heading to in life? I want to make an assurance of this that whether on a wrong or right trail, you are heading for something.

You will finally get the reality of things you have been sweating for. It is good to be true to ourselves as far as what awaits us. You will get more than you went planting yesterday. If you went joking a lot yesterday you should await meeting more jokes and few jokers by the way.

Your jokes were different and so it is practically hard to trace your match there. Our unique view of life keeps clear for a reflection made upon who we have turned out to become. Time reveals secrets we kept to our hearts.

Our perception towards life keeps these secrets alive. You are in this attracting your own piece of work; a blessing to do more and feel attracted to what you do.

This is the biggest trigger to alert our conscience of the need to have more out of store. Without a sense of self attractions to what you believe, is good for you; people that consumed the first products of your work will be there to encourage us. "When should we expect the next issue of the magazine?" consumers will ask. With you it is clear that people around us for the good have known something we did not tell them before. It is the work we are indulged into that makes it all happen.

It is crucial to have a talking work plan to keep talking about yourself for the work you do. However; do not go looking for talking pieces of work. Go out doing more pieces of work to start to talk for themselves. The sense in this holds that we must do better products of our work every other time we attempt to produce more. You are auditing yourself better to keep improving in the presentation of your products that the number of consumers keeps on the rise.

You are a better person already that you deserve to seek meeting your mentor. This is on the view of a shift in the sense of attraction where people start to get attracted to what you do.

I want us to mark that it all started with us getting attracted to our pieces of work, it is now on to other people to feel attracted to the same work.

You will have to use more effort than when you felt attracted to your own work. It is the opportune time that no one has time to demand more products of your work. They are not disgusted with the previous engagements with them per se as a business partner. You have grown to a level of anticipation overflows that the market anticipates more at any time.

You will have worked hard beyond being a smart person to grabbing someone's trust.

Very few of us have accepted to be there since it is a zone of founded resilience and a reminder to people of what they ought to do. You have the capacity to change something around the universe. It is for only a greater cause to know what to do and when to do it. Today most people wish it was them at your current age. They wish they were younger so they realise the good in doing what they want to do at that time.

We have the key to lock regrets outside the room where a foresight of success is manufactured. It is at answering the two brilliant queries of what to do and when to do it. Do not allow people to determine what you want to do and most importantly when you want it done. Even when everybody expects a cake to be served at table, you have the mind to decide which cake and when it is to be ready. You are truly going baking and to the final stage of having the dough on a pan placed in the oven.

A true mentor is aware that they once enabled you to start peddling the bicycle and the rest can be different tomorrow. They will not have to ask how one will tackle any life issues in case something happened diversionary. Innovations and creativity approaches are not started by other people but yourself. In us lies the trust to change what the world shall ask better for the day. Imagine every other person went asleep and it is you to wake them up for yet a specific activity.

This time you can decide to wake other people up because of the novel idea you want shared with them or how life sounds a mess. Look back at the most times you woke people up only to make them learn of how life really sounds messed up.

You talked a lot of things you feared to think about and further ignored to do. In other words you indeed may never survive the double edged sword of having woken them up. It is even worse that you woke people up like yourself. The human mind is designed to store good and bad things as thinking takes course.

I know how weak my brain might be at times. To this fact I must write down new thoughts that I may easily forget probably because it was at night and I was getting asleep. There are ugly facts you much know that constitute who you are. You may not tell the rest of the world if you know they do not deserve to be a part of them at that time. It is your burden and it is worth considering to have for once distorted your success measure.

It is never important to be honest to other people if you cannot be honest to yourself. Start by feeling the weight of this ugly fact about your life and later see how to work it out differently. You can get out of the worst situation only by knowing it was never good for you. You similarly cannot want to run mad having seen where mad people get their food. It is really not pleasant for us but the mad people are comfortable in the discomfort that we all fear. For the sake of a proper expression of where most people have been to see success. They know it is not good to be mad and stop at admiring being mentally sound.

You just should do something about your current situation. We all want to get out of it and be better people but a few work to mean being better than the rest.

This is the reason a mad person will be seen to be healthy and not going to hospital as ill when you have drugs to swallow every day of your life and continue convinced that you are the healthy one.

On the other side, when you are to wake people up and it is a constructive discussion of how their life could change having gone to believe you are a changed person; a lot of actions will take centre stage. Did you know that most mad people act and try speaking to their actions? You may start laughing at yourself for failing to do better than mentally ill people when you have a medical insurance package for the rest of your life. Even for people that have achieved a gold medal in the Olympics, it is possible that they may never go back for another.

I always appreciate what I achieve and want to go for more by doing more. It is merely absurd to spend 20 years of your life training to win such a gold medal and now spend the rest of your life talking about it. There are always more gold medals far beyond where the first one was met. It is not time for us to tire of going great for what we ought to sincerely do. Whenever I went to school it was my parents that sent me there. I offered little of my time to get what they sent me for as far as my ability to perform.

If it is an innovation, I know that I am sending myself and so anything true and ugly is not a source of shame. It is rather an opportunity to correct myself for a better person in me. Allow the rest of humanity to see us fall and have a reason to stand up again. I recall being a challenged pupil in class but I so much loved to repeat that level so that I could correct myself. Most will think you wasted time, true but you simply could not recognise you were going wrong.

Someone in the position of a teacher expressed their intentions for a self-corrected person. They brought out the bitter truth on the first, second and third pages of the report book to reflect a steadily failing pupil. The pupil did not only fail in the first term and second term of the year but also in the third term of the same year.

Had I not known the ugly fact of my situation in class as early as eleven (11) years of age, I probably was going to become a complete failure for the other part of life. If you distinctively choose not to know where you are going wrong, it might be late to correct yourself. You will also never want to meet your mentor again. You feel there is nothing done over time to qualify them demanding of accountability for the time long spent away from them. Consequentially, the mentor under discussion will feel defended wherever you went and so there is no room to offer credit that is worth a recommendable effort.

Merit Grows With Sweat

What extraordinary milestone shall you go attaining around the world without hard work? I want to make it clear that you must sweat for wonders to happen. Being a better footballer will necessitate that you know how different you deserve to be from other people on the football pitch. This difference that makes you who you are pushes you to train every day and take an extra mile for a better person.
There are very few people you can sit with in a hall, stand among crowds of people and believe they are different from the rest.
You will at a point want to know things that trigger differences among human beings. It is mainly two things for me; where you want to go and call a destination and how one must look like to be referred to as successful people.
What did you put in your bag on setting off for your destination? Most reliably you should not forget to pack your bag with the urge to start, courage to move on and resilience to start again with hope to reach a happy woman or man.

There are four main words here; starting, courage, resilience and happy. It was intentional upon the writer to signal out these words.

Most people do not want to go slow for their probable destinations and so choose to have a descending order of these words; happiness, resilience, courage and starting. In such instances you do not treasure hard work, it means more sense to be happy with people that have toiled their path and now drive across the bridge. Did you know why laughing is not a game for the hungry? They have no energy to go making the better laughter everyone would want to get accustomed to. In trying to laugh with other people, you envision the same measure of joy at the end of the day.

This means you want to own the same size of land or strangely go for the same car they are driving. Hardly does such a human being want to empathise for goodness sake. They all know that it makes less of what the other people went through so they will do what it takes, for negativity as far as getting to where these people are. Who these people are is what they worked to become. If you want to sit on a round table with them for the sake of being happy; the happiness will soon be short lived.

You practically have no capacity to be as resilient as they were yesterday before they met us. Standing up with other people today does not mean standing up on your own tomorrow. Spontaneously, you will choose to quit the game and think of having the urge to start alone last. Every person that quit their situation knew they would not go somewhere because they were not prepared to get there.

It takes hard work and over time to reach there, it further takes a memory that goes for better thoughts to be better. On that round table the discussion is most likely sharing memories of how they all could afford to get happily married and well off.

Don't you now believe that you will start to excuse yourself for a stretch over as it comes to your turn of telling the memories? Make your story count by working hard through every beat of life to make it real. It is great honour at some point of everyone's life, for they perhaps get merited upon good work.

You must resemble what you have worked to become for the last years of your life. Successful people exist in few numbers because we all see how they look like with limited knowledge on how to look like them. Most successful people use less for more whereas the unsuccessful people use more for less. Putting this into context, a successful person will work for a shorter period of time with less or no supervision and still earn more money. Unsuccessful people too have their own window where it is about using more energy and take back fewer rewards.

The difference is reflected in what the successful people did to attain success and what the failed people did to attain failure. The rewards serve true for either party that every worker deserves their wage. There is merit for the sweat of the two categories of people. Casting my mind in the past when I was academically challenged in class where the merit for me was repeating the same level the next year. In the same fashion, most pupils received their merit at being promoted to another level.

It was all for what we did to get where we were as successful and failed people. I would soon choose to have where credible merit is achievable. Every other route for my hope would turn out to an area where I solely wanted to work hard for my results.

You could have at some point of the day worked smart to justify hard work. It was never true for a number of reasons embedded in people who want to go that way.

Your effort is coming out of vain to work smart yet it is the results of hard work that should tell a long story. There are many people ready to pull you uphill in the struggle to follow the right paths. How should you get out of the idol practices? Think of leaving the comfort zone now that everything seems simple.

Do not wait to be hard up where you are because your mind has more room to accommodate better practices that will change the whole situation around. Believe of the time you have settled in comfort to have gone wasted. Try to convert that time into what you wish it were used for that is a source of merit. A lot of new and productive directions will open up waiting that you act on taking that direction. Start off with nothing in anticipation but work hard to change every day's picture of your life.

It is possible in holding a more admirable view of your life even when other people go to criticize your steps to that direction. Deep within you it is about making a challenge thought after for every solution to come. We must be part of the solutions that are changing the world rather than enjoying the comfort of our unthought-of scenarios. The first tactic to use preciously in running out of that comfort zone is to assign to you one of the world's biggest challenges. I know it sounds unheard of for most people to want to solve the biggest challenges when the small challenges around them go unresolved for as long as they have lived.

It is with the biggest that you will think different and conform to making the biggest ideas and solutions. When your colleagues go happy with solving small challenges be careful to keep your ground of solving the big ones.
You will be happy for as long as you live tackling the biggest of challenges, the merit to come your way is in the biggest enclosure of success. It will soon be well with you for the battles you chose to get involved in.

CHAPTER ELEVEN
Fight All Battles And Lose To None: Not Even Death

We are all on the battlefield where no one wants to die; there is no reason for us to kiss the soil. There is always a reason for us to fight a winning battle in life where the fighting jets are the human brain. It is for me the strongest weapon humanity has been blessed with to fight winning battles. We have to start getting out of our houses with a winning attitude for anything. This means that for whatever people set their hands on should come to an end. You are requested to better do things you want to finish.

Believably there is a day in a week where we all might wake up on the wrong side of the bed. At times it serves the right purpose of getting to finish what we started if there is a preconceived plan. It is unreasonable for us to sleep in the night without a plan for the next day. You are working yourself out for no good intention. Planning for the next day before you get to bed is part of laying strategies that facilitate the capacity to adjust in life.

Why would someone stop on starting what they wanted to perform upon on a given day? Flexibility is a virtue you can apply when something you earlier wanted to do was rooted in a sketching paper, your mind or spectacularly planned for. Putting this on evidence based perspective, if you wake up in the morning and it is the time you want to meet someone; most probably being disappointed is one thing to expect. Given that you earlier considered making a plan on how to meet these people; an appointment in detail of the plan, these people may not easily slip off your catch.

Well, we cannot rule out all the possibilities of missing these people but prior information might come in to save your time. It is from this that you allow other things to take place from the perspective of formerly failed pieces of work. Often one will lose the urge to do one activity but have the courage to get on to the other. This is recommendable for us to keep on the lane of being active people and accept what it really takes to be there. You will not have to let go of what you have held even for one minute.

There are many people that ever wished to get the opportunity you have but time has run out for them and it is only time for you today to behave different. If you so decide to act their way, you must be aware that you have just passed it on to other people. They will not take another hour to wait but it will be the rest of their life time fighting to protect its fruits. We have a point where lessons can be picked for a better day ahead. In every community there is that person richer than the rest of us and there is another poorer person than the rest of us.

Where do you lie today if this is in your community that a vote is to be cast for people in the category where the richer or poorer person would be got? In sincerity of heart you and I see our positions without indecision. Why then have we often adamantly gone against being flexible to keep moving to where we wanted to be? Is it sheer testing of yourself to see if you can live a poorer person than others and think of jumping out of foul-smelling poverty for a position of the richer people.

I want to distinguish between these two characters in our community for us to see where one might end up that is if we do not see ourselves there yet. The richer woman or man has more battles to fight everyday they are alive. They create the battles for themselves and fight them.

They have a foresight of what is going wrong and how they personally can go about it without crying out loud. For your own information the richer people are scared of other people in the community to notice of what is making everything seem stagnant. Within their making they have a great feeling of making the most selling solutions that will win for them the entire battle. Through this every community member, community leader and human being runs to them for bargain over what the solution should be for the other problem. A few questions will be posed before the community dwellers to see if these are yet to challenge them.

By the end of the day, different parts of the solution will be made by the community dwellers without their knowledge. The richer man is aware that the most important resource is a human being with a human that is put to work constantly. This reminds me of a number of incidents when my mother often told me I was over working my brain by waking up at mid night (12:00am) to write my manuscripts. "You need to rest and relax your brain", she said.

It is worthless to live a hundred and one years with good health because you did not tire your brain. You are as good as a new born baby that every time you are awake you call for attention. Why don't you think it is you with the better solutions for your community? The richer man or woman around you is guided by this question to do everything that unfolds without turning to consult the poor people. They will definitely find their level among the class of richer men and women in other communities.

The poorer woman or man has room to turn around and side to side on their bed every time they are there. They will snore for as long as it is dark within their vicinity. This situation is indeed darkening too and many people's brains have for long slept off.

It is from this mark that they grow vulnerable to the extent of running to the richer people to utter all they see as a mess in the community. They are not attracted to being the creators of the mess and hurriedly go thinking the mess was there before they were born, the same mess is reoccurring today and so it shall be tomorrow. It is not until something is said out to others that a solution can get into a pipeline of their survival. What happens if we are to continue surviving on the mercy of someone?

They will exploit us even when they did not intend to but just feel sorry that they exploited us without coming back to tell of the exploitation. Going forward to be poorer than the rest qualifies you to hate flexibility with the smallest of life's issues. To this note as solutions are finally drawn, you will wholeheartedly take what comes your way. The world is rich in good things and someone is feeling thirst for the riches there in.

The poorer person is simply living in a vacuum of satisfaction. If the satisfaction of the poorer being was real then we would see them do something to quench this thirst with lasting solutions. It is again the poorer person that is contented with what they have; they detest asking themselves questions like; what is most likely to happen if this was gone? Certainly without asking such a question to you, it is less of accepting to take on any battles in life. The moment of your life where you think it is not good to get a scratch on your body for any battle then it is the last day to think of being richer than other people.

With emphasis, you have limited battles to engage in because you cannot create any by yourself. What disturbs you that is from the other side of the family, community or the world over is not that strong a battle? It is measured at lighting up a gas cylinder that is already leaking in your house; you may lose your life there.

Whoever has left their paths unclean shall still find them open. If you think it is not important to make a better day for your community by being a better person yourself, you gradually will have less to take in from it. I want to make you understand that we must fight battles that give us gains or where we benefit.

If there is a battle to engage in and you are losing from the side of gains then it is not worth spending your limited time there. The world is not a scene of people that can but a habitant for people that do. I cannot do something so that someone else will praise me. It is okay if they praise my work at the end of the day. We are not looking out for armchair critics on this battle field; it is people who must act their way through.

Why should you be blessed with words to justify your abandonment of the battle field? What makes you happy to have accepted to settle there?

The realm of your life is ungovernable by practical principles but only to see what goes on and follow. If you admit letting the other part of the world conquer who you could have been at the pivotal point of flexibility, it is your way. It becomes your way of following on fading footsteps of successful people around the world. Where does this get grounded in our life? It is partly accepting to grasp the chorus of songs sung by other artists.

This is not grounded in the truth that one time you must sign your own. We want proverbial things that can be done by people you seem to associate with to manifest for a greater part of your own actions. Human demise should be a shock to us because we are not dying as we continue to live. Actions that speak deny everybody the opening of their door to gradual death. It is one kind of demise that you and I deserve but look, no one will force you to live up to the end.

There are signs that we are not living to die once. Open your eye brows wide to keep safe or even be safer. First, I am not God and not His equivalent to tell of when someone may kick the bucket. Be careful with this lesson. It is not yet our time to accept defeat in the eyes of a dying person when they have breath.

In the disability fraternity most people there are not with the five God awarded senses of smell, sight, hearing, feeling and tasting. Or they have lost control of their limbs or mind. At least they have lost one of these which are out of their control but to live life that way. Most of these people have accepted their disability and still defied all the odds to live a life worth humanity.

On a number of occasions I have seen deaf couples together making family life true and blessing their children with education. They have children who have hardly any disabilities on them by God's grace and owning children. I mean children who own the hearts of their parents never to abandon them for being deaf. We had earlier noticed that the day we wake up on the wrong side of the bed, something should have gone wrong without prior knowledge. Have you and I not seen people abandon the battle field on such a day and say no to work?

Oh it might seem that someone is telling you that human beings have sought refuge in lazy zones of life. God creates strong human beings at birth, whatever; the disability on them. I personally was born to a visually impaired man. The late Mr. Besiga John who did not become blind after my childhood but before I existed he was. This man had vision for greater life not only for himself but also for other people around the world.

Literally he had no sense of sight. Having had his children through University level and witnessed their graduation meant he had done his part.
You ought to do your part every day you realise you are still alive. If today you are dead asleep with sight when the visually impaired man like my late father played his part; try feeling empathy for him. God forbid that you wake up a blind woman or man. Do you have confidence that you will live a better life?

You are having the disabled keep the ability to go where they want to reach. For many years my father has employed sighted people on his farm to graze cattle.
This is not for being blind but the ability to have the sighted work in his enabling vision. To this point there is living proof that he is aware of his limitedness to sight.

The biggest malady is not to notice we are at times hand cuffed by nature. This is the better part of the lesson; it is not time to waste thinking about changing ourselves from who we are. It is the day to accept our race, skin colour, tribe, religion, nationality, sex and physical appearance. Through this you are opened to the truth on how life should be lived to the extent of being flexible for that you are. People who are dying before their natural death are involved in fights with which nature has identified them to be.

You are a better person with better abilities given that you notice your father was a fisherman. That was his occupation; go being a fishmonger that your father spent most of his time on the waters is a point of risking his life so you do better. He is not calling you to the waters to fish with him amidst the waves of the sea. You just have to look for profit off the lake and the sea shores. Be the first person to carry the fish off the shores to the market where price partly is determined by the journey involved to get the fish.

Likely it would not have been pleasant for my father to concentrate on his loss of sight at six (6) years of age. It was pertinent to invest his time in growing visions that make life full of light for himself and other people.
It would sound a weak position of your life to keep where your parents were yesterday as far as developing your community. It is not even for the richer people that their children are to be like them.

The children of a richer woman or man in your community should accept the position of their parents and therefore go being richer than their parents if they so deserve to. It will not matter that your starting point was talking to these richer parents; the essential bit of it is living to the last day of your life. Your pride should lie in having life lived to the full today. Don't you think it is no longer important to think you deserve to be poor that your grandparents were poorer than any other sometime back? Your life shall be determined by fighting your own battles to the end.

Your grandparents succumbed to less and did not believe it was less. They imagined it was more for the next century but it is no more today in the 21st century. If we do not own the less we have, it is obvious that we shall not live for more. Natural demise will find us unsorted and having to bet weather we are the right people to die or not. We all have a day to pass on at some point though most people keep dying gradually till the time life is done with them.

If we get deceived that we are beautiful women and handsome men to attract death every day, it is unfortunate. Your way of life is telling a story like this. The last time you visited the doctor for medical checkup s/he offered pieces of information on what your health looks like. Having noticed it was not for the good of it all they further offered different pieces of advice upon which presumably one would regain their health status.

The entire message from the doctor was left on their door mart as you left the counselling room. What is it to anticipate given that in case of a deteriorating state of our health?

More care will be accorded to us in the Intensive Care Unit (ICU) well aware you have less chances of survival. They certainly will blame it on you as an adamant patient and feel proud to have satisfactorily done their part. In a broader picture of what I wanted to make you discover, the world around us is for us though we often are against the world itself.

You have no one to drag you to courts of law for not living to the dot. However; the world will soon turn against you to make you believe you first went against it. We should dress ourselves in proper armour to fight and win all battles even those we have created ourselves. People in your community will wholly burst into laughter for refusing to accept yourself in time. I cannot be born again (not for my faith) to another man and call them my biological father because Mr. Besiga was blind.

Accepting them in the first place is an eye opener than to enjoy their company and love. I have indeed believed that if someone loves you they go on to love your dog. On a number of occasions masses of people lead us the wrong way but individuals save for other ways. It is not by accepting the entire community in which you are born that everything will fall in line. It is rather by accepting yourself that soon you shall raise to the top.

I tell you this purposely to re-echo to you why you ought to create your own battles. You will by design fight them better and have better solutions in life. If you wait on fighting battles that drag your entire business into a loss side of it, they will watch on you lose as you indeed draw closer to the battle field. We have a marvel in our eyes and should find the mirror to preen ourselves through for it to be real. This shall be the source of your gains to appreciate what you are and for who you are today.

Your life from this point should not be taken for granted by the world around us. It should cross to your own mind not to take yourself for granted. You do not own it all and so stop bragging over who you are saying you did it to the end. The woman or man of the time that is full of wisdom will commend their work into the hands of the Lord. This projects them attributing their success too for God's love.

Without Him you will not live again and again. It is through appreciating who we are that we appreciate people around us; both for and against us and furthermore appreciate God who makes it happen. Have the rest of your life struggle to live better than day dreaming on how you would die better. Death has no formula though it is a battle that every living creature beyond human too ought to succumb to. There is someone in control of your life and so they are aware of when, how and why we are to pass on. I want us to go in the truth of things we have control over and leave the others to those in control.

It is only death that you have no control over when it comes, although sometimes we do things that can hasten death. What is keeping people anxious of what they will leave behind on earth? What did you come with on earth? You should enjoy every day and get contented with how you have chosen to spend your time and the people you are spending your time with. If we are put to task to explain how one wanted to live their last day on earth; a lot contradictory paths would appear.

However, things that keep relevant are being real to a day well spent according to every one of us. I do not see someone who wants to enter their shop and make no sales at all. You solely did not knock by someone's door and tell them to be your customer the next morning. All you did was to have items that sale given customers appear in search for them.

Be always in the right corner and wait for what unfolds, it will most likely be in your favour. Most profoundly is when you and I think it was worth doing well. God is writing our cheques and soon we shall be paid in the biggest currency ever on market. The trick behind this is to promptly fight your battles to the end.

You Did Not Cheat Death: God Knows Why?

There is at least one scenario of human life when we all think we must have cheated death; power over death. Jesus Christ as Lord came in the image of man so that we could notice that every human being shall succumb to life and death. He was on to live as though man could but kept the partial view of God. He was both God and man through His way of life on earth as per the thirty three years he had lived. Everything He faced within this time; good and bad.

Uncountable lessons have been learned from Him since He has always been among men and women to preach the word of His heavenly Father. He was open to great persecution, threats and the bitterness ever known and heard from the mouths of rulers and kings. King Herod was one of these that tried their level best to persecute Christ.

Only for what we are today, Christ cheated death since He was man and God. This was evidenced right from the early days of His life when King Herod plotted to kill him in cold blood among other new born babies as reflected in the bible Matthew 2:16. The Godliness in Him was shared by the care takers that the heavenly father communicated to, of King Herod's intentions. Every other first born child of the time was killed but Christ survived not because of His intellect but God the Father had something to teach human beings of this.

Right from your birth time, years are still counting on as I want to ask; "Where are the other children that we share the same birth day?" They are gone, would be the answer if you dared to ask this. I may have not considered time to ask such a question. The wise people will struggle to think about how to live but death keeps inevitable by all means. In a small collection of thoughts; reflecting upon your past that you did not know we lived is left to the strong hearted.

Why do you think it was not you and me to die prematurely in our mothers' womb? Many passed on at that stage of life. Why do you think it was not you to face abortion in the hands of your parents? Many unborn babies were aborted then.

Why do you think it was not you to die at birth? Many children faced the wrath of death as early as that? Why do you think you and I are still alive? Many people that would be marking their birth day with you are dead. Therefore something in your life should be in query for the love you share from God everyday you live. Do you share the same love to other people in your own capacity?

Carrying the portrait of Jesus to have lived as a human being only to thirty three (33) years of age, would stand a test of what the world must remember about you after you die. We are challenged to try Christ's life style in the name of what He did on earth. What legacy do you and I anticipate to leave behind as we indeed shall die at some point? Today I am thirty one (31) years of age in 2023 I want to feel the pinch for the legacy we must think about.

Replace my age with your current age as long as you can read this book from the previous sentence. If you are a parent try to insert the current age of your youngest child given that they are above twelve (12) years for boys and ten (10) years for the girl child. You start to see where we are heading to as we continue to work tirelessly today. There are more resources to apply today to be better people than the time of Christ two thousand and eighteen (2018) years ago.

The clear distinction between us and Christ is that He knew the kind of death He was to face at the end of His earthly life and we do not know the kind of death we are to succumb to. This is a great sign that He was God too even when He lived on earth. I realise more hope for us because we only carry the image of God which does not qualify us to be in the position of Christ.

However; there is a great deal of events to consider for our legacy left behind for the day we shall not make it any more. You do not have to work to the tune and measure of God but you have to work to the measure of the greatness in you. Everyone that died by the count of yesterday was mature to face death though may have not been old enough.

They had lived their part and you should consider living yours every day. It is only the strong that can read this chapter to the end as I try to break down death to a diversionary thinking. I want to capture the faint-hearted too. Have an hour of your life that you have read this and spare it for the past people you might have met in your first class in school.

In sincerity and honesty my mind does not have the capacity to memorise names called after people. It is only for the extraordinary people in my life that I will grasp their name again. This is more to mean I am full of myself but it is that simple. However; there is no picture of these people further than knowing their name that I recognise today. Where are they today and which trail are they on?

This does not mean that I did not enjoy my childhood with them but there is close touch perhaps for losing a number of them to death, life and uncertainties in there. I will always feel like shading tears to this fact.

This is the time the facets of life lie in peril of people we have lost and indeed cannot trace today. I want to say you are most favoured today that you are alive and kicking.

The power to live against the dead and their realm was only in the hands of Christ through death on the cross and resurrecting after three days. As he ascended into heaven His glory was lived on and on to this present day of human existence. He is known for what He did which is the foundation for His legacy on earth. What are you doing today that your own legacy is in formation? This question comes in at the time you have full knowledge of human levels of maturity with death.

There is a purpose for which each one of us is set to live different from the other. It should be feasible every minute of life for the sort of things we do. Did you know why you are counted among the living today? I will use two cases here for us to have our own life situations fit in the picture. First is Rev. Prof. Peter Kanyandago at the point he shares the unconditional love of Christ for his own life. On the morning of 22nd March, 2016 he was set to return to Uganda from Brussels in Belgium.

On his arrival at the Zaventem airport in Brussels on Tuesday, he saw terrorists blew set off bombs which blew part of the airport where he had just checked in his luggage. This was the deadliest act of terrorism in Belgium's history. The former ISIS fighter one Ibrahim el-Bakraoui and the bomb-maker Najim Laachraoui together launched attacks killing sixteen (16) people. An hour later, another suicide bomber – Ibrahim's brother Khalid el-Bakraoui blew up explosives at the Maelbeek station, killing sixteen (16) people too. A third airport bomb failed to explode, leading to a weeks' long manhunt for the suspect one Mohamed Abrini, who was later arrested on 8th April, 2016.

Today, in 2023 he (Prof. Peter) is 72 years of age and still relatively strong. Many people on the fateful day died in the hands of terrorists and the whole world was in shock. It was breaking news all over the international televisions with estimates of the dead and trying to find out the terrorist group in question. I was not aware Prof. Peter had to travel back to Uganda but I have managed to write about him as a family friend.

Prof. Peter has done a lot of charitable things in his life and I just did this as a gesture of appreciation in my human capacity. We thank God he survived the Tuesday, 22nd March, 2016 bomb attacks. One true story everyone should know is that as a young Catholic priest he managed to meet a young visually impaired man; Mr. Besiga John who happens to be my biological father. With all he had; it meant sharing his love to my late father manifested in paying constant visits to him in school and subsequently paying his school dues. Most likely without his intervention, he (Daddy) would have been a different personality than I have known.

Education to blind people is what expands their chances of a bigger vision beyond sight. You shared to other people when you had less and God intends to share with you more than you gave out. There is nothing that surpasses investing in human beings through charitable ventures. Furthermore, this substantiates the fact that Prof. Peter never cheated death and so are other people that survive in similar situations. In my understanding as a feminist, another case ought to cover a female being.

She happens to be my aunt by the name of Mrs. Kibaju Naome. She was travelling on Mbarara – Masaka – Kampala road with her driver and a house assistant with whom they had lived for fifteen years. On a fateful day they got involved in a fatal accident and in a considerable time they were air lifted to Kampala for immediate attention.

It was my sister that sounded the breaking news on the very evening of the unfortunate incident. I started to imagine what the picture was for the family and friends.

I truthfully did not think about the causalities with prior knowledge of what a car accident might be. In a few days they were said to be recovering steadily which sounded hopeful a situation for everyone. More from this day was the demise of the house assistant who lived by a child. Soon after the burial proceedings, Hon. Naome would soon start her travels to Japan and South Africa. This carried the sense of her relatively stable health. In the light of God's love are people that were in the same car and faced the same causality but one passes on and the other is living.

With the two distinct and unique cases, we ought to concretize the lesson lines of what life means before death. How you intend to live your life to the full is not solely about you but about us? Many other people are capable of holding your position in office, by rank and age. If you feel you do not deserve to be there await your dismissal, sacking and impeachment for a greater cause.

The play field is levelled for us to use our time promptly or never. There is a moment of your life where it must be late. Not even you to have room to bargain over a given price for a commodity you wanted to carry home. Not thoughtfully even for the time wasted on denying better opportunities to managing time. When will death strike and how it will come should be none of your business too.

All to keep in mind is that we have no power over death as we are mortal beings but in the meantime let us live life to the full and aim at winning all battles. I truly know that as long as you and I are living we shall keep blind folded by the clause, "better late than never." This does not count the day a deadline has passed, for it will be other people to benefit from their earlier submissions.

You will have done the panel of interviewers a great opportunity not to waste more time with more interview sessions. The type of life we live is linked to how we meet our deadlines. People who meet deadlines are not people who are really free to be occupied with work. These are people who mean what they say by doing it.

Deadlines are set to measure the discipline of the applicant and their capacity to start and finish what they started. Do you start something for yourself and finish it by yourself? Why don't you start something for yourself and end it yourself? There is nothing you will start for yourself that you want to see put you down. This is the success factor of starting something for you. It is a pillar of setting the deadlines to have it accomplished given that you must start on more things.

Therein is a concept of reproduction for every venture we take on by ourselves. You must have more that will not easily fade. The actions of your life today should not be limited to a hand count. In a broader view you will get more money for having reproduction of your good ventures at its apex. It is with this that your bean counter will have to use a calculator for computation of the gains out of your efforts. The importance of reproduction goes deep to making a productive mindset.

You make a way of seeing success nearer to you than relenting of the past achievements. Well, death is inevitable but where shall we fail to live by ourselves if we must live. It is through self-denial of what you should do today by hating postponement of any activities. Most people have thought of postponement like I have previously done as a way to do work when we are better off. It is not necessarily true that there is the right time for what you want to do other than today.

All that is good in the name of other people held no postponements. If it were for Christ to postpone His death on the cross, we probably were never to be saved by shading His blood. In your human mandate it is not yet to the interpretation of saving the world on the cross. It is about saving yourself on respecting the time you have to do something. Please never consider it for the time you have to do anything. It will be done any way and the results will not be of a legacy worth memorable.

If you ever deferred some activity for two hours ahead of the day, you will not perfectly execute that even in your line of duty. There is a close range of losing with whatever we intended to achieve before the deadline catches up with us. It is coming to someone else's time of moving what they are meant to move. Everyone has something to move for a distance they allocate to themselves. It is as far as you want to go that you will move that you must move.

There are numerous things you will have to move into your life and more out of your life. I see many obstacles that have hindered you from moving something to where you must go. The obstacles, nonetheless; are marked to believing in other people without at all believing you can. You have interpreted life by doing less and sleeping more in the guise of relaxing for the next activity.

We are living for the purpose in us to do better than yesterday and to accomplish our goals. It is relatively flagging off someone and they keep waiting as the clock ticks. They will miss finishing in time and act like it is time to stroll to where they initially had to go. I must live in my world of getting to the apex of starting and finishing what I wanted to do yesterday, it is not okay for you to live in your own world of never starting. Certainly you will not bring to an end that you did not start on yesterday.

In purpose of life, you also will not end what you started without marking the finish line. It grows to mean that there; people will continue doing the same thing not to recognise advanced technology, emerging businesses and therefore new competitors. People are meant to turn on to another page of their life from achievement to achievement. Agreeably, I will be doing more than yesterday month in month out and witness the diverse results that ought to make me realistic in nature. The bitter truth is that we continue closing in the gap of what we have to do on earth.

The biblical view is clearer on age differences in correspondence to human life span; seventy (70) years and eighty (80) years for those who are strong Psalms 90:10. As you grow older their age gap is covering in which does not call upon the highlight of one's failure to do their part right. It will be unfortunate to see most people in their middle age stressed of their old age backed by leaving everything out of control. You will be wide of the mark not to have the knowledge of the law and wait to be in courts of law because you have done wrong. Likewise it is not time to pretend that something is not true.

The design behind every human being is death and the design behind every day eis how you choose to live it. It is you to set the rules of the day and see where they must lead you. Know more about things that should put you up the mountain and believe it is true that you can fall off the mountain too. This will drive us to think it is important to think twice every time God tells us to go on. Once again it is not that we have defeated the trap of death but God wants to know where every one of us will head to thereafter. Recognise His hand in your successes and you will in turn know where to head to.

Where Are You Heading To?

It is interesting to know that nothing is against us from today onwards. All the hell that you could have gone through is proof enough that nothing should have brought you down. There is no limit for more resourceful time that is contrary to the days before. We are acting in full wisdom of a life that must be true to ourselves. Life is not to be lived anymore in speculation of calamities.

A good farmer will run into a virgin piece of land and make it fulfil his dream life of meeting better yields season in season out. They will not easily go for wicked thoughts that go against them. It will not be imagination of what would happen if floods, pests and disease brought his work down. He will insist on the important issues like clearing the virgin piece of land for ploughing. Within, a spirit of a green light that over shadows the red light and he keeps himself set for progress.

Soon the planting season will start only to maintain a positive path for their initial plan. At the end of the entire season, they will feast on their labour and time. There is also a bad farmer who will mention of all the possible calamities and add that they would not want to lose their time. Why do you plan for the bad situations and you tend to forget about the limited time one may have to do their work? What keeps the good farmers moving even when the land originally known as a virgin piece of land loses its fertility?

They have more time to visualise and recognise beauty of their farm lands. It is all valued at adding in fertilisers to make the exhausted piece of land alive again. Do human beings get exhausted like these pieces of land around us? If they get exhausted then, what makes them far much exhausted not to attend to their own life?

We are set not to only conceptualise what we ought to do in life but also to go practical and find someone beyond ourselves. You most probably will want to head to where other people have not considered a better place for adventure. Go your way and make the place accessible for other people to soon call tourists. Time demands that they pay a specific visit with interest of appreciating the flourishing view they will not own.

The human purpose of living a life that must be trajectory of their life built motives is based on where they believe their route must lead them; focus. You often will receive a check on whether you are ready to proceed or not. This is when people around us get better only to realise we are the same age, went to the same school and funny enough we even always beat them in class.

In the scenario for that I was yesterday is not important if competition has come and left without me noticing its presence. What should be the most admirable turning point where competition seems unnoticed for some time? Do not run away from this to its reality; it is embarrassment. Face it and seek guidance on how to make you get on a better track. Never mind they are simply better people today because what made you the best yesterday was not the most important for today.

They have decided to be better people by choosing to do better than you. Several times it is like a baby clinging to their caretaker (not necessarily their parent) because they treat them better than their parents. There are things that will certainly treat you better than the most yielding life situations. They will keep you company of comfort, less stress, more colleagues and family first tracking of a support system. The other person that you see far achieving in life; where you intend to go across, they are accommodative to discomfort, more stress, few friends and limited or less family presence.

They will believe it is possible to go where they want to reach. It is you alone and where you want to head to in life with less company of things that delay success and progress. You are invited to be a machine of your own life where constant checks should be made and the right lubricants applied to the engine of the machine. Every other day of our life demands rejuvenating people not by age but by strength to do better. If it means calculating the number of hours to sacrifice for what you did not have yesterday so be it. Find out where extra time has been spent for several days.

If it was in things that yielded short time smiles like paying attention to people that make less like you, offer less time to them thus investing in other spheres of life. You will most likely have to make a genuine and painful shift in your life. For most cases of my life, I will make people seem less intriguing for me because they are not ready to make a shift in their life. Why do I have to offer time to someone that never wants to be better? People, who are not set for pain that teaches us the way to accommodate ourselves resiliently, indeed want a smile for a while.

You will need to shift from who you were that we all know to who you know you must be. It is true that everyone around you reads a wrong picture on your face. People cannot determine where you are heading to if they have a mind that contradicts your own paths. Do not make a shift of trial rather make one of focus. You are now resolving to lead your own life in a visionary perspective.

On one hand we are redesigning who we should be and on the other accenting to everything with a reconciliatory tone. It is no more of working under false pretense in acknowledging a turning point in life. It must be feeling sorry for previously wasting ourselves and time doing things that were not meant to make us leaders. If you cannot lead your own life you will not follow the right leaders.

It is easier to lead other people the wrong way than to lead yourself the right way. The shepherd will stand looking for the one wolf among the sheep because they are not seeing it. As the evening draws nearer one will certainly go counting their sheep to see who is ill and who could be missing.
It will not be far from over; the wolf will be fought and killed mercilessly in a bid to safe guard more sheep. You and I should deservingly know that it is not worth the position of this wolf.

Many people have lived as wolves among the sheep with obnoxious trends of hurting other people they lead.
You can alternatively choose to have a redefined life of who you always were and make of a game changer. The game changer will not be self-seeking and selfish with what they are doing. The perimeters of work mandate you to be honest with other people so that they can offer a helping hand. Make your true colours be seen among these people that if they are to go useless, the existent loop holes are keenly noticed.

It serves an introduction of who we are so they will know us and push us for that we must go for. The most obsolete part of a life that intends to be transformed is inner silence. What is inner silence for humanity? Inner silences are things that are not seen in your actions because we are not readily available for our own transformation. If you are not willing to see yourself transformed from who you are to what you ought to be, await stronger winds to sweep you off.

Why have most people lived to the test of time and not gone transformative of their own life? I will tell you that they did not pick lessons of what transpired in their life where all was in a mess. Casting my mind back, there are situations where God has indeed become my refuge and shielded me from accidents and committing crime. I have talked about how Rev. Prof. Peter Kanyandago and Mrs. Kibaju Naome survived death.

If someone will not pick any lesson that would make them transform from who they are to whom they ought to be, the rest of the story should still fall on their shoulders. In other words no one should be blamed for our own rigidity to being better people. Dubiously, such a person may stand to dance to the tune of their wrong and previous traits. This gives them false courage to think they cheated death. If you got involved in a car accident for being a drunken driver, your point of survival from death should make you stop drink driving.

Our God is a merciful God but there is a lot people may not understand by insisting on our path even when signs keep coming to mean calamity. I have seen people die a non-shocking death; where people around them insist on saying that the deceased person did not conform to the pieces of advice issued by the doctor. They were told to stop drinking alcohol excessively but all was a waste of time.

What would justify keeping stagnant with where we are and strangely keep engaged for the deadliest acts? Nothing at all would make us free when everyone notices hand cuffs confining us for a better part of the day. We should often feel the freedom to get out of the confinement of our own life led initiatives.

CHAPTER TWELVE
Set Out For An Action Plan

Largely for many of us a lot has gone astray in the past and small successes have gone unnoticed. There is nothing wrong that goes unnoticed both in the nearer days of life and in the days ahead. It is incumbent upon us to thirst for success that one has to get out and make things happen again. You are not alone for things that went unexplained but today it is an individual's role to stretch alone and reach for your success. It is all about you and you for you to become you.

What do most people do to measure where they have reached covering a specific journey? They easily start work and easily leave it hanging thus abandonment of their success stories that would reflect ups and downs of one's life. We want to hear about your journey differently from narrations to self-assessment. I should be able to assess myself for whether it is true or false of what I have done so as to move on or do something different. The reality would be that in your work you deserve a credit or a pass mark that is based on the results due assessment.

I will encourage the entire universe to be true to themselves during personal assessment sessions. Do not credit yourself where you ought to get a pass and keeping all factors constant the reverse is true. In contradiction to the truth about your projects, life led interests, mistakes and milestones; it will be the best drawing of an action plan meant to please the eyes of other people. Someone will absolutely thank you but it will not be true indeed and it may have an indelible and painful mark on your entire life ahead.

I prefer sharing to you a bit of a personal action plan that should prove what the future stands for.
It is to highlight the paintings on the wall and spread out meaning with less questions but more work. It is not time for accountability to ask yourself a hell of queries for the assessment done in line with the truth served better. It is rather the day the entire world and its peoples out there to draw away the curtain with intentions of unleashing work. It is work that is tangible by the end of the business day.

The action plan you intend to have should have the muscle to explain who you are, where you are coming from, why now, who is to take charge and where you are heading to with the actions there in. You are creating room for people to understand how far you intend to go with the truth in your heart. I want to say that no one is against you for what you make of yourself as far as what you want to achieve. Most individual actions might seek criticism and this; positive criticism is allowed to help us keep on track.

It makes sense in seeking what one can do based on what they want not necessarily their current capacity. I advise people who approach me not to limit themselves for where the want to go. My personal Action Plan to shed light on what you want to do to get better with making up your mind in life.

Model of Bruno's Action Plan

Goal - Publish my second book at 23 years of age
Target - Writing a 300 paged book about domestic violence
Action - Self publish the book
Responsible Person - The Author, Bruno Asiimwe

Time scale/ deadlines - End of August 13th, 2015
Resources - Time, Pen, Three rims of Paper and a laptop computer
Success criteria - Prayer, Research, mental discipline, Sacrifice, determination, Accepting to create a challenge and create a solution, Hard work, Prayer and resilience
Monitoring - Proper allocation and usage of the limited resources
Impact - Ending domestic violence for every person that shall read the book and access the information there in from any other form; from the horse's mouth
Future Action - Talent realisation and skills development (Write book 3 about an in impacting time in life)

The ascending order reflected in either column from the word go should be respected. I was very clear at setting my goal because without it I was never to fulfil my dreams, however hard it was to put pen to paper. Goal is the hinge of an action plan that everyday stands a reflection towards that goal. I chose to have my book worked on and published at twenty three (23) years well aware that every new day would appear a reduction to the life span of the project.

I ought to repeat myself as many times as possible to make you understand how a goal under my action plan would serve a hinge. It is the foundation of the work yet to get started on for which reason I would never alter it. Whatever, reasons; nothing should justify changing your goal for anything.

Within the goal you are saying to yourself it is a do or die activity. The necessity for your work to be complete is hidden in your goal. I went telling a few concerned people about my goal though they did not know all about the action plan. You may have previously had your mind set to do something unusual around the world with a goal yet you still could feel it speak out. It should be detected to be a realistic goal considering where you have come from though also relying on where you want to go.

It is impossible to receive a healing miracle if you were not sick. Likewise it is wrong to be deceived that you will operate a patient as a doctor without knowing the past history of the patient especially about the disease you want to treat. To avoid administering a wrong package of medication in the long run, I will encourage you to look at where you are coming from to gather the strength to go over. I personally would not wake up to write a book with a goal set in 2015 if I did not know the time I started writing. Within my mind there lay a clear picture to have started writing small back in 2005.

The opportunity to get right your goal is based on the revelation of a gradual growth in what you want done. From drafting letters in 2005 at the age of 13 at St. Mukasa Preparatory Seminary - Mushanga, I was writing articles for the school magazine in 2009 at the age of 17. Within me, I never knew money was an important issue as time went by to start valuing my work. Nevertheless; the pupils I was drafting letters for we getting payment from their parents inform of favours rated at making constant school visits with loving and appreciating hearts. I was losing out of the market as early as 13 years but still did not give up.

Similarly, my articles going to the school magazine at St. Francis Xavier Minor Seminary - Kitabi went without financial payments. Sooner than later I noticed that the school was selling these magazines to students, old boys of the school and parents among other groups. This was a strange issue that bothered me that I vowed not to write more articles to the school magazines. Why would I pay for what I manufacture? It is like today's civil servants who work to earn income in working for money to first pay taxes, see their earning face a reduction in docility and start to spend without question.

I was very sensitive to have withdrawn from submitting work for publication only having been exploited for a one article's submission.

I am not bragging about but for the fact of my life, I would not stand exploitation as early as 17 years of age and five (5) years in the field of writing. This is yet to explain never to change your goal.

Though I was not writing to school magazines again, I did not give up on writing even when I did not know it was my goal then to be a writer of all times ahead. That was where I rested for a winning side that would soon weigh heavier than the losing side of my work.

Winning side	Writing as a goal
Losing side	Paying shillings for my writings

In 2011 at the age of 19, I started writing articles to a few of my class mates who grasped them to the dot while at Eden International School. In other words they were very fascinating to read that they would earn those good marks.

This was done surreptitiously to continue paying myself at measuring the gradual growth of my writing abilities and the talent therein. Day by day I reassured myself of being recognised as a writer. It was not on my mind to know the kind of writer I was then.

With the growth margin in view, in 2012 I was a student at Namirembe Hillside High School - Gayaza and at 20 years. I met a young student one Mark Mao who told me he had a friend that would see my articles get published in The New Vision one of the leading newspapers in Uganda. I finally could not see light even when I often told the school bursar; Mrs. Kajura Rose as a family friend about the yet to be published articles in the paper. It was true that I also started informing my first editor in life Mr. Ssebunya Christopher who was a teacher of literature in English about submitting articles to the newspapers. I do not know if it was a writer with a loose tongue.

All through this I was not a student meant to attend classes of literature in English for I detested literature. I was better positioned and way practical than students that attended classes of literature in English. It was not time to give up too that I went on writing more articles and having got an editor that I did not pay I was stronger. In 2013 I talked to the students' leader in charge of entertainment; then Hon. Male Solomon to allow me use one of the school notice boards for my writings.

In light of being a student leader too as a dormitory leader, it was a sail through on a lake on a calmer day. Within, it was a blessing in disguise that I conquered the notice board for my pieces of writing.

Having missed to appear in the New Vision, I formed my own newspaper at school with a broader view of the school notice board. There were sections I made for articles in politics, religion, culture, sports and business. All these articles had one author with an inscription of their name at the bottom of every article; Bruno Asiimwe.

This taught me to always insult people with positive work to seek genuine criticisms. What went strange beyond criticisms was that most students did not read my articles but teachers did. This was because the writing was so artistic to identify a philosophical writer even when the readers then and I could not tell.

However, the teachers appreciated saying I had extraordinary pieces of work. In 2014 as a student at Makerere University Business School, I had gained just enough courage to write my first book. This was at 22 years of age, a clear manifestation of the paths I took to write my first book. Who knew this would appear after 9 years of hard work with a never giving up self-drive mentality. It would not be late again that the next year in 2015 at 23 years I was writing my second book.

This book you are reading is my third book at I largely wrote at 26 years of age and the release is appearing at 31 years. The goal to publish my second book at 23 years of age had a foundation. It was rooted in the past which communicates the possibility of it being a realistic goal. In the end I would not have a goal and fail to get where I want to be with it. You could have had a greater goal than mine if you decide to draw your action plan today and never change your goal.

I met many obstacles and some I created for myself to make better of the solutions in my world of writing. Today schools still exploit students like they did to me for just one article. How sensitive are you with your goal for whatever you want to do? Are you fitting among the crowds around your world of work better to be exploited? Speak out with your actions where you feel vulnerable.

I knew that verbally speaking out against what the schools were and still are doing was to put my academic life at an uncalculated risk. Still it was not time for me to drop out of school even when I did not live the life of an academic built up setting. You should therefore not incite the sleeping masses around you to cause mayhem. Incite yourself to cause change in your world of work. They probably have their own world of work hidden to you. Your goal is the overall channel where you are saying "no retreat no surrender" for your future boyfriend, girlfriend, husband, wife and children.

Look at your goal everyday as a law that should never be amended even in the United States of America, the laboratory of democracy. What can we change in our action plan for us to make it a point to achieve the goal there in? You can only change your target in the mapping of the action plan. Measuring your action plan should start with a target which tells how far one wants to go with a given piece of work. The target of 300 pages of the book would certainly start at a level of a manuscript.

As time went on I keenly realised my time for writing was running out. The better part to attain my goal was to change my target by reducing the pages by 1.

This would soon reassure me of my position to have the book ready for publication. You must create your own world of work that is different from mine to have a target that can realistically change. What happens in instances where a given target is not bound to change? There is a possibility of an abrupt collapse of the entire project hence no reality to meeting one's goal.

This is not to say that you must change the first target set prior execution of a given project. I would be in a better situation where my target was not changed. Why did I have my target bound to change in case it was necessary to? In my life, I have tried to be true to myself than any other; I live in imperfections.

Here my target would under construction serve as space left in between the walls of the bridge to allow expansion and contraction as times ought to change. One is already prepared and they will not see the bridge crack at points of contraction and expansion as a matter of fact. You probably did have the same work to do; there is a reason for being in position to adjust your target accordingly. As this happens go for areas where it must change for work to continue. Rigidity will pose big threats to the entire project work.

Life demands to see your bold position which is the action you and I intend to put forward. From today hence forth you must avoid being an armchair critic in life. You and I have better accomplishments where actions are more than mere words in utterances. Without action all would just keep on a piece of paper as an action plan.

In the end it would serve no justice to me and the world around me. Without acting upon what we say, we are as good as an orator that does not do what they say. It was not up to my task to present an eye catching action plan on paper without the passion to act upon it. It was my life's principle to make actions make the loudest sound for other people to listen to the message I was carrying. Today, it is my way of doing things to act with distinction in my work. You will not have time to waste if you are more of a woman or man of actions than simply sweet words.

The trick behind the overwhelming unemployment rates facing the governments all-over the world, is young people that ask for jobs when they cannot show practical work for their words. You should never be given an opportunity to work as a mechanic before you have demonstrated being one beyond your academic documents. I would soon start to move from one position to another due to my actions. Growth of your work is seen at how much you act for a better day. You will never do less for more if you did not try acting yesterday.

In the same sense, you will not spend less effort to yield more results given that you were never bothered by transferring work from paper to the ground. How do you get to results without doing work? It is not factual to keep waiting on someone who is not ready to produce results. I attained the position of the Founder and Executive Director of Domestic Peace Foundation Uganda at 23 years of age. Holding this position made me appreciate people who act contrary to a lot of words.

I did not have to hear a lot of words from an employee or a volunteer for me to see work done. I was so much fascinated by people who proved who they were through their actions.

To that effect we would easily measure the results of someone's work at the end of the business day.

Short of this most people lost their jobs and it was never a regrettable act behind the mind of the organisation to dismiss and terminate contracts of such people. If you do not want to do your part, then who is for you? There is a time when the whole world is against us; the day we are not there for ourselves.

Independence and largely a stand-alone person can attract other people to sail through with. Either way you are not good enough to tell people what you cannot do. Imagine what a teacher of theoretical work does to the environment of academia. They poison the entire education system and bring down three quarters of the entire country.

As a theoretical person in the academia wastes someone's time and enables them to bring down a nation, so is a life built on speeches without actions. You can decide to waste your own time by speaking more and kill yourself by doing nothing more. My action was clear; to self-publish the book in question. With whatever the action, you mustn't beat about the bush. It calls for utmost openness and use of a direct approach that fits your capacity to see work done.

The only reason in principle as to why people do not act at all or act limitedly is having an overwhelming task than they should do. Again you should be real to yourself. There were many other options that would soon see me publish the book, among them visiting a publishing house to have all the work of publication done there.

Acting within your means is a blessing meant to help you grow. The bitter truth was that I had meagre resources to have the book published in one of the giant publishing houses in Uganda. I want to back this phrase with the day I met the proprietor of Fountain Publishers, Mr. Tumusiime James in 2015. He was clear and said, "It is way expensive to publish a book, where will you get the money."

I would soon look around for more financial support but the truth stood out later that I did not find more money. In defense of my goal to publish my second book, I stood firm to make sure the book came to light from the dark side of a manuscript. It was always on my mind by the way to meet my goal. Without knowing my financial fault lines I would certainly not see my inner strength telling me there is a goal as your ultimate solution. Make sure you design a goal that serves as a reminder, for it is never time to give up or end there.

The fear to see your faults expands the fault lines to make you more vulnerable to the extent of not seeing the inner abilities in one's life. It is better a deal to correct your paths in making a working action plan. We have the capacity to design an action plan but you must go an extra mile to have a workable action plan. The way a person acts matters hence explaining the same way it would reflect of how much the harvest will last.

Most importantly, I would have not seen my passion grow to keep me chase my life dreams without a sense of ownership. As an author this would soon carry an inscription on the front cover page of the book reading, Bruno Asiimwe and at the rear part of the cover page another inscription; about the author. If you trust your work and feel it is worth defending so you must take responsibility for the image it makes around the world. This is still relevant to defend your actions and the measure to reflect your yields.
There is great honour to know how much I invested in the book to the point of owning it.

This held me on the issue of copyrights for the book that no one had permission to use my work different from the right way. In case of any other way someone would want to use my book; they would have to certainly seek permission to avoid penalties from the courts due to infringement.

Why do people hate what they do and do not want to own it in the light? Is it worth ownership in any case? The better part of achieving your goal-led mind is to keep within the confines of the law.

It does no harm to be legally binding with the work of your hands and mind. You are the only person that knows the price you paid to have your work complete and ready for public consumption. I solely knew the amount of time I had invested in writing the book. I really deserved sole ownership of the book and the inscriptions therein. If you do not want to take full responsibility for what you do, it is simply wrong to own it.

Away from ownership of the project or work in progress you risk good pieces of work into the hands of undefined people. This happens on several instances due to failure to respect time. My timescale for writing the manuscript was due end of August 13th, 2015. Without setting a deadline for my work I would delve into procrastination leaving one piece of work incomplete for another day. You have no crew of the ending style of the other piece of work you are taking on since the previous one is pending.

I found myself drawing my other plans on a broader board accommodative of future intended work. Ideally from August 14th, 2015 it was time to look out for a better editor for my philosophical work. Why do I ask you to find deadlines very interesting in your daily life? There is more to completion of work allocated to you and in turn you have time for other things including yourself. It makes a strengthening guide to mental health due to limited stress at meeting deadlines.

People also derive satisfaction from the feeling of getting to the end of their work. You are happy to notice a positive change like in your work. In my life there was constant growth of relief to go wherever I wanted to make a better life.

Prior to every timeline in your action plan, consider what you are doing currently such as your job and career. There is no productive human that is not multitasking. Even when I had a specific time set to have the writing part done, I was a student of Makerere University Business School. This meant that I soon would return to school business alongside my personal business. If you have a family it should not collapse because you have more work to do at the workplace.

This is how relevant timelines keep us an important part of a complete story yet to be told. The linkage between ownership of work and timelines is a complete story. How do you accumulate resources for such kind of work? Is it wise of someone to make an acute accumulation of resources needed for work? We must look for the long lasting resources that are within our work stations and limits.

Every unemployed youth and elder person will justify their current situation with lack of resources. These are greedy people who have nothing and want more every now and again. Your resource base should be for things you will easily reach for. I chose to use Time, Pen, Three rims of Paper and a laptop computer as my resources for the project. These were within my means, accessible and cheap. You need to not over stretch people around you with what they want to see you do.

I did not bother my bread winners as an undergraduate student who had less money to spend. What are the most important resources in your work? Why do you need money as a resource for places it is not necessary? I could not get stressed up for not having enough money as a suiting resource for me. I needed to first finish writing the book as fast as possible and due completion find the money to have the manuscript ready for editing.

It is also aching for someone to look for money to go printing the book before it was under editing.

Many people are idle because they dream during broad day light as purported to be very ambitious people. They have more and forget that they have started at zero for their work. An action plan should entail only the resources you cannot do without.

Maximum resource utilisation is dependent on the success criteria applied by every other human being. You should have clear success criteria for your action plan to be sound. The success criteria are meant to comprise of the things that will push you through attaining your goals in life and for other activities. I was very systematic in the choice of what would constitute my success criteria. The items that included Prayer, research, mental discipline, Sacrifice, determination, accepting to create a challenge and create a solution, hard work, and resilience to make me a sound action plan that would soon have more meaning.

Why would I start on the work God has guided upon without prayer? It is a divine sign of thanks giving and seeking further divine instruction based on insights of the work one sets out for. Through this start button, it will all not be by you at the end of business time. The rest of items on the to-do list were for my case and you can decide to have your own different from mine. We want to get to success and not easily lose out.

You are thinking through projects with urgency of reassuring yourself of things that often back up your achievements. Every milestone is not falling from the skies like manna. It is because you are fully involved in seeing the actual paths of these milestones. The pay measure is equally defined in the success we attain. You will conquer with me to have full payment for work done.

There is nothing as hard as monitoring yourself. It is much easier to be blind folded by what seems good for an activity to cover the entire project.

If it so happens; monitoring to make us serve right for the appropriate mandate it holds, proper allocation and usage of the limited resources is paramount. Within your mind it is important to consider the limitedness of resources and thus proper allocation. In instances where it is different from this, you certainly appear midway the project work with no resources at all.

You may have the capacity to get around searching for more of the resources but it will not be you for the picture in the drawing. You will in other words tell the whole world that you are not good at planning, for the very reason you could be good at failing yourself. In a bid to avoid such embarrassing circumstances we need to carry out monitoring independent to highlight individual weaknesses and project weaknesses.

The distinction between the two will make you carry out monitoring at every stage of the project. For this purpose you will have a follow up of what you did the other day to support the project or bring it down. Are there things that are not worth doing in life? For me it is a big yes. Things that do not make an impact in human life are not worth doing.

If the monitoring plans in your action plan start to reflect no impact with what you are doing; have those indicators as the saviour of our generation. I knew that my passion for my work lay in the impact that was strategically going to the world over and my personality. The impact of my work was to end domestic violence for every person that would read the book and access the information thereafter from any other form especially from the horse's mouth.

The impact must clearly put the picture of what you are holding in view of a challenge and where the solution was to come from. Indeed without solving a specific problem in question for my project, I would feel a gap in my action plan. The reality of my intentions would not carry the right sense for which I would offer all my time for something.

There is power sustainability of your project with impactful practices where you stand to do work. This will date from the day the project starts to run for impacts on you and move on to other people.

Talent realisation and skills development went for my future action because of the great impact scenario. I now know that what I want to see in the future will be less to offer to the current world. This goes for a complete decision to have a goal reached and served through consistent performance. The service of my action plans ranges from what I want in life to when it must happen. You have all the time to decide on when to see what you want to happen come true in consideration of when it must see the light of day.

If we always set out action plans that are realistic in nature, it means that we shall see ourselves from one good day to another. You should desist from living your life like other people do. You must stop having very good action plans on paper which never face the true world of your life. It is rewarding to go practical of the world you choose to have on paper from the writing on the face of the paper.

Time To Elevate Yourself

In sight of a realistic and practical action plan, every one of us should elevate high above the sky. People might at some point in life want to see your elevation which will not necessarily come your way though it happens. You are the first person to see your seat on Elijah's chariot all for having gone right about your action plan. Why do I keep rotating around the action plan for an elevation? Most people see themselves where they could have failed to be at some point.

Every other day it seems it was the wrong way through which you got to the seat.

There is nothing to look at for your success upon which with the value of time other people can see themselves similarly there. You have a few things to do for your life to be better today than yesterday. Yesterday you did more things which were untimely and obsolete. The small things you have to do are the most important to see you somewhere in life.

Start by being in places where fewer people want to reach. Well, there might be pain because you are yet to be hardened to the facts of life. Endurance is for people who are successful before they actually get work done. I have come to believe that it is true in seeing you are deceived and in dreaming you believe. Human eyes see what is happening and may not feel it is not true for them.

Better things are not meant for people as the worst come our way. You have to dream in the position of an elevation and work for the reality there. The way you work for a better life situation is absolutely different from the way you work for a deteriorating life situation. No elevation comes by luck for people who are already there, it is rather by work. If it were luck, why does luck keep in one direction of the highly placed people in politics of a nation, some among the religious women and men, some civil servants and a few business people among other categories of people?

People who wait on luck never work and have kept waiting by the way for the last years you knew them for the lines that define them. People who work find luck which is a step away by the on lookers. This is the picture for you and me from today and onwards. There are three lines that illustrate things your neighbour will call luck when you indeed worked hence the lucky person you are today. First is the line of one's background being academic, family or greatly ancestral under illustration.

Your neighbour will openly say, "They often held one of the last three positions in class during their school going days." "I know it is by luck that they now are the president of Uganda or any other given country where you come from", they will add. This is no more of them, people have changed and they have succeeded in life outside class.

For the sake of family; "the entire village can testify of the poverty levels that defined their family background" the neighbour asserts again. These people have chosen the path of work and are therefore out of poverty. Another neighbour will have this to say, "Oh, well from their ancestral origin, the entire lineage was atheist by word and deed". It must be luck that they are now church goers. Please come on, someone has turned from of old and they are new in Jesus Christ.

Surreptitiously, know about them by who they are today through a closer observation of who they are and what they do. They will open up to you the working pattern of their life, from which you will know of the real work contrary to the state of luck you wish them that you think you do not have. People will attribute our success to be luck depending on a line illustrative of our current jobs. Your neighbour having noticed that you have purchased a new piece of land, they will make various utterances about your current job. They will easily say she is working in the president's office; the reason they have had luck to purchase a piece of land today.

Otherwise how would they have afforded to have their own piece of land in town? They will have purchased the piece of land not because of luck but for the work they do. We must remember that there are many other people in the same office without their own piece of land. Your current job is probably an elevation in itself. However; you and I should believe more in elevating ourselves beyond what our neighbours know.

There is something you will have to indulge in for more work that other people have feared to do. Within the context of our jobs it is never adequate to give what we are. For better for worse, it is not luck for all by a self-sustaining job. The third line of illustrations to hold luck from the view of your neighbour is partnerships. With the view of current partnerships especially channeled through friends, people feel a sense of luck for us. It is not necessarily luck, because their partner that has walked with them for where they are today that is lacking for you.

You have not been in position to trace friends like hers or his own. This is an impression that a very unique factor brought these two people together for better practices they share; not luck. If it were for luck drawn from the three lines of its illustration, every human being would absolutely be lucky. This is based on the fact that you can not miss out on all the three lines of illustration for luck. You perhaps have a good background in line with academics, family and ancestral link, you had a good job at some point and we all have had friends that should have been engaged for partnerships.

Do you find room to say people are lucky without working to be where they are or attain a specific level of elevation? That kind of elevation is done by the beautiful works of people which puts them where we are seeing them today. Someone is also seeing you at an elevation and they should know you have worked to be there.

You can always work to see yourself at an elevation where your work is considered important and relevant to a given situation in society. I know people do not seek elevations but they deserve to be where they are. You are richer than other people involved in real estate business because you are playing your cards better.

What is that pushing people for an elevation according to the magnitude of things they have achieved in life?

Like many other people want to get elevated so are the people we may consider successful. To this understanding people have gone changing their work stations in order to attain that. It is the step they are taking for their life to get better.

You have one thing to do; carry yourself high. You do not have to change your jacket to elevate yourself.
Why do I want to believe in keeping your true self for such an elevation? There are people already on that stage set to perform. They are seeking the attention of the audience and the judges for a better day. If you want to change for the fact of only reaching the stage; it will be about change all over.

You will in the end lose concentration because you think changing before the audience is okay. There is no good thing in changing yourself from time to time. It is sensible at realising where the problem lies before going on to camouflage. Don't you think there is an environment where you cannot camouflage and be accepted? Every human being deserves a point of elevation because they are working towards it by themselves.

We have on several occasions missed a step by acting someone's position. Keeping yourself in a suit of which you really are, makes you assess the necessary time to invest in yourself. It will certainly be more time to take for your rehearsals than time to be there; on a stage full of lying to yourself in the long run. Since you have admitted to the fact of more time for better results, you will juggle better for times ahead. We just need to be equipped to take on things beyond the training session we have attended.

With specialty, yes you are to go but you are not better to stay for other areas better suiting for your service. Specialty even for its own is not a stand-alone obligation per se to us, unaware of things making change around the world. You may be a dental specialist in a given hospital but this is not enough for an elevation.

I constantly work on myself for peace and conflict analysis as a specialist in that field of work but it is never enough. Diversity of the human conscience is what must be enough as far as reaching out for an elevation. You have no reason to make yourself subconscious because you feel better for where you are today. This does not hold only for good things, it goes as far as bad things that we experience in life. I know one day I believed it was okay when in actual sense it was not. It is not nice at all to say it is better then.

You must get out of it and face the truth to see your scattered bones and start at gathering them. You do not need the flesh to attach to these bones because you know it is a skeleton. In other words if it is a broken relationship that has dragged you back; be true to its reflections in your life. We must live to what we face every day with the right approach. Look, for you to get better with yourself act on getting better with the approach there in.

What do you do when things go wrong for example with your action plan? Someone else might have come to tell you with expertise; drop everything and start afresh. No, it never works that way. In that thought where we must elevate ourselves with such a missed step of harsh forces within the problem. It should be as simple as turning on to the past page in search of an error or mistake for that matter.

This is meant to help you not to repeat it ahead of the practical path of the action plan. The practical path could have been marred by your husband, wife, boyfriend, girlfriend or children. People you always have around you in times of sorrow. It is possible that your business partner is painted red in reference to making everything go astray.

Most people are liable to losing their own intentions because it all seems okay. That day, we all wasted time when we believed it was okay when it was not.

The day your friend told you to stop being faithful to your marriage partner or dating partner. They stole our conscience to believe it was okay. Make a recollection center in your life; embrace your attitude towards work that makes you better than luck that stops you from working better.

If you hate work for us to notice a point of elevation around us, seeking luck should make you settle for unexpected things. It is exploitation that I know is unexpected, nonetheless; it is what luck provides before you work. In the event that you will not easily realise you are hurrying out for an exploitative agenda, it all goes on swiftly. Unexpected things for people who think they are lucky are systematic. I know how painful it is to set yourself as the prey when you are not aware of the whole truth of the matter.

Most young girls have fallen prey in this scenario in Uganda and countries all over. Why do you get convinced beyond doubt that a job must be yours when you do not suit its qualifications? These hooks are not necessarily set for a specific girl but for those looking for luck without work. An old man the age of your biological father meets you in a party and asks only one question, "Where do you work these days?" This is an indicator that this probable perpetrator works under a systematic laid network.

They work under sheer false pretense imagining that the lazy ones will easily give in. True, the lazy people hunting for luck ultimately will give in. The young girl takes time to notice they are soon falling prey of their thirst for luck without work. They calmly and supposedly reply, "I am not yet working". Suggestively one makes herself clear; I have been looking for work all over this town but all in vain.

Well, this man in question or other accomplices who might be women since they will easily be understood, take it for a deal worth taking indeed. They now know that their mission is over.

Sooner than later, the two parties exchange contact addresses and wait for the day when they will meet. It becomes clear that it is true there is a job to take on. Without knowledge in that field of work, the young girl gets to believe it will work out right by the close of business day. The man aiding her to suit the placement arises to demand for sex and it would soon appear a joke.

The girl also rises to suspicion of what she is giving in for but there is limitedly power to say no. They are convinced it was a golden chance to have run into this man and subsequently the job. It is time for them to work hard to keep around in a bid not to lose the job since they have been elevated. Why do you expect other people to elevate you if you cannot elevate yourself at some point?

It is related to attending a class without a pen and a few minutes later you realise everyone is writing down something. It is okay if you want to continue seeing other people write with an assumption that you have no pen for yourself. However, it is not okay to believe one of your classmates has more than one pen so you seek to borrow one from them. There is one question to make sense out of this. Why do you expect your classmate to have got two or three pens in the event that you do not have any?

This expression drawn to make you understand that we all have the capacity to get where we wanted to be. They have worked to be there and so we ought to do the same. As the young girl starts to see the levels of exploitation being elevated than her, she will be at the mercy of their perpetrators. With the aspect of exploitation wherever it is done in the world, it is always the victims to prefer it being okay when it is not okay.

As the externalities of the working environment appear vivid, it is time for abandonment of the victims in this case.

We all know that what goes up must come down; it is not the way to go up and not the way to come down. Luck attained before work positions you for emptiness only to elevate the rate at which you are being exploited and consequently bring down your body and mind full of emptiness.

You must treasure a better path to take through your action plan to get up. This means that your action plan deserves you alone or you and your partner either in family or business setting. Where do we see wrong people in our practical path of life? They come when we know within ourselves; worthless beings reside. Every time you hate yourself to the extent of waiting on luck to find you, wrong people will proclaim the opportunities for the lucky people.

Certainly the unlucky people will be engaged already with their own ventures, however small they might be. As early as 2014 in first year at the university several people tried to email me, raise me on phone in the intent to exploit me. I want to say it is not easy for young people to say no but I said no. It was all built on the principle of a self-engaging person that I had to say no. Do not think of devaluing yourself against your own work and own self.

My small pieces of work as a writer expounded everyday to feel the resonating passion of being enough to myself. I wanted to prepare for self-employment than go working for people that would exploit me. You must know that you are enough in working hard and for yourself. There is more meaning for which you must live a diversified life to pick on that sense of elevation free of exploitation.

I always said no to opportunities that seemingly were from the backdoor which opened my conscience to further walk away from luck before work. I would rather spend more time elevating myself believably that I have a unique sense of self-esteem, taking on my talents and appreciating my gifts in life.

To work better that other people will see as luck, calls us to define ourselves first. People might define you to suit their own intentions and analysis of your success. The definitions that people around you have are not necessary what you might be. Accept you alone to define yourself through actions that elevate you from time to time. It is not supportive of these actions where you live in confinement of negative utterances that you would not want to hear of. Words have power to make us strong again and power to deny us room to notice the greater worth in our being.

Living Out of Confinement

Imagine a life where you are not confined by human beings and the rest of the world around you. It will be a day for us all to celebrate and more to make merry of given what we do during such a day. This is the day you open up to oneself about things yet to be fulfilled in the action plan. The ball has been set rolling and everything must come to pass.

Things you decide to do on this day should spread a glimmer of hope around the world. It is no longer a moment of your life where people should determine your fate literary speaking. From this year on you have perhaps chosen to perform without tight supervision and control. The very clear issue you are avoiding is a wrong character dressed on with a human face. You should beware of moles and all of the people that live with us.

It is normal that human beings are imperfect but our shortcomings and imperfections are not a guarantee to see other people at war with us. No one is mandated to ill advise you to justify their level of imperfections. There is often a complete dissonance between living a confined life and being open to freedom in life. On average, over 98% of the people's experience goes both for a confined life and a life of freedom.

Most people cherish openness to freedom but what they do is the first point of seeking self-confinement. It sounds queer for us to throw ourselves into prison cells. We shall always take home what we work for and what we are readily making on our own. Considerably for acting in good faith not one would want to be the fool of circumstances that are under such a nature. In any scenario where things go wrong, be careful to your reactions.

I will have to make you know that there is always fire where smoke is the only thing you are seeing. In the same manner, you will soon find out of the triggers behind our actions on a presumably better day. I want to single out of the use of technology to make advancement that is visible in life or lose it all to your ways. In this era many people have had access to technological gadgets especially cell phones.

I held my first phone at the age of 21 in 2013 which was after my high school days. It was okay with me for all the past 20 years of my life to exist without a phone. You know when you first held or even owned a phone. The first phone I used was not my own but given to me by my parents. This phone did not have supported operations for internet use and so I would soon work out of the box to purchase my own that would be different.

I was able to buy a smart phone mid 2014 that had supported operations for internet use. Within me I was trying to venture more for what I would use the phone for. You too could have sold off a phone or computer for a better one at some point. With a very dynamic world, I soon started using Facebook which I got introduced to by my youngest sister one Moreen.

With this social media platform I wanted to get to be a better person with the use of my phone. How I would use my phone to arrive at this, is the best path to go over technology.

Every time I run on Facebook was to attract better people who would make me appreciate life. Remember you can only attract people that share with you certain things in common. At some point it was not true because I noticed some sheep among the wolves.

For the sake of how I was to use this platform; it was easier to unfriend and unfollow these people. Amidst these changes millions of people were accumulating friends on the same social media platform. My youngest sister was one of these people. I did not change my ways to become like many other people but I insisted on using technology my way. It is about getting to be someone by the way you use something, in this case technology.

Do people have better relationships because of thousands of friends on Facebook? Are other people growing richer by spending all the time they have for workshops as time to attend to Facebook? Social media platforms like Facebook, X and WhatsApp are the only avenues where we should use less to attain more. You should invest less time in opening up your browser in order to login to Facebook, X and WhatsApp.

It is only one thing to make us prosperous over using less to attain more. Appreciating small things for big ones is the secret behind using less for more. Be grateful for the few things you have, your smart phone is small in it but many other people will want to see how you grow with the small things. Let it be the first time you are proving to people that a seed can yield into a shrub. It is true and possible since we will not have access to bigger things with the small ones.

Most people have thousands of friends on Facebook but are still unemployed. What is the logic behind many friends that cannot make you a better person? It is also true that a few people have a hundred friends and still go empty handed and spend the night on hungry stomachs.

You can choose to be among the fewer number of people with tens of friends and have yourself a hand full of treasure. The discussions you are always engaged in with friends matter when you have them engaged and when they have you engaged too.

The time you accord to each other is not a blowing wind that will sweep away everything. It is that time that will gather around better jobs and solving your personal problems. How many of your friends ask whether you are well placed for a given job or not? If none of them are doing you such a deed, you are already wrongly placed. This could stand out to be the first reason you have not been employed for the last number of years you started using social media.

In the long run you are being confined by social media not because it is dire. Technological innovations mean development with the innovators themselves and the users. It is rather unequal at the expense of the users. We should open our eyes from technological confinement that hinders you and me from getting where we wanted to go by yesterday.

The truth lies in your heart over how you are using social media; at losing yourself or gaining over. It does not stop there; it starts to restrict your attention to very important ventures and responsibilities. I have seen and heard of marriage couples that have had to divorce or separate due to misuse of technology. In other words it is a reality that we can get addicted with, just for wrongly being placed. These are issues we can avoid and no one will blame us.

Having hesitated to misusing them, it will for a longer period of time enslave us and make us humble to its service. These platforms are artificial and have no interests against humanity. How about people that may have specific agenda against their society and fellow human beings? You must know that there are people that work around the clock to hurt and trap you for danger.

They will want to control you and your work for a number of reasons mainly known to them. Considering that competition in business is positive, is the positivity margin realisable every time competition is at its apex? Have you not seen counterfeit products on the market of late? People are ready to invest their time to have you in confinement.

It is relatively true that we want to keep in the open corridors of freedom every day we wake up alive. What did you do yesterday to live out of confinement both posed by people and the world around them? Are you pretending to be safe as though there are no security guards on your gate or at your office? Is it not becoming a trend to have escort cars for highly placed people among governments all over the world?

Is it not useless to protect your externalities and leave the interior corridors marred by your own practices? We all have an urgent agenda to pay heed to for a more resilient person that hates being controlled by other people. You also have control over your children and ultimately you do not want them to control others in future. Just stop it now; start guiding them as you guide yourself to run out of self-confinement. If you ever tell your child not to make a call past 9 o'clock, it is okay.

It is also okay for you not to make calls past 9 o'clock. It is never okay to tell your child that they will be kicked out of the house if they attempt to make calls past 9 o'clock. Beyond this child trying to make a phone call past that time only to wait for what may unfold; you are confining them with change. In a bid to change them they will go with that today. You must be aware that you are making them subconscious of what is right with blasting them with fear.

In great fear to be beaten, they will tentatively conform to your expectations of them. It is likely that they will have an encounter with a friend who would like to reach out to them at 10 o'clock in the night.

Likely your child will not want to lose their friend in question. It will be the question of when to submit to their pieces of advice that are in turn contrary to what your child did. With fear surrounding this relationship, they will change again to adhere to their friend.

This symbolically tells of more parties ready to change us for what they want to see in us. They do not consider who we are and what we have seen them do. It will be unfortunate to recognise a constantly changing being because of fear to lose something or fear of vengeance.

If it is the case where this child saw their parent, do the right thing from of old, the same will most likely be done by them. It is truthfully about influence and not change. It is about openness to freedom that will allow a child to grow and live out of confinement. It serves immensely the same purpose that we had better start to live out of confinement.

You cannot have a realistic action plan if you still believe you should be confined for one reason or another. I know it does harm you to pretend that people should control your life to the dot. For that matter you will certainly submit to these people whenever they appear in and around your life. You will not see time aiding you to change the world around you for the betterment of all.

Everybody is set for what they want and you should not be set for what they want that you hate. You should not waste time explaining your position; rather have time to stand alone in the truth of what you cherish. We are at times better people for who we are and not for what other people want us to become. From this point on, you will go for things that pay you better; may be defending property rights for my scenario and through the earlier action plan.

CHAPTER THIRTEEN
Property Rights Are Our Future

Today we must acknowledge that less knowledge of property rights has continually dragged cohabiting men and women to false comfort. Cohabitation is not legally recognised anywhere all over the world. For a greater cause it is one of the practices that go in recognition to be against legal marriage. I see cohabitants exist after family break ups as far as divorce and separation.

It is a flash light of ignorance which has found roots in enabled domestic violence cases ever on the rise in such situations. One thing that hurts most is treasuring short lived events that will soon be disregarded by the laws and justice systems around the universe. At the age of 31most men like me are expectant of a family life ahead. Property is one thing and property rights is another for both women and men.

You should know that property rights are not about claiming something in a strategic position to creating something. Most people often claim property upon which they have no property rights to defend them. Why would you claim a piece of land as property yet you are not part of the creation of the property rights for the land? Value for land is okay but only with the knowledge of property rights.

For men and women still cohabiting, time is so demanding that they get into legal marriages.

Stop being friends by cohabiting and get to understand the necessity of picking the intriguing path created under the law. I want to enable mature and conscious women and men not because I am a feminist but for time worth accounting for in marriage. This is what will distinguish between the right people in marriage and the falsely comfortable people in cohabitation.

I should put this reasonably through real life scenarios that have seen women and men at war of ignorance of the law. It is this that deprives us of the worth, enjoyment and freedom got from property rights to define the future. I will totally conceal the true identity of the parties but drive the nail into this piece of wood. Patrick meets Patricia for an encounter yet to be identified as a turning point for the two. They are truly a match and soon they get involved to go for marriage (FIDA Uganda, 2012).

They legalise their marriage as husband and wife through church marriage as one of the legal requirements for marriage in Uganda. A few years down the road, Patricia gets into discussion with their marriage partner to travel abroad and with her aunt for business engagements. They easily come to an agreement and Patrick keeps around with the children and looking after matrimonial property. Soon Patricia started the transfer of funds to support the family back home especially with the children's school fees.

As time went on business grew in the United Kingdom (UK) and Patricia was remitting funds for construction of houses. One of the houses was put up on the ancestral home of Patricia's husband and the other on their private land. It was intended to have them serve as commercial houses to sustain family income. The first house was put up to completion and the other was already roofed up but not finished with interior works.

The family side of Patrick seemed silent ever since the construction works went on, however; signs of an eruption of words were soon to be seen and further heard in the UK where Patricia lived. It was not long enough; Patrick started to cohabit with Sumaih even when all these developments were going on. The ears of Patricia started shaking too in the UK at listening from different people over the cohabitation in question.

She called home to Patrick to ascertain the crux of the matter. The husband opened up the sad news which was a reality for him to have been cohabiting with Sumaih. It was a big blow in the life of Patricia. You too can imagine what Patricia was going through at the time, strange indeed. Patricia arranged her travel documents in the UK and soon travelled back to Uganda in quest to save her family and children.

On her arrival, she got into her matrimonial house within her understanding which was set up on the ancestral land of Patrick's family side. It was not convenient for Patrick that he forced her out of their home. One month down the rough side of the wall, she was running out of solutions. All she resorted to was to seek legal guidance and intervention especially for the family and in specificity to have rights over their matrimonial property. It is true every human being has the right to own property which is way different from having access to property rights.

Considering the struggles Patricia endured to support her family, we all feel sympathetic but the law maintains its position. In the same sense you must know how important it is to understand property rights. The ancestral home is legally own by the whole family of Patrick's origin in this case. You do not require rocket science to have you think through this. If Patricia could afford to put up these houses, she definitely had the strength to purchase another piece of land away from Patrick's ancestral home.

There is something most important that we have to learn amidst such a scenario in life. Every young person out there should have legal guidance alongside other forms of guidance prior marriage. It is much better for women like Sumaih to find out where they are going to reside.
In turn this prompts an argument over who made it happen at some point, Sumaih should know it will not be her property rights to own at the end of the day.

I would advise Sumaih to ask Patrick to go outside his matrimonial home to purchase her a piece of land on which to build her a house. Through this the chain of cohabiting that was started by Patrick may come to an end with her. Short of this, Sumaih will certainly fall prey too and it will appear late to be seeking property rights over Patricia's matrimonial home.

You have to distinguish between private land and ancestral land for that matter. This affects every one that may have access to their ancestral home land. It is not wise to put up a matrimonial house on your ancestral home. Go out work and have a private piece of land to stop expecting the unexpected in future. Property rights offer to you sole control over your property.

You absolutely will never have sole control over your ancestral home unless otherwise. Imagine you are engaged in a business on a piece of land where you have lived for 20 years and someone knocks at your door asking you to leave. It will be a fortunate situation if they come without a bulldozer to clear the land on which your house is. "I want to set on this piece of land a shopping centre," they will say. Title of land is the only proof of ownership of any given pieces of land.

Through the power of title of the land in question, you will be operating at a freedom guided approach which gives you choice to sell off or stay put on the same piece of land.

My father at some point was a civil servant working with Mbarara District Local Government. Through this he was entitled to house benefits where we lived in a government owned house for some time. You know working for the government is tricky to the extent of accumulating deductions on your salary like rental fees and pay as you earn and so on.

The government had property rights over the piece of land where the government owned house existed. Rumours held that some pieces of land were being set for sale allegedly as per the subsequent district council resolutions. One Monday morning, I saw a bulldozer with my necked eyes come as if it were to pull down our rented home. The initial plan by the property rights holder in this case Mbarara District Local Government was to pave way through creating plots of land from the bigger chunk of land in question. All this happened without prior notice and it was okay with the government.

As sitting tenants there was no reason, whatsoever; to have us served with notices prior redevelopment of their property upon which they enjoyed property rights. Deep within everyone around us that could have been affected in one way or another was not infringed upon. In other words no one would demand for compensation through any courts of law. I personally was there to watch the bulldozer put down banana plantations on government land.

I scratched my head for some time to know how this was done and for what reasons thereafter. This was an eye opener and a point where I picked a lesson over my future. This is not to say that my father did not have his private property around Mbarara City and far at his ancestral home in Kazo district. From this point on, I would soon believe in property rights as our future in time.

Three-quarters of the world's population do not have property rights. This means there is no proof on the pieces of land they are using for farming. It is the same land we live and work on. In Africa 90 per cent of the land is undocumented which increases the rate at which you should defend your property with property rights. This meant to support you to like a stronger life and healthy life with less worries over your property; a tactic to save time.

It goes on to become strange as in most parts of the world women are not allowed to own property or even inherit property. What does it mean since women enable production of half of the world's food? It is systematically breaking the patterns of productivity as men continue to distance themselves from farming. In a more scaring position that less than 20 per cent of women own land.

You better invest in your future due to proof of ownership through documentation. You were free to go anywhere in the past but times have changed. The next morning your neighbour will have fenced off their pieces of land because of creating property rights for them. Property rights give the right to exclusion where other people will not have to interact with your property. In this you will grow your muscle of privatisation as far as being productive for the rest of time is concerned.

Did you know that old proprietors of property did not privatise it? This in turn gives the late comers room to go as far as using the property to trade in it? I know of many people who originally owned big chunks of land but are being rented out on where to stay today. In the first place they had a lot of property rights, falsely knew they were rich and started to apportion the land for sale. Whatever good or bad thing starts small. Under this situation land is apportioned into smaller pieces of land till one realises they have sold it all.

The late comers have wisely taken over since they have legal knowledge and guidance on property rights. They reward the old proprietors by fencing off their property in question that they start to enjoy the right to exclusion. According to Jason Brennan, a Professor at Georgetown University; this late comer will enjoy more rights on whether to modify, use, destroy, sell, transfer ownership or rent it by making money off of it (Brennan, 2016).

By this far you should know that morals and ethics for registration are so much involved in property rights. How come you have a big chunk of land today and you insist on not having it documented for registration?
This serves beyond property rights on land that is tangible to intellectual property like copyrights, trademarks, patents and trade secrets. To a greater extent we live with property rights to shape our morals and ethics at the point of ownership.

Why are you eliminating property in time? Do you have a right to property or right to life? At birth we all have a right to life though we cannot fight our own battle considering the vulnerabilities of a baby. If you are alive today someone fought this battle for you; bringing the right to life true and attainable for now. Nonetheless, you do not have a right to property if you do not have the property itself.

Broadly you and I must first work to acquire property and assume the right to property. It is way different too with property rights, having acquired the right to property you should go ahead to create property rights pre-eminently through registration as a piece of ethics and morals. Life reassures us to create property thus finding the rights therein. Noam Chomsky recommends that intellectuals should speak out over property rights like I am doing.

He adds that what constitutes an access to evil is not giving your work patents, copyrights, trademarks, and trade secrets (Chomsky, 1967). Through this we shall have freedom of thought that mostly controlled by democratic tendencies right from America the laboratory of democracy to other countries in the world. In 22nd March, 2018 the president of the United States of America Donald Trump signed into law a document that was to protect its property rights from exploitation against China.

He called it a reciprocal though economists called it tariffs imposed on China. His Excellency Donald Trump claimed that China for a long time was conscious with their property rights where America paid in taxes which were not applicable in the case for China (CNBC, 2018). The USA and Britain are dependent on controlling the gulf region for material prizes and a strategic source of power. If the super power countries are fighting to retain and increase their revenue through property rights, why not the developing world and individual persons to respect and value property rights too.

Away from extremes of the poor and the rich; prosperity for the poor is a reality given that they embrace property rights as a very essential issue. Make the little you have your own by the truth in property rights. You mustn't imagine you are living in a vacuum where competition is unheard of. You have the better path of making working solutions by seeing who might want to control you. Today the United States of American and Britain control the world because they have a vast ownership of property rights.

Competition is a normal game for governments and individuals. I surely have seen and heard my father tell us as children about competition. At around 10:12 pm on Wednesday, 28th March 2018 he told us that we ought to compete amongst ourselves and still keep brothers and sisters. He wants to see all of us well off in the near future.
Good enough in the earlier hours of the day I had contacted the office of the Intellectual Property Rights Initiative to have my books copyrighted. I had gradually vowed to grow wealth in my life that is sustainable for my future.

Intellectual Property

One thing is supposed to support another for us to say sustainability has been achieved. Property rights have been held from time immemorial where the worlds' super power countries have had to engage themselves for a war. This has ranged from use of words to signing of new laws into place in order to see their positions felt all over the world. In the same sense Intellectual Property (IP) can better be addressed from the same perspective depending on which country has held more courage to implement their laws for that matter.

What does it mean for master countries like the United States of America, Britain and China to see the worth of Intellectual Property this far? The developing world has to feel the pinch and the world truly gets divided for an economic war. From today and onwards, it is you and I to choose on where to go by what we do and attain for the rest of time. It is time to find the most precious mineral in life so that the competitive edge gets to favour you.

It is not any more sensible to look like where you came from for development and self-transformation. It is okay to be born in the developing world, go to third world schools and stay in the developing world. Notwithstanding, for all reasons it is not okay to fail yourself by not competing with the rest of the universe. Your achievements should be labelled different to stand better than the people you may silently admire in the developed world.

All I can say is that civilization, respect for property rights and the sensible path of Intellectual Property have put the difference. It will start with you because to this point you have attained a remarkable step in life.
This book has by far redirected your position to appreciate what time means and how to dribble your football better.

It is less of what your country must offer; all is about you by starting on what other people are not doing.

You do not have to consult anyone for that matter; you have the better acknowledgement of where you must go that is far beyond USA and China. Why has IP gone unrecognised in your life? Which planet are you living on for that matter? What do you have as an asset in your life? All these questions have a force behind them to mean you must have underrated what you are doing today. No one is placed to believe in your work before you stand out for yourself.

It is not time to attract sympathy for real. Every day you think you will attract sympathy; waking up late is first thought after, innovations are not your way, creativity is not put up by the human brain and women should not do better than men. In other words you become the laboratory of negativity which deters you from valuing your little pieces of work to thereafter pick on for bigger things.

I personally did not know of IP as an asset though I was there. I worked hard every day and night and people around grew sympathetic. Can you imagine this situation that people see you work on your life day and night, but fill pity upon your brain being overused? Put your brain to use but strategically with improvement on your assets. The rich are not bragging for being rich but they are shouting all over the universe, "We ought to defend our assets and encourage more innovations and creativity amongst the citizens".

It is not normal by the way for us to imagine it is a war for the developed countries. As USA and China wage an economic war on everyone's property rights and IP, the developing world seems intact. True, that is what it is on the look of things for you but not for me. Today at 31 years of age I am not bragging but I am better off to know the price Uganda is paying for not having room to get involved in this battle. As someone in ownership of Intellectual Property, I am fully involved.

I waited to hear if the developing countries around the globe were to feel the pinch over super power countries waging war against their own for IP and Property Rights. There was no one whispering even in the corridors after the 22nd March, 2018 exchange of words between USA and China. If you are not bothered by your own future, it gets uncertain to get concerned with that of your neighbour even when they are well off. We have to uplift our national practices and self-driven mandate to compete for a better world.

The war has indirectly been waged on the lazy people and the developing world. As they defend the respect for their property rights and IP they strive to grow more assets for their survival. In reality here the developing world is growing their liabilities and the dependence ratio between nations will grow from security to education to health care and ultimately to currency variations.

I am well aware that if you are set to encourage IP in your country, you hate inventions and creativity for all. First there is self-hate at knowing what technology should be meant for because you cannot depend on your own at some point. Year in year out the dependence ratio is shooting high even when a country's annual budget is entirely self-financed. Is it any better to entirely finance your entire annual budget when the health care, security and education are not fed by the country's own IP by far?

You just have changed the face of dependence as a country perhaps for people who simply went through school and the entire population of illiterates to feel comfortable. The masses like these will be okay with this relented approach for some time but not all the time. I have to that effect decided to value my IP way beyond my environs to suit the super power states interpretation. This is the kind of war that is worth individual involvement to the last dot of every detail therein.

Intellectual Property goes beyond your ideas to protecting them from other people who want to take advantage of your work. It was on 22nd April, 2017 when the Principal of Makerere University Business School, Prof. Waiswa Balunywa together with a team from the Business Incubation Centre visited the regional study centre in Mbarara District – Uganda. Prior to their intentioned visit pieces of information were passed around the school campus for students to be part of the audience.

I vividly recall it was a Saturday during a period for course test where a few students were at school and more away to their hostels.

I was among the few that run into this activity by hearing students' leaders; Jimmy Mwesigwa, Emmanuel Byamukama and Felix Atungye who were the minister for education, guild speaker and minister for sports respectively. I was just a student but way intrigued by their talk to join the audience ready for what the Principal had in store for students.

I was not contented however; with the information given to me which prompted me to ask the campus director Pontius Byarugaba over the intentions of the Principal for his visit. He replied calmly, "The Principal, Prof. Balunywa is here to encourage innovations and creativity among the students' body." "Oh yes", I quickly said. He already knew my assets for IP and it was a smooth path as I asked on whether to come with my two books then or not. He was very encouraging and said, "It is the reason he is here, please do".

I had not travelled to school with them but it was a one kilometer stretch from home to school as a commuting student. I hurriedly moved home picked on my books from the display shelf and back to school. I entered a room where I was the only student with IP with specificity of authorship to the two books. It is not about what you know and what you have that will sell you over and over again.

I had authored books, never heard of the word Intellectual Property in a business school where I was in the evening hours of my program. You should surely be mindful of the struggles you go through every day of your life. The School Director made introductory remarks as he welcomed the Principal to speak but key was, "We are blessed to have one of our students who is so creative and they have written two books".

"You are meeting the right group Mr. Principal", he added. Deep within I grew joy and time to present my mind in a few seconds away. Prof. Waswa Balunywa at 12:27 pm started introducing his team from the Business Incubation Centre among which included two ladies Rehma and Diana. He further asserted, "We are here to enable your future as students". In his communication key was that he wanted students to create business ideas upon which the centre with support from the World Bank would help make these ideas come to light.

At a later time, I was the first student to speak from the students' body forwarding my books. It was a very realistic moment for my life. As a writer it is important to speak out to people over what you know for the success of the world through your works. I had quest for the school's support towards publishing my books. This did not see the light of the day though I was encouraged to move on with my work for the future was bright.

All this happened as the Students in the room grew dead silent and the visitors were nodding their heads in agreement as though they knew I already had such assets while at University. The School principal too was in quest for novel ideas from students to be submitted to the Business Incubation Centre for rewards upon winning. However, students started by lame excuses with instant growing fear over the safety of their ideas.

Today information is one of the biggest rewards someone can offer to me. These students offering different programs ranging from Bachelors of Commerce, Bachelors of Business Administration, Bachelors of Procurement and Supply Chain Management to Bachelors of Human Resource Management did not know of what Intellectual Property would mean in this capacity. They had no knowledge about trade secrets, patents, trademarks and copyrights.

Intellectual Property is what would best protect the ideas of the students in question. Who knows, if they knew probably the competition would have been stiff with more competitors?

Today is meant for actions and yesterday was the better part of your life to make excuses like these, sorry yesterday is gone and so look at only acting your way to IP. Through IP great ideas can be encouraged and so those in ownership of the great ideas shall benefit from them. Do not sit back with your idea and get deceived that you will attain the better part of it in your bed room. Move it out to the world and seek protection wherever.

The idea you have today is what you are exactly going to look like ten (10) to fifteen (15) years from today. In that idea you are going to get wiser, healthier, pour out more love, experience greater love, go spiritually stronger, do more charitable works and grow wealthier. I will also write more books in addition to this. This is indeed a true reflection of where your idea is yet to lead you in life, for hope there, all will appear sooner than later.

Also make an analogy of that future you really deserve to attain and what you are doing today. It is simple, are you sleeping in your 20s, 50s and 60s like you marked your a hundredth (100th) birthday yesterday? Are you having discipline of hard work or you have discipline of listening to everybody?

It is not paying 10 to 15 years from now to sleep at 10:00 pm from watching TV all day and wakeup at 8:30 am in the morning. You mustn't work for your funs but your future and family. In this regard discipline stretches as far as doing work by yourself when everyone says no, where your editor is not demanding for books to work on, your coach is not around, your mentor is asleep and you are awake making the future realistic bit by bit and day in day out. IP is greatly making my life better sooner than later.

I want to say having such a great idea is not enough, protect it with trade secrets. Seek registration for your trade secrets and start to get better to make it part of IP. According to Peter Davis a Patent lawyer, trade secrets are any pieces of information that by virtue of its secrecy gives the owner the information and competitive advantage. A trade secret ought to be generally known, there should be reasonable efforts to maintain secrecy and it must offer to the owner competitive advantage.

Trade secrets live infinitely which should reassure the lazy people life like the earlier students of the safety of their ideas. You should not run out of solutions as long as you have something other people cannot see. The absence of my novelty in other people is why they look out for me. I hold the uniqueness in a given aspect and it is what they want not me.

People want your idea and not you, so hold it as long as you are protected by trade secrets especially after registration. If you hold it just to yourself it is not bringing out the reasonable efforts to maintain secrecy. Underneath you will not understand the employment agreements, building security and network security that are important for reasonable efforts. Failure under IP may not bring you down but put you higher than you ever thought one would get you.

The good bit about this is that your idea may be totally new under the sun; it then qualifies to be registered as a patent. Patents are inventions and compositions of business methods. Patents take more time to develop which makes it very expensive in the long run. If you have a loose tongue you may lose it soon prior registration. It is even expensive to protect especially with legal fees involved.

You will need to get help from a Patent Attorney to fully work better as far as safe guarding your work not to lose out to wrong people. It will most likely take a longer procedure than other parts of IP to have your patents recognized and registered (Juetten, 2013). Filling a provisional application is important because from the word go you are safer on the road of patents. It lasts for one year whereas the standard application lasts for 3 to 5 years.

Within this time you can choose to keep on the road or abandon the idea. Right from registration of patents you are conscious of the time involved. Publication must be after 18 months from the time of filing. You still can decide to withdraw your application or not, entirely at this level it is the standard application.

Ultimately in this process the Patent Corporation Treaty (PCT) for USA may serve to widen your market base after registration. PCT creates a link between the US application and other countries if you want to extend your patent in other countries. It covers one year at standard application. You realize that the entire process to register patents may cover ten years in total. By this fact, United States of America still takes control over the biggest part of the world. If you filed under PCT, you can fill any application be it provisional to allow your point of public disclosure all over the world.

Among key requirements for patents is that the invention ought not to be obvious (obvious things will fall under trade secrets), no one ought to have ever done such inventions or written about them and there ought to be full disclosure. Through patents there is contract with the government which certainly involves disclosure. Short of disclosure and someone happens to infringe on your patent and you file a suit against them, where the court system finds out that you did not disclose your invention in the first place; you lose the case.

This is how important it may serve for us to ensure disclosure of the idea under patents during registration. According to Bitlaw Guidance, the expenses incurred in having patents registered from the initial cost range from $15,000 to $20,000. This should not worry you and make you create excuses for not having patents recognized tomorrow. It is controllable as far as making reduction in view of your bargaining power between you and the lawyer. This could even reduce to $5,000.

There is examination of the application which cost $5,000 mainly caused by backlogs in the patents office that takes one to three years. This counts being examined till one gets the offer of the registration certificate for USA. With clear terms, the US patent is 20 years from filing an applicable to having filed the standard US application. In case you notice that there were delays of the patent office due to backlogs created from the initial stage, an extension is granted to you beyond 20 years.

If the extension is not granted, you still can request for an extension by yourself. Maintenance fees are also involved payable with a three and a half months period. However, you ought to be in the know of what disclosure carries with it. By the way you have one year to get a patent application filed from the day of first public disclosure.

Contrary to this, what you disclosed will be considered dedicated to the public and certainly you cannot take it back. In a greater sense of reason you will be the first person to lose out and not have your idea pay off. Through all this, Is it worth what you are doing today to hold patents? Do you think one day you will be recognized as an inventor? Inventorship has similarly a lot in common with ownership for patents.

An inventor is one who contributes to the conception of the invention. Ownership is explained where each inventor has undivided interest in the patent. If you are five inventors holding a patent and one of the inventors decides to part ways; they can still exploit the invention as far as having a license, start up their own company. With this nothing can be done to stop them.

There is a lesson to pick from this; it is way costly to get a patent and way expensive to litigate a patent. The entire process is indeed for people that deserve it and people that have worked out their discipline away from the sight of a mentor. First you should have a beam of light start to spread in your life, if you have just found out that you are an inventor by reading this book. Mundane business will not stop competitors anywhere in the world. Patents are potential barriers to market entry by competitors.

It is only through IP that you can put an end to competitors, short of this you are a mundane business operator to me. With this margin you certainly will start to harvest revenue especially in terms of license fees. It is important to note that more to the benefits of patents is serving as a marketing tool having demonstrated the inventor's commitment and attention to IP.

Over and over again you will through Intellectual Property have a defensive tool against other patentees. Where are you not to have IP as your first asset?

It all calls for your time to believe you can do it. Look at what you are doing today and imagine if you are set to compete with billions of people all over the world. You could be involved in business that does not change from time to time. Have you known why you do business like other people? There is something missing to make your business idea from growing in whatever you do. Trade Marks (TM) is one thing non recognizable for every business that has failed. Trade Marks identify the source of goods and services.

TM is categorized under word, name and symbol or a combination indicating the source of goods or services like a logo and signs. Trade Marks must be used in commerce and should not be generic and by far descriptive. However, TM should be fanciful, suggestive and distinctive in nature. For the accrual rights of Trade Marks; it is automatic prior registration with simply the symbol of TM on the commodities involved with the exception of unpacked fruits like apples. TM under registration helps to effect enforcement of infringements upon registration (Durham University, 2016).

In addition to this, registration of TM avails evidence that you are the first owner of the work. Trade Marks at registration carry the symbol of ®. If you are already in business it sounds better to register your TM. With a clear understanding of this you would not get protection having not registered your Trade Mark. The costs therein are less than $2,000 under the US IP office.

This will prevent others from copying your brand identity as they transact business, or if they copy you, you can defend your rights legally. To a greater extent Trade Marks contribute to what the business looks like today and offer more value in turn. Coca-Cola is the most paying Trade Mark valued at $84,000,000,000 in the whole world (Durham University, 2016).

Like its value kept growing, so the value of your Trade Mark shall grow starting with registration and putting in place better practices than Coca-Cola It is possible to get there; if you keep in business and definitely continue to renew your registration mandate.

It is my pleasure to have enabled you before enabling myself. Most important for me however; is Copyrights represented by the symbol ©. This symbol was first introduced to the United States Copyrights Act of 1909. Copyrights essentially cover original works of authorship, art, literature, architectural and music. This goes as far as books, soft wares, manuals and company documents and DVDs among others. The accrual rights of © are automatic that if somebody copies your work, it is an infringement. Important to note is registration with the Copyrights Office which is greatly required for statutory damages (ibid. 2016)

This means it makes sense to have your Copyrights registered through the guidance of an attorney. It is as good as finding out that someone is infringing on your Copyrights; for you can even register a day prior to suing for damages as real infringement occurs. Each act of copying is considered a separate infringement under enforcement issues. In a greater sense even for modification of an existent Copyrighted work resulting in a derivative is an infringement of the original work.

The process is not so hectic though at the end of the day it is already paying off flourishingly. According to the U.S. Copyright Office an application document has about three pages and the cost for filing this application in the US is $45. This is very cheap compared to the past incidences of costs highlighted for Patents, Trade Marks and Trade Secrets.

All this offers to you and me as a writer and importantly an author a more ownership mandate which is more personal than the rest. I am making more emphasis of authorship because I love it and it makes me proud of myself. Furthermore, the duration of © is determined at the entire life of the author plus seventy (70) years after their death (Durham University, 2016). In other words through writing my books and every time I put pen to paper, I am not being selfish to the world around me.

My great grandchildren are yet to benefit with God's love. They will have full mandate to earn from my sleepless nights of joy and untiring efforts. For anonymous work and pseudonymous works made for hire, it means 95 years from publication or 120 years creation. In the event that I am alive and 70 years after my death; my work in such books shall not be rented, copied or performed without my permission even if it is on the Website.

I and the people I may transfer my authorship to like my wife and children in future even after my death can recover all damages from anybody who infringes on my Copyrights. For that matter permission to Copyrights can be met usually in return for payment of license fee or loyalty. You know what Socrates said about Copyrights; very important and he said, "Copyrights will implant forgetfulness in human beings' souls; they cease to exercise memory because they rely on that which is written, calling things to remembrance no longer from within themselves, but by means of external marks" (Brennan, 2016).

This is true only to someone out there that may try reading because they will find new things and discover a lot in there. It is so unfortunate that Socrates was not talking to most of you. Many Ugandans and Africans at large go to bed the same way they woke up in the morning.

It is the same story from parents to their children and grandchildren here in Africa. Why do you hate yourself this much? Recall you get what you deserve in life and not necessary what you want. If you do not invest in yourself then you have no worth to invest even in your children or other people.

I always told my staff at Domestic Peace Foundation Uganda to treasure reading books for them to get better informed and act on an informed point of view in life. On day I place UGX20,000 an equivalent of $6 in my display book which was placed on the first shelf of our small library in the office. For two months not any of the staff members opened the display book first for themselves and certainly for our visitors.

After two months I said to them, you still haven't found some treasure because you do not want to read. And I tell you; systematically they all would soon fail to support the organisation thus being fired. If you have absolutely nothing new to add to someone, do not talk to them. Why do you intend to bring someone's life low to who you are? Subsequently, this tells you that if you cannot read a book or two you will never tell other people to read.

Upon which reference can you make of the book titles and the relevant authors? Parents, make your children better by influencing them to read books because you can read too. You must have respect for people that create Intellectual Property. In this it is not about do as I say but as I do.

I must fully get involved in my pieces of work for you to be able to read them. Intellectual Property is not for the people who want to give up but for you and me ready to see what we get done. You must desist from telling people what you like to be that they never see you become everyday of your life. As a philosophical writer, I am seen in my pieces of work and my authorship pays off through IP.

Where are you seen and what are you seen doing? If you say things to please your girlfriend, boyfriend, husband, wife, children and friends you are lying to yourself and time will soon file a suit against you. You will certainly lose this case. On the other hand you well know that it is you living your life like I live my life. No one was born strong but the strength has entirely been drawn from our weaknesses. If you make up your mind today, time ahead will still pay off.

Respect time with all its values in this book and I will soon meet your success in a letter headed, 'from failures we get successful people'. I was once a failure but I did not look down on myself. I did not know how to spell my name before my Primary Two teachers but I did not accept to keep stagnant. Today I own assets and Intellectual Property is my game. Find your game in valuing time for there is quality of it somewhere.

CHAPTER 14

Our Parents: The Inspiration We Carry

Messages to recognise the late Mr. Besiga John. Blessings to Mrs. Generoza Banooti Besiga for loving Daddy. Our parents, friends, mentors and relatives influence our success.

My husband, my companion. I thank God for the gift of my husband, Mr. Besiga John. He died at a time we least expected. I also thank God for the opportunity he gave to me having lived with him in holy matrimony for 30 years. There is nothing hurting and painful than talking about the beloved that doesn't exist. First but not the least he loved God and his fellow men. His love for God was manifested in giving support to the church, and by fulfilling the commandments of God. His love for taking readings at the holy mass, his pleasure when amidst the church choir on many Sunday and other big occasions made a statement.

Blind as he was but his disability did not mean inability. A husband and a friend to me and to multitudes of people of course plus his own lovely five children. He educated them and told them that the sky was the limit. He was always ready to render a hand outstretched to the needy especially through paying school tuition for the less privileged children. My husband was strong hearted, courageous, hardworking, cheerful, smart, brilliant and God Loving indeed.

People could not understand how he managed to study to the extent of becoming a teacher and afterwards an inspector of schools since he got blind at six (6) years of age. Very generous to others; trying to pay back to God. One day he told me that we should always visit the sick in hospitals, take the sick people from the village to hospitals especially those that could not afford taking care of themselves and his frequent visits to the prison cells saw many people become our friends after they were set free.

Relatives and non-relatives of course without forgetting parents (his and mine) were consoled and comforted to have passed through this life at his watch. A man of truth and openness, his yes was yes, his no was no, he lived by his word, ready to give his views when in meetings through proposals and his words always emerged the best. I remember one time he was invited to attend the meeting as the chairperson of the Disabled People of Mbarara District; in that meeting there was the President of the Republic of Uganda His Excellency Yoweri Kaguta Museveni, then my late husband Mr. Besiga John raised his hand in order to suggest and offer pieces of advice.

The President allowed him to speak; when he finished what he wanted to speak, the president made a remark and told the enormous people that had assembled there; "Do you see this man who has been speaking? He sees Uganda far better than many sighted people gathering here". As a wife who was close to him for 30 years living together I could sometimes fail to tell whether he was sighted or blind. One day he grinded millet grain on a grinding stone, slaughtered chicken, cooked the meal and we ate (when I was of course sick).
His intelligence from God was always extraordinary telling us that it was abominable for him failing to emerge as the first (1st) in class (always the best). Children and students could go to him for help. All that he did was followed by his remarks jokingly and full of vibrant and heartfelt laughter.

How he would read with his fingers to read braille and use the braille machine, how he would differentiate between people by calling each his or her name left many wondering. He would even know and tell the footsteps of people including myself. One day when we were walking to Nyamitanga cathedral to attend the Sunday mass in 1997 few years after our wedding, I had forgotten some money which was meant for offertory back at our residence. I had to go back home and left him by the roadside; I rushed back home which was not far away. On my return, I tried to bypass him trying to find out whether he would recognize me, then all of the sudden he spoke in a loud voice, "Mummy, why are you leaving me behind?" I had to come and hold him by the hand but I was amazed at his intelligence. God is always good and does miracles.

To sum it all, our children and I had an opportunity of caring for a great and a generous man whose humor lived on both in health and sickness. He got all his rights and respects in life and death respectively. We heard him singing when he was healthy and happy, he also sung when he was sick and sad. He sung on his death bed a song that we will never forget that goes, "I have asked the Lord for one thing; one thing only do I want: to live in the Lord's house all my life". Translated from Rutagwenda; "Ekindikushaba Nyakubaho Kandi ekindikuronda nikiimwe kyonka, n'okutura Omunju ye ebiro byoona". Psalms 27:4 *MAY THE SOUL OF MY HUSBAND, FRIEND, AND GUARD REST IN PEACE.*

Children's Choir:
Memories of our late father and the love of a mother
Our Father's Legacy:
Thanking Mr. Besiga John for a Life of Resilience

Mr. Besiga John was a remarkable man who worked hard to provide for his family and was an inspiration to many. His legacy will be remembered for generations to come as a reminder of strength, resilience and the power of love. Even as a blind man, he exhibited an extraordinary spirit that presented a brilliant mind and unwavering love for his family thus a beacon of inspiration. Daddy's union with Mrs. Bainomugisha Eunice created a foundation of love and strength, giving me the support I needed to thrive.

Tragedy struck when Eunice faced mental illness, causing Mr. Besiga John to marry another woman, Mrs. Banooti Generoza Besiga in 1988. The circumstances called for adaptation and Mrs. Generoza stepped in to provide a nurturing home. This shift wasn't easy, but it was a testament to the resilience of a family bound by love and determination. She reintroduced me to my biological mother, Mrs. Bainomugisha Eunice, at the age of 16. This reunion marked a profound chapter of reconnection and healing.

I wished a world where my late father could witness the accomplishments of my family. With a heart full of appreciation, I honor the man who shaped my path. On October 20th, 2019, Daddy departed from this world, leaving a legacy of love, resilience, and unity. He serves as a reminder to all of us to never give up and to keep striving for a better future.
Mr. Byamukama Bernard

Memories of you remind me of what a great father you were. The love you gave to all of us was heavenly. Every day has now become so hard without you. Every father is a hero to her daughter but you were no less than a superhero to me. I had lost my happiness when I lost you. I still miss you every day of my life.

I love you Mom. I thank you for everything you've always done and continue to do. You are an intricate blend of gentility and toughness. You are loyally fierce and ethical; and I admire you so much mom. There are so many things in life that are good but mom you are great.
Ms. Musiimenta Emily Besiga

A blind man with a vision Mr. Besiga was. The President of the Republic of Uganda, His Excellency Yoweri Kaguta Museveni first met my father in 2007 at Mbarara University of Science and Technology; after Mr. Besiga's speech the president concluded that the man had a vision. He always asked us what our eyes were meant for after searching and finding lost items that the sighted people would fail to trace.

His mouth was the strongest tool on his body. If you gave him an opportunity to express himself, it was a sure deal that he would make his way through and get all he wanted. The only way of denying him something was not to allow him speak. Up to now I still imagine what his last words would have been if he had not lost his speech a fortnight prior to his death. He had a great memory in addition to his power of the tongue and great command of the English language which helped penetrate all the barriers that were associated with his disability.

Up to the time of his death he was a Human Rights Defender and I remember when he urged with and won a seasoned Human Rights lawyer (Mr. Opio Nicholas) and what the Constitution stated on the emoluments of the parliamentarians, he was declared the winner after confirming that his citation was enshrined in the Constitution of the Republic of Uganda as he had stated.

Rest in perfect peace Mzee Besiga (a brain power)
Mr. Agaba Benedict

I wrote this poem to mark the 53rd anniversary of Daddy's visual impairment and the 30th anniversary of holy matrimony, ceremonies that were held on 23rd March, 2019. We did not know he would later succumb to stomach cancer on 20th of October, 2019 (the same year).

The Mark was set
The mark below which Daddy and Mummy never gave up, as life opened up to them.
Meeting the challenging and memorable times together, as marriage opened up to them.
Child bearing and the responsibilities thereof became real, as priorities opened up to them.
For them; failure was not an end in itself; as reasons for reconciliation opened up to them.
Like a beggar; their last option is never to give up, the reason for them to return tomorrow.
The optimism you exhibited ahead of our journeys to school, riches to return tomorrow.
The nurturing of peace you made in us and other people, peace to return tomorrow.
The ceremonies of today's successes serve a reminder, joy to others to return tomorrow.

The woman you refer to as wife is a unique one; it is vision not sight, in God's choices we lead.
Did you choose for everyone a blind man? In God's choices we lead.
The man you worked hard to meet chose you too, in God's choices we lead.
Daddy's vision for us; to influence the world extraordinarily, in God's choices we lead.
We did not find it a crime to be your children, parenthood speaks volumes.
It is with joy that we call you our biological parents; everyday of nurturing us speaks volumes.
You failed because you tried at something, your success speaks volumes.
Knowing how to fail different without giving up marks this day, God's love speaks volumes.
Rest in Eternal Peace Mr. Besiga John. Mrs. Generoza Banooti Besiga never wean us off your love.
Bruno Asiimwe

There's so much to say about my beloved Dad, Mr. Besiga John. Dad loved us so much regardless of his disability. There's no day I missed out on anything either a basic need or a luxury. I remember when I had just started working; one evening he called me out of the blue and said, "I might be broke but anything for you. I have sent you some money go spoil yourself." You should have seen my face; it became so radiant all of a sudden. Dad went big on education and took us to the best schools in the country. He pushed me to enrol for my professional course to become a Certified Public Accountant after getting a degree which I did and was about to complete. I am forever grateful. Dad, I wish you were around to see how successful we have become. Dad, I wouldn't have been who I am today without your endless support. It hurts that I get lots of dreams about us having conversations only for me to realize you aren't here. I miss you so much.

And to my beloved Mummy, Mrs. Banooti Generoza Besiga; it feels nice having to spend my life with you. Thank you for loving Dad so much and for creating such a beautiful family that has enabled us to bond. Mummy, I love you so much.
Ms. Musiime Moreen

Memories of the late Mr. Besiga John from mentors, friends and relatives

In the 1980s when I was a young priest, I got to know a man called John Besiga, He was visually impaired. What struck me most was that John was not seeking self-pity. He was on his feet and whatever advice or assistance he got he would convert it into something that would propel him forward. He would never accept any obstacle to stand in his way. He had a high sense of tenacity and endurance. Having known him well, I often ask myself why we people without impairments or disabilities do not achieve more than our present performance.
Rev. Prof. Peter Kanyandago
Episcopal Vicar for the Laity in the Archdiocese of Mbarara and Deputy Vice Chancellor of Ibanda University

John Besiga - A Star Shining in the Darkness
A Celebrity and a Star
"In that way you may be blameless and innocent, children of God without blemish in the midst of a crooked and perverse generation, in which you shine like stars in the world," St. Paul writes (Philippians 2:15).

The excerpt from St. Paul's Epistle to the Philippians quoted above, paints a picture with which probably a good number of us are familiar – a challenge and an invitation, to emerge from the shadows and emit light amidst the dark environment around us, to demonstrate the willingness and determination to overcome hardships with potential, disability with endeavour, and overcome evil with good. We are certainly familiar with some individuals in society who, even though they were born and raised in lowly backgrounds, managed to gradually ascend the rungs, have attained high ranks and are eventually counted among celebrities; they rose to the category of being considered stars. Such people positively respond to the invitation expressed in the adage: "Light a candle rather than curse the darkness!" Remember, if you are light there won't be darkness around you. Again, as the saying goes: "A quitter never wins and a winner never quits...".

It is to such a category of personages that I want to place the Late John Besiga, a man who, having been visited by blindness in his youthful years, insisted on being light amidst the darkness around him, and hence deserves the rank of a star! Here is a man who loved truly, and lived to beat all odds in life and won the hearts of many including mine. Why do I dare count John Besiga among the celebrities and stars of our time? In the ensuing reflection, I wish to highlight certain dimensions of his life that lead me to believe that John Besiga deserves the title.

God-Fearing and a Devout Christian Believer

"The fear of the Lord is the beginning of wisdom: and the knowledge of the Holy One is understanding," says the book of Proverbs (Proverbs 9:10). John Besiga was endowed with the gift of faith, which made him a remarkable believer and an active participant in the life of the Church. This gift did not just come to him by chance, but was born out of his closeness to God, to whom John learnt to fear and give honour; as a result he was rewarded with the gift of wisdom and understanding. Armed with these rare gifts, John learnt to put God at the centre of his life and activities.

John was a regular attendant in whichever Church he found himself. He was even courageous enough to volunteer reading the Word of God during the celebration of liturgy, of course being totally blind, he read using Braille scripts – with great eloquence and clarity, to the amazement of the beholders! At the local level, he was an active member in councils of the out-station of the Church, and a resourceful contributor at meetings, planning Church events and activities. I remember him coming to my office where by then I worked as Diocesan Chancellor in the Archbishop's office in Mbarara, to solicit for financial help, in the endeavour to support the church that was being constructed in his home village of Mbaba, Kazo District in Western Uganda.

Surprisingly, he told me that he was a member of the building committee; and actually he intimated to me that the building of that Church was a result of his initiative. That's how much he loved and served his Church, blind as he was! John was God-intoxicated, and an exemplary Christian, serious with Christian values and moral principles – all of which steered him to work hard and support his family.

Bernard Byamukama, one of his sons, rightly remarks, "His legacy (John's) will be remembered for generations to come as a reminder of strength, resilience and the power of love."
Love is Blind - the Testimony from Real Experience
In order to appreciate the dictum, "Love is blind," and to enter into the real spirit of this sub-section, it is of paramount importance to first give it a scriptural background. St. Paul and Jesus insist on the centrality of love among humanity, and most especially in Christian life.

St. Paul dedicates a whole chapter in his First Letter to the Corinthian Chapter 13, on the said virtue - popularly known as the Pauline song of love; which supplements St. Paul's teaching on the same subject reflected in some of his other Epistles like the Letter to the Romans, Ephesians and Colossians. It is sufficient that these texts are only mentioned in passing, since there is need to keep within the scope and limits of this piece of writing. Considering the significance of St. Paul's doctrine on love, it is worth quoting from him en masse. Here is what St. Paul teaches on the virtue of Love:
"If I speak with the tongues of men and of angels, but do not have love, I have become a noisy gong or a clanging cymbal. If I have the gift of prophecy, and know all mysteries and all knowledge; and if I have all faith, so as to remove mountains, but do not have love, I am nothing. And if I give all my possessions to feed the poor, and if I surrender my body to be burned, but do not have love, it profits me nothing.
Love is patient, love is kind and is not jealous; love does not brag and is not arrogant, does not act unbecomingly; it does not seek its own, is not provoked, does not take into account a wrong suffered, does not rejoice in unrighteousness, but rejoices with the truth; bears all things, believes all things, hopes all things, endures all things. [Emphasis added].

Love never fails; but if there are gifts of prophecy, they will be done away; if there are tongues, they will cease; if there is knowledge, it will be done away....But now faith, hope, love, abide these three; but the greatest of these is love" (1 Corinthians 13:1-8, 13).

Turning to Jesus Christ, from whom St. Paul takes the courage and strength to speak so eloquently about love, we ascertain that, Jesus is the true embodiment of God's love for humanity for, he summarises all the Ten Commandments (and Jewish Customary Laws) into two Commandments which are alike, namely the love of God and neighbour. "'Love the Lord your God with all your heart and with all your soul and with all your mind.' This is the first and greatest commandment. And the second is like it: 'Love your neighbour as yourself.'" (Matthew 22:36-40).

He even names love and elevates it to the level of a New Commandment: "This is My commandment, that you love one another, just as I have loved you" (John 15:12, 17). The Song of Songs adds even a more serious nuance: "Love is as strong as death!" (Song of Songs 8:6). What is not mentioned in Scripture though, but which is implied, is expressed in the English dictum: "Love is blind!" – Literally translated in the Runyankore language as "Rukundo n'empumi!"
Turning to John Besiga's in this regard, I must say that we have the said dictum exemplified in his lived experience. Somewhere along the path of life, providence brought a woman of his life, with whom he would eventually get married and build a family.

He wooed Generoza Banooti, the girl that came into his life and loved with all his heart, took her out on several dates, till the time was ripe enough to be introduced to her parents. The parents of the girl also did not mind that their daughter was engaged to a blind man, even though deep down they may have had some fears and reservations, who wouldn't? Then came the Give-away ceremony and then the wedding in Church.

John Besiga and Generoza Banooti, tied the knot, and were officially pronounced husband and wife.
Throughout the years of their marriage, John never got the chance to look into the eyes of his wife, nor know the complexion of her skin, whether dark or brown. Perhaps he could guess her height, and the feel of her body; and maybe he could tell her size, but that is all. It was not the external beauty of his wife that mattered to him; His was the kind of love that is commonly described as "skin-deep!" the kind of love based on internal beauty and inner qualities. John admired in Generoza the type of wife described in the Book of Proverbs as the 'perfect wife' (Proverbs 31:10-31).

I must now lay more emphasis on Generoza, John Besiga's wife and children. Let me re-echo once again the image of the perfect wife mentioned in the Book of Proverbs, whom, in my opinion is reflected in Generoza: "A wife of noble character who can find? She is worth far more than rubies. Her husband has full confidence in her and lacks nothing of value. She brings him good, not harm, all the days of her life" (Proverbs 31:10-12)

For, even though Generoza had and still has her full sight, to date, she did not mind about getting married to a blind man. She instead loved a man, who would be for her a loving husband, with all his inhibitions and imperfections. She was enlightened to quickly realise that there is no "perfect" husband on planet earth. As the famous writer, John Gray rightly says in his famous book, "Men are from Mars; women are from Venus", totally different planets, but who are meant to complement each other, in spite of their individual limitations (Gray, 2004).

Thus, my assertion is that she too embraced the adage, "Love is blind!" - Blind to external looks and capabilities, while concentrating more on inner beauty.
External beauty, which is usually excessively emphasised, more especially in contemporary society, but which is in reality quite deceptive and elusive because of its transitory nature, is the last thing that the Book of Proverbs mentions, also in one line or two and in passing – probably as a pointer to its minor role in family relationships.

John Besiga, and Generoza likewise, did not consider bodily beauty as priority in family life, as long as they fulfilled the requirements expected of husband and wife.
As we all know one of the key roles of married couples, apart from mutual love and support, is engendering children to increase the human race on earth in the Church. And John did produce children, all bright and good looking. But, being blind, John Besiga never got to see or know how they looked like. Yet, he lavishly loved them with unconditional and endearing love, so much so that some of the children would only discover later in life that he was actually totally blind! He could only tell their gender and differences by the sound of their voices.

Together with his wife, he nurtured them, fed them, raised them, and worked hard to educate them all, so that by the time of his demise all of them had graduated to the level of university.

"Disability does not mean Inability": A Highlight of Some of Besiga's Achievements and Successes

It is said that at his birth John Besiga, the Late, was born a normal baby with all his senses, including his sight. But at some stage in his infancy, some calamity befell him: he was struck by some mysterious ailment, which left him blind - the beginning of his misfortune of losing his sight the rest of his entire life.

It is said that during his childhood, a certain Missionary priest, by the names of Fr. Edgar Trembly, a French-Canadian belonging to the Society of the Missionaries of Africa (popularly known as White Fathers), made a Safari (pastoral visit), to an outstation near the home of young John Besiga. As he came out of Church, after celebrating Mass, he saw this child who was groping, trying to feel the body of Fr. Edgar's vehicle. The priest asked around, curiously inquiring who this could be. Fr. Edgar was told that it was a child, who could not attend school due to his blindness. From that day the priest made some arrangements and had John Besiga registered at St. Helen's Primary School, at Nyamitanga Hill in Mbarara City, which had the provision of the school for the blind, to date. It is in that school that John Besiga completed his Primary School, reading and writing using Braille. On completion of Primary School, he was helped by good-hearted people from the Catholic Church, so that he was able to pursue further studies to advanced levels; this set the ball rolling for future achievements and success.

It might be his academic career, or simply his natural personality that shaped John into a disciplined, principled, and no-nonsense man, who fearlessly spoke and spoke the truth, and a passionate defender of justice and human rights. His level of education, moreover, gave him the opportunity to act as a school teacher in various domains. He served on many committees in local, regional and national levels, for the cause of People with Disabilities (PWDs), and related sectors. He strongly believed in the axiom, "Disability does not mean inability!" He even won several awards, because of his tremendous achievements. John was a hardworking and competent man, who managed to emerge from humble origins, to the status of a renowned and respectable member of society. He and his wife lived and worked together in mutual cooperation. Through their hard work and determination to succeed in life, they managed to build themselves an executive house (semi-storied), which John never had the opportunity to gaze upon either. And the family also managed to acquire a vehicle! Did John cast an eye on it? Never! During the eulogies at their father's funeral one of his children caused laughter to the mourners that "those with their full sight and bodily capabilities, would often solicit financial help from John who was blind!"

A word about the children. They too did not care about, nor be ashamed of the fact that they were sons and daughters of a father that was blind. What they needed was a caring Dad. But even if they cared, they couldn't change anything about their situation. There are certain things in life, moreover, that we can hardly choose: we never choose our parents; we don't choose the place or country in which to be born; we do not choose our race, and sometimes not even determine our religion, especially if we are born into it. We can choose to change our colour and religion later in life, but such choices usually run contrary to our original natural upbringing.

So, John's children too loved their father, without paying too much attention that he was a Person with Disability (PWD). Often they were their father's guide in showing him directions on the roads, streets, and roads of life. However, in one of the son's testimonies again at the funeral, he indicated that John was such an intelligent and intuitive man, that he would sometimes walk alone into buildings and offices unaccompanied! At first the family was nervous about letting John go alone, but they soon realised that he would go and come back safely, even without guidance. At other times he would be the one to tell his guide that the path he led him to was not the correct one.

Scripture talks about two types of blessings: the first one is the one described in the Book of Psalms we have just quoted - whereby husband and wife and their children sit around the table and enjoy the meal and rejoice in each other's company. Having a successful family life, is in Scripture, is considered a physical/material blessing; that dream was realised in John Besiga's home. The second type of blessing is the spiritual one, as described in St. Paul's Epistle to the Ephesians. This is how St. Paul describes it: "Blessed be the God and Father of our Lord Jesus Christ, who has blessed us in Christ with every spiritual blessing in the heavenly places, even as he chose us in him before the foundation of the world, that we should be holy and blameless before him"(Ephesians 1:3-4 [1-6]).

In raising his family, John did not stop at grooming his wife and children into responsible citizens: he had that strong desire and urge, to instil in them true human values, of being humane, people of uprightness and dignity; individuals capable of standing on their feet and defend the truth; and most of all be courageous amidst life's ups and downs. He also inculcated in his family the love for the Catholic Church, faith and trust in God. He always remembered with gratitude, how instrumental the Church was, in elevating him to the pedestal he stood on in his life. He wanted to have his children always to hold onto that same faith, and uphold the teachings of the Church, plus the values of the Kingdom of God.

All in all, John Besiga's entire family survived through life on the conviction that love is indeed blind; and it is! By and large, John's children got that message loud and clear - they are decent young men and women, thank God. Isn't that the kind of material and spiritual blessings that the Book of Psalms and St. Paul respectively talk about?

After all these achievements, I am sure that whenever John and Generoza, his wife sat with their progeny around the table to eat, and enjoy the fruit of their labour, they would rejoice in the spirit of the family recounted in one of the Books of the Psalmist: "Your wife shall be like a fruitful vine in the inner part of your house; your children will be like olive shoots around your table. Thus shall the man be blessed, who fears the Lord" (Psalm 128:3-4). I suppose John managed to achieve all that because "he loved without seeing!" His was not "blind love" though. Even without physical sight, he was well focused. Instead, his were inner insight and love. Indeed, John is a living example and fulfilment of the idiom, "Love is blind!"

Till we Meet Again - A Decent and We'll-deserved Send off

I got the rare blessing of being privileged to preside over his funeral Mass and burial: listening to witnesses that gave testimonies about his outstanding personality and successes, even though he was totally blind, I couldn't but be moved to tears. Even the majority of temporary able-bodied people would not be able to do what he did in his limitations.

Lessons to those with all their Full Senses, and the Need to Express Gratitude to God

The advice of this writer, is this: none of us should take our lives for granted, especially when we find ourselves living a life that is healthy and strong. We all have our lives from God our Creator and Provider. None of us should be proud, or boast because we were blessed to be born and raised without being handicapped. I am often taken aback by some men and women who lead their lives showing off, simply because they have a nice figure, good looks, and are sleek and slender, real paragons!

Again, as the Runyankore saying goes, "Omuto tasheka burema" ("The young should never scorn or laugh [at the person with disabilities])! Life can take an about turn, as John Besiga's did. Besiga was born as normal as many babies do. But misfortune befell him, and he had to put up with the disability of sightlessness throughout his entire life.

Moreover, people who are not disabled should learn to acknowledge and respect the dignity of the disabled, the handicapped, and treat the PWDs with reverence. We should all love them with the spirit of magnanimity, sticking to the example of John Besiga's shining testimony that "love is blind!"

Finally, I thank God that John Besiga came into my life, and became a gift and gift to me, and certainly to many others who were privileged to know him and associate with him. St. Paul reminds us, as he did to the believers in the Church at Corinth, that we should never forget or be oblivious of the fact that "that they [who] seek God, [ought to know that] He is not far from each one of us; for in Him we live and move and exist, for we also are His children" (Acts 17:17-28). John Besiga had a sip of life's challenges, but he stuck to his guns, determined to succeed against all odds, trusting in his Lord and Master, our Saviour, Jesus Christ. And he succeeded in being a star shining in the darkness around him! If Besiga could do it, why not us? Yes we can!

Rev. Dr. Bonaventure Turyomumazima, PhD.
Former Diocesan Chancellor, Mbarara Archdiocese

The John I knew
John Besiga was my brother-in-law-turned-best friend, my big-brother, who fended for and connected me to big people, offices. Although he was totally blind, he could 'see' and do what many temporary able-bodied, well-placed and educated people could not. Then one day he shocked me out of my wits when he cautioned me thus; "You guys are careless with your sight!!" This was after I asked and wondered how he looked for and found my wallet which I had misplaced and could not locate in the room of his house where I had spent the previous a night.

Mr. Muhanguzi Justus Kampe

Author – Eyes of a Journalist and Former Public Affairs Officer at Uganda Human Rights Commission.

Dear Daddy.
Farewell thee Daddy as you continue to rest in peace. You are still remembered as a daddy to the disability community, champion of change and an inclusive society. It's what you always wanted and indeed you played your part well; disability rights were well addressed. I was blessed when I became part of your family and work; there is no single day that has passed without saying, "Rest peacefully, Daddy."

I am proud that you mentored me to mentor many other people through the love you left within the deaf community which has always made us to remember your spirit of hard work and your motto, "Breaking Barriers". Indeed you were cherished by many because you meant what you spoke and you stood for the truth so that disabled persons should not be left behind. You were a freedom fighter and I am sure you are still happy with us.

I remember the sweet memories we last had on his death bed; he touched my hand and said, "yes Betty, I will soon be okay", he was so strong that he would not let sickness take away the love for his people. I am happy that I held his hand though I didn't know it was his last time. He used to ask me about the girls especially Anne, it's sad they have grown up without him now. I have cried and come to relax later, it is part of the healing. Daddy, Daddy continue to rest with the Angels, we loved you so much but God loved you more than us. Fare thee well daddy and my mentor. Psalms 37.4
Mrs. Kyogabirwe Betty.

CEO – Support Disabled Uganda and Deaf Disability Inclusion Champion

An epitome of love and a gem of life he was. One of whose worth we will forever make a toast. Mr. Besiga John was a man of great wisdom and knowledge who did many small ordinary things but with extraordinary love. Not letting disability define who he was, Mr. Besiga chose a path of success and wrote his story. Unlike many other people like him, he definitely walked his talk. We know that stars can only shine brightest in the darkness. Surely, with perseverance, hard work and determination, this great man overcame all hindrances in his way so that he could achieve his dreams. He believed that we can only rise by lifting others. With so many charitable works and service above self, he won the hearts of many and is an inspiration indeed.

His presence always brought in an abundance of joy and love. The warmth of his smile always embraced the hearts of whoever came in his reach. The radiance of his face defined real happiness as one that originates from the heart. He cherished and valued all his relations and always put his heart at everything he did. For the time one spent with Mr. Besiga, he was a father and friend to me and always saying wise words. He taught me to always believe that I can do all things and raised in me the confidence to take on any opportunity that comes my way. Above all, I learned from his great example: to know my worth and not let anything define me but rather that I should tread my own path as long as it will lead me to excellence.

I will forever live in loving memory of Mr. Besiga John, being grateful for the opportunity to know a great man and warrior like him. You are forever loved.

Ms. Atengorit Anne Grace
Senior Four- Maryhill High School
His friend and a daughter to Mrs. Kyogabirwe Betty

References

Brennan, J. 2016. *Why Property Rights?*
https://www.youtube.com/watch?v=Ec2BH82t5vE

Chomsky, N. 1967. *The Responsibility of Intellectuals.* The New York Review of Books. https://chomsky.info/19670223/
CNBC. 2018. *Trump slaps China with tariffs on up to $60 billion in imports: 'This is the first of many'*
https://www.cnbc.com/2018/03/22/trump-moves-to-slap-china-with-50-billion-in-tariffs-over-intellectual-property-theft.html

Durham University. 2016. *What's Intellectual property got to do with you?* https://www.youtube.com/watch?v=EQsZf2G4Sdc
FIDA Uganda. 2012. *My Story – Women's Land and Property Rights in Uganda.*
https://www.youtube.com/watch?v=Bo4sGN3eneY

Gray, J. 2004. *Men Are from Mars, Women Are from Venus.* A Practical Guide for Improving Communication and Getting What You Want in Your Relationships.
https://lookingfortruth.org/wp-content/uploads/2018/04/Men-are-from-mars-women-are-from-venus.pdf

Juetten, M. 2013. *Understanding the 4 types of intellectual property.* https://www.youtube.com/watch?v=sMos5Dx-9CQ

Robert K. & Sharon L.L. (1998), Rich Dad Poor Dad: Why teach financial literacy? PP 73-105

The 1995 constitution of Uganda. 1995. Cap 4, Article 29, Se 1 and subsection (a). P. 46

The Nation. 2015. Vigilantes and infighting are the new narratives. https://www.thenational.ae/opinion/vigilantes-and-infighting-are-the-new-narratives-1.37318

U.S   Copyright   Office.   2023. https://www.copyright.gov/about/fees.html

The New King James Version (NKJV). https://app.logos.com/books/LLS%3A1.0.30/references/bible%2Bnkjv.65.17.22?registration_source_host=biblia.com

BOOKS BY BRUNO ASIIMWE

1.   Speaking Volumes for a Moment in a Seminary

2.   A Family for Us: Together against Domestic Violence

3.   The Quality of Time: From this Moment Onwards